WHISKY WARS

Also by Malcolm Archibald:

A Sink of Atrocity

Glasgow: The Real Mean City

Ancestors in the Artic

Fishermen, randies and fraudsters:
Crime in 19th century Aberdeen and the North East

Liverpool: Gangs, Vice and Packet Rats

WHISKY WARS

*Riots and Murder in the 19th-Century
Highlands and Islands*

Malcolm Archibald

BLACK & WHITE PUBLISHING

First published 2013
as *Whisky Wars, Riots and Murder*
This edition first published 2019
by Black & White Publishing Ltd
Nautical House, 104 Commercial Street, Edinburgh EH6 6NF

1 3 5 7 9 10 8 6 4 2   19 20 21 22

ISBN: 978 1 78530 239 8

A CIP catalogue record for this book is available from the British Library.

Typeset by RefineCatch Ltd, Bungay, Suffolk
Printed and bound by CPI Group (UK) Ltd, Croydon, CR0 4YY

For Cathy

'The north of Scotland is in a state of virtual insurrection against the local authorities on account of the attempted intrusion of unpopular Ministers upon reclaiming congregations'

The Belfast News Letter, 10 Oct 1843

Contents

Introduction

A few years ago I was on the ferry from Uig in Skye to Tarbert in the Isle of Harris. As we approached the island, a young man standing near me was enthusing about everything to his girl while his fellow passengers were listening and smiling. The man obviously belonged to Harris, but despite his exhilaration at returning home, as I looked at the low cloud that smeared the rocky hills and the breaking grey sea, I wondered what sort of place I was coming to. Within a few hours I realised I was somewhere special. I knew most of Scotland fairly well but the atmosphere of the Outer Isles was something I had never experienced before. It was autumn: wet, windy and wild, yet strangely beautiful.

While I was there, I toured the twin islands of Harris and Lewis and came across a memorial to the land struggles of the 1880s. Now, the Clearances are well known and justly condemned, but outside the Highlands less is known about the resistance of the later nineteenth century. The subject intrigued me and I planned to investigate further, but life intervened and the intention was pushed onto the back burner. I began to work on other projects, including some study on crime in

Landscape of the Highlands

Dundee. That led to a book on Dundee crime in the nineteenth century, which in turn led to a similar volume about Glasgow and then another about nineteenth-century crime in the Highlands and Islands.

The wheel had turned full circle and at last I could look into the Land Wars of the 1880s, but that also led to a dispute of conscience: the men and women who took part in that struggle had broken the law, but was it a crime to fight for what many people believed had been illegally taken from them? In the bigger picture of things, how should crime be defined? Certainly the landowners saw the actions of crofters and cottars in occupying land as a crime, but history is more lenient in its view. Crime seemed to be period, culture and even class-specific in some respects. For example, those people who attempted to prevent grain from being exported from a starving countryside were viewed as criminal by the authorities, while others may view them as desperate people attempting to keep body and soul together.

In this book, crime will be defined as much as possible in line with the view of the law in the period. Some actions were reckoned as criminal in 1813 as they are in 2013, others are less frowned on now and the sentences handed out by a possibly biased judge could be viewed as excessive or even appalling. The young man from Wick who got sentenced to eight months in jail in 1847 for merely being on the street after the Riot Act was read was one case in point. Even at that time there were those who protested the sentence, but sometimes Scottish courts were perceived as being heavy-handed when dealing with those who threatened the status quo. The rule of Law, and particularly the rule of the establishment, had to be seen as unchallengeable in a period when the French Revolution was still remembered and there was always fear that European republicanism could spread to Britain.

Types of crime have also undergone some alteration. Some, such as theft, assault, murder and rape, still darken the Highlands, but others, such as infanticide, breach of a promise of marriage, and bigamy, are less common. All of these were known in the reign of Queen Victoria, possibly because of the stigma attached to illegitimacy and the expense and difficulty of divorce. History has thrown a cloak of romance over other crimes that were undoubtedly traumatic at the time, so that highway robbers are viewed as romantic, poachers have achieved the status of folk heroes and smugglers are seen as laughing desperados rather than the dangerous if daring men they undoubtedly were. Perhaps in a Highland or Hebridean context, nineteenth-century poachers and smugglers wore a different plaid to the cloak that concealed the truth elsewhere.

Certainly crime in the Highlands has certain aspects unique to the area. Where else would second sight help solve a murder? Where else would a piper lead hundreds of poachers in a two-day raid? Where else would men sound a horn so they could break the law? Highland crime could be tragic, such as the triple family murder in Benbecula;

violent, such as the assault on the Excisemen near Dufftown; or poignant, such as the doomed protests against the Clearances. But whatever it was, it also helped define the culture and attitude of a people and place. For that alone it is worth examining. Although there were the usual suspects of murder, assault, robbery and theft, Highland crime had many unique aspects that this work intends to reveal.

This book is split into a number of thematic chapters. It starts with a brief look at the geographical and historical background of the Highlands and Islands, then moves on to the whisky wars, where the Excisemen tried to control the huge number of illicit stills. Next is a look at some of the more interesting robbery cases of the century, followed by a view of some of the rioting that was periodically endemic. The nineteenth-century police forces that tried to look after the area have their own short chapter, and then there is crime at sea and some of the murders of the century. Chapter 8 focuses on crimes committed during the Land Wars when the crofters struggled to gain security of tenure. Chapter 9 looks at relationship problems that were as relatively common in the Highlands as anywhere else. Chapter 10 features assaults, Chapter 11 some of the difficulties that religion caused and Chapter 12 the widespread problem of poaching. Chapters 13 and 14 are about children and women respectively, while Chapter 15 looks at a whole medley of disparate crime. The book finishes with two of the major murder mysteries of the century, the Goatfell murder in Arran and the death at Ardlamont.

In common with the sister volumes on Dundee and Glasgow, this is not an academic work that attempts to analyse or explain the crimes; it is a book that hopefully portrays something of the realities of criminal life in Highland and Island Scotland during a volatile and traumatic century.

1
The Geographical and Historical Background

Geographers know it as the Highland Boundary Fault as it bisects Scotland from Helensburgh in the west to Stonehaven in the northeast, but historically this division was as much linguistic and cultural as geographical. To the south and east lay the Lowlands, the home of Robert Burns and James Hogg, of Edinburgh with its court and trade links with Continental Europe. The Lowlands were cultivated, with neat farms, and were dotted with cities such as Dundee and Aberdeen, as well as market and cathedral towns. Foreign visitors commented on the breadth of Edinburgh's High Street and the neatness of the town of Glasgow, but few ventured north of Perth, for here rose the mountains of the Highlands.

Today the Scottish Highlands are synonymous with beautiful scenery, tourism, wildlife and outdoor sports. In past times, mountains were considered ugly and the Highlands were thought inaccessible, with terrible roads, rivers that could be crossed only by oar-powered ferries, low ground that was liable to flood and hill passes that were often choked with snow. The very name 'Highlands' gives a clue to the most essential part of the geography of the area, the granite heartland of mountains that acted as both barrier and guardian to the people. These were the highest mountains in Britain, and the oldest. The Ice Age scoured them to great mounds of grey granite unable to hold a decent soil, with Arctic conditions prevailing on the howling plateau of the Cairngorms, while in the north-west the mountains are dropped like giants' playthings from a bitter winter sky. In between the hills were glens and straths, some deep as the cut of a hero's claymore, others broad and wide, home to countless generations of Gaelic-speaking people. Most had thin acidic soil, but some were fertile and bright, sweetened by the dung of thousands of rough-haired cattle, and much contested by land-hungry clans.

There were various passes that penetrated these fastnesses and which connected the areas of lower ground. Of these Drumochter – Bealach Druim Uachdair – was the main pass that snaked across the Cairngorms between Inverness and Perth. At 1,508 feet [460 metres] high, it was and is subject to closure through snow. There are many others such as the Cairnwell in Glen Shee between Blairgowrie and Braemar, Bealach na Bà in Applecross, Corrieyairack south of Fort Augustus, the lonely Lecht on the borders of Moray, or Killiecrankie in Perthshire. Before the days of motorised transport and metalled roads, each was a place to be respected and feared.

In the Highlands of the eighteenth century, wheeled vehicles were scarce. People moved along tracks rather than roads, and kept to the hill flanks above the often-flooded bottom of the glens. There were many tracks, and sometimes the traveller needed a guide to show him [or more rarely, her] the way.

Augmenting the high altitude difficulties were rivers and lochs. The rain in Scotland has been known to ease from time to time, but it can be persistent. The west coast in particular can be a damp place, and all that water has to go somewhere. The result is a plethora of burns, waters and rivers, each of which acted as a barrier to travel. Some had fords, some had ferries and a few even had bridges. It was not until October 1733 that the first road was built over the River Tay, at the historic town of Aberfeldy. This bridge was the crowning achievement of General Wade, who built over 250 miles of road in the Highlands in the 1720s and 1730s. As one allegedly contemporary rhyme put it:

If you'd seen these roads before they were made
You'd lift up your hands and bless General Wade

William Cauldfield completed much of Wade's work in constructing a Highland road network that eventually extended to around 1,000 miles. But these roads were not created to assist the indigenous Gaelic-speaking population; rather they were military roads, built in the wake of the 1715 Jacobite Rising with the intention of providing the military with easy access to the heartland of the clans. It is ironic that the first army to properly utilise them was that of Charles Edward Stuart, the enemy of the contemporary king.

But even when the roads were built, there was little transport on them, and the first coach service to Inverness did not start until 1811. The local people were delighted with this innovation, and probably even more so when, in 1819, a coach ran daily from Perth to Inverness and even further north. Inverness was no longer on the edge of civilisation; by the second decade of the nineteenth century there were coaches and mail gigs as far north as Wick.

If anything, the west coast is even more difficult to access than the Central Highlands. Here sea lochs hack into the mainland like the teeth of an irregular saw, with each one forcing the earlier traveller to a detour that could be scores of miles long, or to venture on a perilous ferry journey across a loch whose waters could be anything but calm. Travel here was arduous, slow and plagued by morose rain that could slither from the sea like an ever-present depression. Add a lack of accommodation, save for a scarce number of King's Houses or government inns, and only the fabled hospitality of the Highlanders remained as a salve for utter frustration.

To the west of the mainland, stretching like a shield that protected Scotland from the worst of the Atlantic gales, were the Hebrides. The island names have the golden ring of glamour about them: mystical Skye; Benbecula; Uist; Barra, where the piratical MacNeils once held sway; Lewis and Harris, along whose western coast stretched a fertile belt of arable machair land; Tiree that was famed for its grain. However, access depended on the often-fickle weather – mostly their soil was acidic and bogland provided only bog cotton and hazards. Life was hard. These islands are famed in song and story, but only since the magic quill of Sir Walter Scott turned bleakness into romance and remoteness into a virtue with tales and poetry, such as his 'Lord of the Isles':

Tis known amidst the pathless wastes of Reay
In Harries known and in Iona's piles
Where rest from mortal coil the Mighty of the Isles

When winter clanged shut its iron door on the Isles, they could be cut off for weeks at a time. Mist smothered the seascape, gales lashed the coasts and the inhabitants turned inward for solace and survival. For much of the eighteenth century people saw nothing romantic about rugged terrain, a plethora of rain, wind and the black houses with floors of mud and walls of unmortared stone. When the autumn gales blew, or the bitter winds of winter howled, the Hebrides were as inaccessible to the sail-powered ships of the period as was the moon, and the lives of the inhabitants as little understood as those in Africa. The advent of steam power in the nineteenth century opened up the Isles.

At the same time as Scott was praising the historical Highlanders and Dorothy Wordsworth made her 1803 Romantic tour in search of 'wild' scenery, at the same time as tens of thousands of Gaels donned the scarlet jacket of courage and marched to fight the French, industry was changing the face of Scotland and the Highlanders faced a harsh economic and social future. The tall chimneys and ugly bulk of factories mushroomed in Lowland towns and cities, canals and railways thrust across the countryside and old methods of agriculture vanished before mechanisation and modernisation. Highland chiefs donned the mantle of mere landlords and many lost interest in the people who scraped a living from their marginal lands. Sheep farms and sporting estates became more important than kelp farming and cattle raising; the people were seen as a burden and many were swept away to Lowland slums or across the cold emptiness of the Atlantic Ocean. The hills may have wept for them, but that was little consolation to broken families and the destruction of a culture that had endured for centuries.

These then were the legendary wild lands, the home of the untamed. Historically, these were the lands the Romans failed to conquer. Here was the Gaeltacht, the land of the Gaelic-speaking men and women whose allegiance to the authority of Edinburgh was marginal at best and non-existent at worst. Secure behind range after range of granite

Rocky terrain in the Highlands

peaks, the Gaels developed their own culture and lived their own lives. While the Lowlands had dukes, earls and lords, the Highlands had chiefs and chieftains; while feudalism evolved into industrial capitalism in the Lowlands, the clan system controlled the glens and while the Lowlands bred inventors, philosophers and mathematicians, the Highlands produced poets and scholars and warrior men. The two halves of Scotland could sometimes combine in time of war and English invasion, but the major power of the Gaeltacht, MacDonald of the Isles, was as likely to support one side as the other. In the far north, clan Mackay survived by hiring out its active young men to Continental wars. The Hebridean chiefs sent generation after generation of young men to fight for Irish potentates; many settled in Ireland, for the land was more fertile and life easier than among the rocks of the Outer Isles.

Those Highlanders whose home was closer to the Lowlands had other methods of survival. The men of MacGregor and MacFarlane or the clans of Glenshee would raid south, lifting cattle and sheep and sometimes women, so the Highland frontier was as dangerous a place to live as was the border with England. In 1493 King James IV had begun a long process to curtail the power and majesty of the Isles, and over the next two and a half centuries Gaelic culture was gradually eroded, as much by trickery, deceit and suggestion as by martial prowess and Lowland logic.

The sixteenth century saw some ferocious feuds as clans competed for land at a time of severe climate change. Cattle raiding was endemic; the youth proving their manhood in the old, traditional manner. The seventeenth and early eighteenth centuries were times of heroic warfare as a succession of Stuart kings recruited clansmen as warriors in their dynastic squabbles. Although many clans supported the rival Williamite and Hanoverian monarchs, when the British government decided to finally demolish the Gaelic culture there was no differentiation made between loyal and rebel. All suffered under the Disarmament Acts, and the old loyalties lost their importance as clan chiefs transformed into faceless landlords at the stroke of a politician's pen.

Throughout the later eighteenth and most of the nineteenth century there was terrible social upheaval in the Highlands and Hebrides. With the demise of the clan system and the sale of clan lands that were now merely huge estates, the indigenous population became largely expendable as the glens and hills were exploited for sheep farming and for sport. This was the time of the infamous Clearances when landlords, both native and incomer, removed the indigenous population, who were forced to learn new skills on the coast, relocate to the cities or emigrate.

So at the turn of the century the Highlands were at a crossroads. The old days of the clans were gone. The future of deer farms, large sporting estates and mass eviction was looming. A bevy of landlords old and new would try and bring industry to even the remotest of glens. Some industries worked, others did not. However, some of the old patterns of the land remained: there were cattle drovers and farmers, crofters and shepherds. There were also thousands of fishermen and seamen on the coast, soldiers going to or returning from the furthest corners of the Empire, carters and coachmen, factors and gamekeepers, ghillies and teachers, tailors, doctors and tinkers. But this was not a land of despondent victims, waiting for the demise of the culture that an industrialising world had rejected. The Highlanders were a spirited and vibrant people who fought back with every limited means they could. There were riots against Clearance and riots to prevent grain ships leaving harbours as the population faced starvation. Sheriff officers bearing eviction notices were ambushed and repelled so the police, army, navy and marines had to be used to control an angry population. There were upsurges in illicit whisky distillation and whisky smuggling; there were huge numbers of Highlanders involved in the fishing industry and a trickle of returned emigrants trying to install new life into the glens.

Hidden among the scattered population and infesting the dark neuks of the towns, waiting in lonely townships, huddled in black houses and crowded clachans, were the criminals. Every community and every age has its share of the ne'er-do-wells and the unsavoury; the nineteenth-century Highlands were no exception. The glens and islands were home to thieves and rapists; there was assault and poaching, sheep stealing and embezzlement, cruelty and deceit and sorrow. There were some dark and sordid murders and some high-profile killings that were reported in all the national press.

This book cannot tell all the story of Highland crime in the nineteenth century, but it will attempt to draw a picture of the underside of Highland life. It will not cover the great sweep of history that is well catalogued and documented, but the small personal day-to-day tragedies that added to the life burden that ordinary people had to carry. For the sake of this book, the Highlands is taken to mean the geographical area north and west of the Highland Boundary Fault, the area in which the majority of people spoke Gaelic, and not the present day, much smaller political area known as the Highland Region. Each tale and anecdote is true; each one was vastly important to the person or people concerned. Most can be mirrored in today's society, for although technology may alter standards and styles of living, crime, like people, basically remains the same.

2
The Whisky Wars

If one was to mention smuggling, probably the most immediate image to spring to mind would be a darkened cove with a band of men carrying kegs of brandy ashore by moonlight. That was probably fairly accurate for England, but in nineteenth-century Scotland smuggling was just as clandestine but much more home based. The practice of illicitly distilling whisky in the Highland glens and carrying it across great tracts of lonely hill and moor to the customers was so widespread that at times it was a boom industry. Naturally, the government was opposed to this practice, as every gallon of illicit whisky – known as 'peat reek' because of the smell of the fuel used in the distilling process – robbed the exchequer of taxes. There was a small army of revenue men based in the Highland towns and patrolling the glens, often backed by military or naval forces, and sometimes there were armed encounters between smugglers and the customs officers, or Excisemen. Robert Burns' poem 'The deil's awa' wi' the Exciseman' caught the public spirit of the times perfectly, although he wrote in the late eighteenth century rather than the nineteenth.

The geography of the Highlands was perfect for illicit whisky distilling. The area was remote, tangled and rough, with a plethora of clean water and fields of barley for the raw product, and peat for boiling the copper still on. Add to that a great number of under-employed people with no great love for governments that had mistreated or neglected them for generations, and it was no wonder that many Highlanders paid no heed to the Excise Laws.

Taxes for War and Whisky Distilling

The first excise act was passed in 1644, with a tax of two shillings and eight pence Scots on 'everie pynt of aquavytie or strong watterie sold within the countrey'. As a Scots pint was the equivalent of around four English pints and Scots money was considerably less than its English equivalent, the tax was not quite as burdensome as it might appear. There was a political reason for the tax: the Scottish parliament had become involved in the civil war in England and the tax was to raise revenue to pay the Scottish armies that helped defeat King Charles I. However, when that war was over, the tax not only remained in place but was increased by stages. Although the tax was partly intended as a tool to try and curb excessive drinking, it succeeded only in driving distillation underground.

The history of whisky distilling in Scotland is long and complex. Many books have been written about it, but suffice to say that legal and illegal distilling thrived side by side in the Highlands. At the beginning of the nineteenth century it was possible to buy a copper still of ten gallons capacity, complete with the worm or coil, for £5 in Campbeltown. Illegal stills could be sited anywhere, in caves by the sea, in the midst of peat moorland or in a cottage in a township, and nearly everywhere in the islands. Distilling was a co-operative operation with women often heavily involved and, in the Isles, the crofter-fishermen carrying the produce to the mainland towns.

Although they were often hampered by an inability to speak Gaelic, the Excisemen eventually became expert in tracking down the stills. However, finding the stills was not enough; the Excisemen had to destroy the cooling coils to really deal a shrewd blow to the distillers. During the French wars between 1797 and 1815, the tax rose again; recession followed and illegal distilling became a necessity rather than a luxury. In 1814 duty rose again and much larger wash stills – the containers in which the whisky was distilled – were made compulsory for legal distillation. It became much harder for small-scale legal stills in the Highlands, so illegal distillation flourished.

From that date onward the Highlands became a battleground between smugglers and the law. The distillers could make large profits, but from 1822 they also faced frightening penalties with fines up to £100, which was about twice a year's pay for a skilled man. That year the Illicit Distillation (Scotland) Act virtually declared war on illicit

Whisky Still

distillation, with the huge fine plus new powers for the Excisemen. The following year duty was decreased and a license system for legal distillation announced. Legal distilleries began to flourish.

Travellers and visitors to the Highlands often commented on the practice of illicit whisky distilling. For instance, in his book *A Tour in the Highlands and Western Islands*, published in 1800, John Leyden said that 'the distillation of whisky presents an irresistible temptation to the poorer classes.' In 1814 Walter Scott visited the Hebrides. He thought the people of Eigg were unfriendly until they realised the vessel he was on was a Lighthouse Commission yacht and not a revenue cutter. But spare a thought for the Excisemen; they had a rough job and the natives could get restless where whisky and their livelihood were concerned.

A Venial Crime

In the Inverness Circuit Court of October 1807 the Lord Justice Clerk gave his opinion on whisky smugglers: 'Smuggling is too commonly considered a very venial crime. It is considered only as cheating the King but in truth it is theft of a very aggravated kind and is attended with consequences much to be deplored.' To paraphrase the words of the Lord, he said that 'smuggling can only be committed by gross perjury by the traders or by hiring or suborning his servants to commit perjury. In other cases it can only be committed by acts of falsehood and forgery' or by 'outrageous and determined violence, often attended with bloodshed and murder'. Smuggling, he claimed, 'tend[s] more to corrupt the morals of the people than perhaps all our other vices and passions put together'. His Lordship may have had a point.

In January 1809 John and Donald Robertson of Blair Atholl realised that the local Excisemen were getting far too close to their illicit stills, and they took direct action. John Robertson was the principal as the two attacked the officers, but he could not stand alone against the forces of the law. At the Perth Circuit Court in May that year John was fined fifty shillings and imprisoned for three months and Donald was fined twenty shillings and imprisoned for one month, with neither man being released until the fine was paid.

A few years later, in October 1812, the Excisemen made a determined attempt to stem the flow of illegally distilled whisky by holding special excise courts in the towns of Inverness, Tain and Cromarty. The Justices of the Peace hit the accused with a succession of fines of £20 and more, which was an almost unbelievably high sum for ordinary people.

Fighting the Smugglers

In the early 1800s the Excisemen's pay was enhanced by the amount of seizures they made, so it was in their interests to keep a steady flow of seizures but not to destroy the industry completely, or they would lose a lucrative source of income. There were various difficulties involved in catching the smugglers. Firstly there was the terrain, for the Highlands are notoriously wild and in these days of few roads and sparse traffic the whisky was often smuggled over the hills on the backs of ponies. The second point was the danger, for the whisky convoys were often guarded by men every bit as rugged as the countryside. The third point was the clientele, for the whisky was bought by even the highest in the land, so a sheriff judging smugglers might well have a keg or two of peat reek stored in his cellar.

There was one celebrated instance where an unnamed professor at St Andrews was given a present of some illicit whisky by a student of divinity. The news spread and an entire convoy of carts set out from the glens of Perthshire, with their whisky cargo concealed by freshly cut peat. The smugglers disposed of the whole cargo and left with £60, more than a year's wages for a skilled man.

The guardians of the stills and convoys were so eager to defend their charges that Excisemen in the early period were often in danger of their lives. Whisky could be distilled in virtually any part of the Highlands but in some areas, illicit distilling was just a way of life. At the beginning of the century Glenlivet was probably the area most renowned for illicit distilling. At its height, there were an estimated two hundred small stills working openly in the glen. Nearly every cottage in Glenlivet harboured a still and the Excisemen were apprehensive to enter. If they tried to make a seizure, the entire population – men, women and boys – would attack them with sticks and stones. Parties up to twenty strong would leave the areas in broad daylight, travel to the Lowlands and go into the towns and cities at night. They carried horns of whisky and stout cudgels for defence if the Excisemen should chance upon them, but there was also a code of loyalty that seemed unique to the Highlands. Once a man had drunk with the smugglers he would never betray them: it was unheard of.

There were also rumours that some Excisemen were open to bribery. The distillers imported barley from low country farms in Banffshire and Moray so there was employment for men and horses, and rents for small farms rose as the distillers made large profits. The trade was at its greatest during the French Revolutionary and Napoleonic wars when the government was occupied with foreign affairs and had little time or money to expend on domestic matters. At times there were up to 200 nine or ten-gallon ankers a week being sent from Glenlivet to Aberdeen, Perth and Dundee.

Further north, in Ross there was an underground movement with the wives of illicit smugglers passing whisky and farm produce to the wives of Excisemen in return for information on future operations. In August 1826 the Collector of Excise sent a letter to a meeting of landowners at the Court House in Inverness. He said that illicit distilling had 'greatly increased' in the country that year with the

Strathglass area particularly notorious. The Collector also said that without the support of landowners or their factors it was not safe for his officers to attempt a seizure. He said that when the duty was reduced, sales of legally distilled whisky rose but when duty was high, legal sales slumped. At that same meeting there was mention that the revenue cutter *Atlanta* was stationed in the Moray Firth and had helped to cut smuggling.

There was no knowing when the Excisemen and smugglers would meet face to face. For example, on 16 February 1821 John Mackenzie, the farmer at Drum of Clunes, was walking with his son and a cart near Nairn. Neither was very happy when they walked straight into David Munro and George Mackay, because Munro was an Exciseman and Mackenzie's cart contained barrels of peat reek. Munro demanded to search the cart; Mackenzie refused and there was a scuffle as the Excisemen pushed forward their case and the farmer and his son resisted strongly. Sometime during the struggle Mackay took his stick and delivered an almighty crack to Mackenzie's head. The farmer collapsed and died the next day. When the case was brought to court the jury found Mackay not guilty.

The Redcoats Are Coming

With whisky smuggling endemic throughout Scotland, the government realised that the Excise service was not able to cope on its own. The military was once more sent to the Highlands to support the civil power in the attempt to erase the peat reek from the braes and glens. The army was stationed at various places in the Highlands and on the Highland border with, for instance, a body of cavalry at Coupar Angus to watch the traffic from the Angus glens to Dundee. It must have been an unpopular duty for the redcoats, stationed in lonely garrisons among the hills and knowing the locals did not want them there.

One of these garrisons was at Corgarff Castle in upper Strathdon. Today Corgarff is easily visible to drivers on the B973; if they are misguided enough to take their attention from one of the trickier passes over this stretch of the highland hills. In the nineteenth century this was a wild and lonely place, with great rounded hills and rising moorland, mile after mile of bleak heather where the smugglers drove their packhorses from still to market.

The castle was built around the middle of the sixteenth century, modernised in the eighteenth after the Jacobite troubles, and then rented to a local farmer in 1802. By 1827 the army was based at Corgarff and patrolling the passes and hills in the war against the smugglers. Two officers and fifty-six men of the 25th Foot were based there for four years, some in the old barrack rooms in the castle and others in the cottage nearby. The very fact of their presence shows how seriously the government viewed whisky smuggling.

There were also bodies of men known as 'cutters' or 'excise detectives' who acted as the hired muscle and information gatherers for the Excisemen. Yet all these precautions were useless until the government passed a law that fined the landowner or farmer on whose land illicit distilling was carried out. Another wild area was the Cabrach.

Battle at the Cabrach

The Cabrach is still a lonely area tucked away on the borders of Moray and Aberdeenshire, sparsely populated and wild when the weather is rough. In the eighteenth century it was still mildly dangerous to cross, while even in the nineteenth, when Great Britain was the foremost industrial nation of the world and a leading light of civilisation, the Cabrach had a reputation for lawlessness. The area was close to Dufftown, set at the northern fringe of the Grampian Hills and at the very heart of the whisky smuggling business. Not only was it an excellent area for distilling, with desolate hills and an abundance of good water near good farmland, it was also where the smuggling routes began to the southern cities.

In 1827 the whisky wars were at their height. In February of that year the Excise decided to have a detailed examination of the hills around the Cabrach and Dufftown to crack down on the many illicit stills. Donald McKenzie, the Riding Officer of Excise based at Elgin, was the leading man, and he called in nautical help in the shape of Peter McIntyre, who commanded the revenue cutter *Atlanta*. The Excisemen based themselves in Dufftown and shortly after nine in the morning of 6 February McKenzie mounted his horse and led them toward the Cabrach. McKenzie and McIntyre were supported by the boatswain and nine men from *Atlanta*. Six of the crewmen carried muskets; the others had to make do with cutlasses. They were crossing the bridge over the Water of Dullan when they noticed a party of about twenty men on the opposite side. Some of the men were armed and were flitting around in a small patch of woodland. McKenzie advised his men to take no notice but to continue with the task. They marched into the parish of Auchendoun and were approaching Laggan farm when a local man called out that they had best return, adding, 'There is hot work before you, lads.'

Again McKenzie told his men to carry on and not even to reply to the man. A few moments later a young girl also gave the same advice, saying the Excisemen 'had better go back as they are waiting for you in the wood', but McKenzie refused to listen. That decision proved to be a massive mistake, as the men in the wood launched an assault.

The attackers were all local men. They included James and William Gordon from Mortlach near Dufftown, James Grant and James Mackerran. With no provocation except the presence of the Excise, they lifted their muskets and fired. The shots crashed out, with the balls passing so close the Excisemen could hear the whistle of the lead. There was instant pandemonium. The cutter's crew were seamen, brave in the screaming nightmare of a high seas storm but lost here in the whispering hills; some stopped dead and refused to go any further, but others were more determined and loaded their muskets for retaliation. The gunfire had unsettled McKenzie's horse so the Exciseman had to fight to retain his seat, but he was a brave man and was determined to press ahead and complete his duty.

McKenzie called to McIntyre and two seamen and led them in a splashing foray across the Water of Dullan, possibly hoping to outflank or ride around the attackers, but somebody shouted out, 'There he is!'

There was a volley of six or seven musket shots. Some passed very close to him; some kicked up fountains of earth around the legs of his horse and one ricocheted from a stone on the ground and knocked off McKenzie's hat. Already skittish, his horse reared and fell. McKenzie was thrown and for a second he thought he had been hit. Another volley followed the first, with the shots hissing past and thudding into the ground. The horse recovered. McKenzie pulled himself into the saddle and re-crossed the water as jeering voices came to him.

'McKenzie and his horse are all blown to atoms!'

The attackers were only about sixty yards away, well within musket range. The two seamen returned quickly to their shipmates, but McIntyre was not so lucky. He threw up his arms and shouted, 'Mr Mckenzie, I am hit!' A musket ball had hit Peter McIntyre on the right side, passed though his body and emerged from his groin.

McKenzie watched in horror as McIntyre fell. 'For God's sake, desist,' he shouted out to the attackers, 'for you have shot a man!'

However, rather than desist, the attackers reloaded and fired a third volley. Somebody shouted, 'Shoot the whole of the bastards!'

Helping the grievously wounded McIntyre across the moor to the nearby Laggan farmhouse, McKenzie hoped they were safe, but the attackers followed. They surrounded the farm, pointed their muskets at the windows and threatened to finish the job they had started by burning the building down with the Excisemen inside. The smugglers eventually withdrew but with McIntyre wounded and an unknown number of hostile armed men in the neighbourhood, McKenzie thought it best to forget his search and return to Dufftown. Once his men were safe, McKenzie alerted the local authorities to pursue the attackers.

The case came to the High Court in Edinburgh in July 1827, where the two Gordons appeared. Grant and Mackerran were summoned but failed to appear and were consequently outlawed. The Gordons may have wished they had also absconded when one of the judges, Lord Mackenzie, said this was 'the most desperate and lawless case he had ever heard of' and Lord Pitmully, the presiding judge, ordered them transported for the term of their natural lives.

King of the Gaugers

Although most accounts of whisky smuggling have the smuggler as the hero, there were also strong characters among the Excisemen. One of the most notable was a man named Malcolm Gillespie, who was one of the very few Excisemen to enter local folklore.

In Scotland the Exciseman was often known as 'the Gauger', which may be from a Gypsy word and is probably the origin of the slang Scots word 'Gadgie' today. Sometimes known as the King of the Gaugers, or the Gauger of Skene – although it is likely that the smugglers had other terms for him – Malcolm Gillespie had a varied career even before he came to work in the Grampian and Moray Highlands. Born in Dunblane in Perthshire, Gillespie had originally intended to join the army, but he could not afford to purchase a commission so he turned his love of action and adventure into a career as an Exciseman instead. He started his work at the salt pans in East Lothian and moved to Collieston in Aberdeenshire, where he broke up a smuggling ring that was landing a thousand ankers of spirits a month. From Collieston he shifted along the coast to Stonehaven, where the problem was once again goods coming in from the sea. He was mentioned in an advertisement in the *Aberdeen Journal* of 25 February 1807, where he was involved in licences for game duty. Finally in 1812, after thirteen years of experience and triumph, Gillespie properly came against the whisky smugglers when he moved his theatre of operations to Deeside.

These Highlands of Aberdeenshire and Moray were dangerous, with the Cabrach and Glenlivet seething with illicit distilling and the Excisemen hard pressed to keep a lid on things. Distilling here was on a nearly commercial scale, with the product sent in convoys of packhorses to the towns of the Lowlands. Often the smugglers carried weapons and were prepared to use them to defend their whisky from the Excisemen. Naturally, the Excisemen were usually armed with pistols and swords, and had the incentive that they got a percentage of the value of their captures.

In August 1814 Gillespie came into direct conflict with the Deeside smugglers. He had moved in on a cart that held around eighty gallons of whisky, but the four men who escorted it were not inclined to give in; they retaliated strongly. Gillespie was kicked to pieces, but managed to pull out his pistol and fire a single shot. The sound alerted people in the neighbourhood, who helped arrest the smugglers.

Gillespie's twenty-year career saw him collect forty-two wounds and account for some 6,500 gallons of whisky, plus 407 stills, over 160 horses, eighty-five carts and an amazing 62,400 gallons of wash, the raw liquid before it was made into whisky. There was violence on both sides. In one fight near Kintore near Inverurie in July 1816, Gillespie slashed a smuggler named Hay across the face with his sword, while another Exciseman was unfortunate enough to shoot himself in the groin.

Gillespie had his own methods for success. Leaving the garrison of Corgarff and other military to concentrate on searching for the stills, Gillespie preferred to hunt down the smugglers as they transported the produce from the stills to the customers. In 1816, he bought a bulldog. In his memoirs, which were published after his death, Gillespie said the dog was trained to bite: 'the horses one by one, till by tumbling some, and others by dancing, in consequence of the pain occasioned by the hold the dog had of them by the nose, the Ankers were all thrown from their backs'. Not surprisingly, the smugglers took their revenge. In an encounter at Carlogie near the River Dee, they shot and killed the dog.

There are many other anecdotes about Gillespie, some perhaps even true. Local folklore tells of a farm called Seggiecrook near Kennethmont in Aberdeenshire, where a farmer named Donald Taylor, his wife, two sons and his daughter, Janet, mingled farming with whisky smuggling. At the time that Gillespie was on the prowl, the daughter was eighteen and well favoured in looks and figure; two attributes that could serve to distract even the most dedicated of Excisemen. There were also a couple of servants, including a herd called Peter Jamieson. On Banff market day Janet and Peter were left in charge of the farm when Janet saw a sheet hauled on top of a neighbour's peat stack, which was the signal that an Exciseman was on the prowl. The illicit whisky was hidden beneath the floor of the bedroom, and Janet pushed the bed on top and moved a chest to the foot of the bed. At the same time she had Peter pile an assortment of farm tools against a door in the byre to make it appear as though she hoped to block any entrance there.

Eventually Gillespie barged in, full of suspicion and bile. He poked in the chest at the foot of the bed and was on all fours looking underneath when Janet called him a 'nasty ill-bred lout' and threatened to throw the contents of a chamber pot over him unless he left her bed alone. Gillespie withdrew and searched the byre instead, finding nothing. Although the story is probably apocryphal, it serves to show the impact Gillespie had on the neighbourhood; he became a Sheriff of Nottingham character, with the smugglers as the heroic Robin Hoods.

In March 1824 Gillespie got involved in a major battle with smugglers near Inverurie. According to Gillespie's memoirs, there were twenty-five smugglers in the party, while he had only two men with him, although there were others within call. Gillespie shouted out to the smugglers to give up but they ignored him and carried on. In return, Gillespie shot one of the smuggler's pack ponies. The smugglers retaliated with a rush at the Excisemen; one smuggler raised his club to batter Gillespie to the ground, but Gillespie shot him through the shoulder and within moments other Excisemen had collected and both sides set to in a major battle. Again in Gillespie's own words: 'Bloody heads, hats rolling on the ground, the reports of firing and other noise resembled the Battle of Waterloo, but in the end the lawless desperadoes were obliged to lay down their arms and submit to the laws of their country.'

Both sides suffered casualties but the Excisemen won that encounter. However, each victory was also a small defeat, for as the number of seizures fell, so too did Gillespie's income, so he could no longer afford the lifestyle he enjoyed. Rather than tighten his belt, he began to break the law and turned to forgery to supplement what was in reality a poor wage. On 30 April 1827 John Fyfe, a King's Messenger, arrested Gillespie, who said, 'Good God, I am a gone man. Let me out of the way for a short time and I will put all right.' Unfortunately he was imprisoned instead and on 23 September 1827 he was tried, along with his clerk, John Skene Edwards. There were eight charges of forgery of bills for the payment of sums of money that varied from £15 and 15 shillings to £38 and 10 shillings. Mr McNeil, the defending solicitor, said that there was a great deal of prejudice against Gillespie in that part of the country; he asked that the trial be moved elsewhere. However, the judge refused and the trial continued.

Knowing that conviction meant execution, Gillespie pleaded not guilty. In a trial that lasted fifteen hours, bill after bill was proved to be a forgery, with Gillespie having signed other people's names. In one case a man named Joseph Low, who apparently signed the bill for £38 and 10 shillings said he could not write. In every other case but two, the real owners of the names denied all knowledge of the bills. Of the other two, one man had died before the date he was alleged to have signed the bill and the last man never existed. Gillespie had to wait for the verdict as one of the jury went walkabout, but when it came, it was guilty. Lord Pitmully said he was to be executed in Aberdeen on 16 November 1827. As his final days ticked past, Gillespie wrote a short account of his career; these memoirs remain as a reminder of the reality of an Exciseman's life.

However, Gillespie was not a man to go with a mere literary whimper. In 1896, nearly seventy years after his death, there was some controversy over the disposal of his corpse. It was supposed that his coffin was buried in the churchyard at Skene near the west door of the church, but there were rumours that the coffin was filled with stones and Gillespie's body had been handed over to the anatomists for dissection.

The Picture in the West

Smuggling was also prolific in the western side of the Highlands, with Glasgow as the magnet. Open boats from Campbeltown sailed to the Broomielaw to take whisky to the city, while parties of armed men marched from Aberfoyle to Cowcaddens. It was thought that by 1820 about half the spirits consumed in the country had been smuggled so in 1823 the duty was reduced from six shillings and two pence per imperial gallon to two shillings and four pence three farthings to encourage legal distilling and discourage illegal smuggling.

Although the situation cooled in the middle decades of the century, there were still occasional arrests, such as that of John Cameron from Knockandhu, who was fined £100 at Elgin Sheriff Court in July 1845.

The kindly sheriff offered Cameron an alternative of six months in Elgin jail.

The Later Years

In October 1875 a large-scale smuggling operation was discovered, originating in Pitlochry. The first the excise knew of it was when some casks of Pitlochry whisky were sent without the required documentation. Two senior excise officials travelled north from London and inspected the local distillery. The manager, Alexander Connacher, appeared honest as he showed them around and handed them the keys to enter the warehouses where the whisky was stored until it was properly aged. The officials were quite happy with what they found, until they entered the bonded warehouse and checked the barrels. The first cask they inspected held only water, as did the second, so they searched for Connacher, who had left them to their work, to ask for an explanation. By that time, however, Connacher had gone, taking the books and accounts with him.

At first the officials were unsure how barrels within a padlocked warehouse could be drained, but they persuaded Connacher's assistant that he would be safe from prosecution if he told them how it was done. The assistant told them that rather than be seen entering the officially secured warehouse, Connacher had made a hole in the roof by unscrewing the protecting iron bars, and clambered down. Once he was inside the warehouse he bored a hole through the wall, inserted a tube and siphoned the whisky into an empty cask, which was buried under the ground outside. Connacher and his assistant refilled the empty cask with water by the same method.

The officials found the cask of whisky underground, and more than thirty casks of water in the warehouse. Connacher and his assistant had been stealing whisky for about three months, selling the whisky they siphoned off and sending the kegs by rail but without any documentation. The officials checked the railway records to find to where the untaxed whisky had been dispatched, but as Connacher had absconded with his books, they could not find out the addresses of any future clients. A number of people, chiefly in Glasgow and Perth, were fined for receiving the stolen whisky, but Connacher vanished.

There was a revival in illicit distilling in the 1880s and 1890s. Perhaps the activities of the Highland Land League had encouraged the people to once again challenge the law, but there was no doubt that the process of illegal distilling was once again widespread. The distillers followed the same pattern of selling their wares in local villages and towns as well as in the more major population centres of Scotland. The northernmost counties, the crofting lands, seemed to be the heartland of this new breed of illegal distilling.

Even as late as the 1880s Applecross in Wester Ross was fairly remote and, as such, the inhabitants may have believed they were secure from the Excisemen. In 1886 the men of Alligin were less lucky than most as the Gairloch Exciseman and Mr McDonald, his supervisor from Dingwall, made a sweep of the area. They found a bothy concealed above the township of Alligin, and when they probed inside they found a large mash tub with 250 gallons of wash, as well as peat for a fire. The next day they found a second bothy at Lower Alligin with another forty gallons of wash.

As the illegal distillation continued to grow, on 1 April 1887 the excise service established a preventative station at Bonar Bridge. Officers were based here to patrol the surrounding area, which had become a hotbed of illicit distilling. The Excisemen found they were struggling against a wild terrain, a people with close kin connections and a distinct dislike of paying the revenue. On the first week of the month, Mr Reid, the supervisor at Brora, backed by William Hughes and William Brown of the Bonar Bridge station, searched the hills above Fearn in Easter Ross. They found a large still only 300 yards above the main road from Ardgay to Dingwall. The distillers had chosen an excellent site, with a cleverly manufactured contrivance of zinc and wood bringing an abundance of fresh water from a nearby burn and easy access to the road. This was no small-scale operation; the Excisemen found two mash tuns, one capable of holding 350 gallons; the other 250; plus fermenting tuns of sixty gallons and a whole collection of equipment which would not have been out of place in a legal distillery. To ensure privacy the distillers had canvas to erect as a makeshift camouflaged tent around the still. There were also extensive piles of draff, which revealed that it had been in operation for some time. However, it was not all success for the excise. They failed to find the copper cooling coil, the most important utensil of all. They also found no whisky.

Later that month the Excisemen launched an assault at Kilmachalmaig and Achnahannet in Ross. They came ten strong and found a number of illicit stills hidden in the hills. They returned in May and found nothing, which convinced them that the distillers had either been completely discouraged by the loss of their stills, or they had moved to another locality. The latter conclusion was correct. The more determined of the distillers had lifted their equipment and carried it, bag and baggage, into the neighbouring Rosehall area of Sutherland and were attempting to carry on business as usual.

Two of the Bonar Bridge based revenue officers, William Hughes and William Brown, travelled the eleven miles to Rosehall and patrolled the dense woods. As it was approaching midnight on Saturday, 28 May 1887, they were on their usual searches around Ravenrock Cottage. They had followed the narrow path down the west side of the gorge at Allt More, stepping carefully in the dark by the glint of a shaded lantern. The burn at the foot was low but still noisy as the two Excisemen moved on. They stopped as they heard two men talking loudly in Gaelic not far ahead. The Excisemen watched as the men descended the eastern side of the gorge, and then they splashed across the burn and walked along the eastern side before climbing up the slope, zigzagging to make the ascent easier.

The two smugglers soon vanished in the dark, but as their voices faded, another pair suddenly emerged, walking in single file along a narrow path. The smugglers and Excisemen met each other head on, but the element of surprise was all with the Excisemen. They lunged forward and grabbed a smuggler apiece; Hughes' victim carried a cask and fought back. Brown left his man to help Hughes, and the second smuggler fled into the dark.

The cask that Hughes' man carried was full of newly distilled whisky, which the Excisemen commandeered. They forced their prisoner to take them through the wood to the nearest road, where they saw another pair of smugglers. As soon as the Excisemen challenged, one of the smugglers ran, but Brown threw himself on the slower of the two and wrestled him to the ground. There was no doubting his occupation as he carried a copper coil on his back.

The Excisemen questioned their prisoners and searched the area. They found two large fermenting tuns and a variety of pieces of equipment, as well as oatcakes and other essentials. The Excisemen destroyed everything except the coil and the whisky, which they took to Bonar Bridge. Brown and Hughes had caught the smugglers when they were at their most vulnerable, in the act of moving from one distilling bothy to another.

In December 1889 the Excisemen were busy in Sutherland. They raided Flinchary, a few miles west of Dornoch, and found a coil and still in the house of a crofter. The equipment was taken to the excise headquarters at Dornoch. A couple of days later they found a still capable of producing forty-five gallons of whisky at Clashnagrave, again not far from Dornoch. The parishes of Dornoch and Creich were still noted for whisky smuggling in the 1890s. However, unlike the earlier decades when the Excisemen arrested culprits, the courts now only imposed small fines that were no deterrent, as friends and family quickly collected the amount so there was no time spent in jail. In October 1896 Inspector Willis of the Brora district subjected the areas to a vigorous scrutiny. He was aided by three excise officers from Bonar Bridge, Andrew Harper, Donald Mckenzie and William Brown. After many hours of intense searching and after probing dozens of people for information, they found a complete still, with a copper still hidden in the woodlands above Skibo Castle.

There is still illicit whisky being made in the Highlands, but not on anything like the scale of the nineteenth century. The old days of smugglers rising en masse against the Excisemen or ambushing them with muskets are in the past and history has cast a romantic gloss over those days. Now whisky is a major and legal industry and a large employer. Times have changed.

3
Theft and Robbery

Although the large-scale whisky smuggling of the nineteenth century was a distinctively Highland crime, robbery is a generic condition to the entire human race. The Highlands had their share of theft and robbery of different types, from simple theft to an international robber who targeted guests at hotels. The prevalence of theft and robbery often depended on economic conditions. When times were hard, petty theft increased as people often stole food or small items to sell in order to live. Even the quietest roads and the most innocent of travellers could be at risk.

Highway Robbery

The Reverend David Wilson must have been a happy man. It was Tuesday, 3 October 1809 and he was bowling along from Perth to Crieff in his gig. The Reverend was the minister of the Associate Congregation of Antiburghers at Balbeggie, which was a very independent-minded sect who refused to believe in any union between Church and State. He was not alone in his gig, for along with him were two young ladies, who must have felt secure in the company of a distinguished and respectable churchman. However, nobody was ever entirely safe on the roads in the early nineteenth century.

The two ladies were family friends, Helen and Barbara Barlass, daughters of the Reverend James Barlass of Crieff, and they were enjoying the Highland countryside as the horse clipped along past the wood of Cultoquhey, near Gilmerton. All three were completely at ease until a man appeared from the shelter of the wall that protected the trees. He wore a greatcoat, had a hat pulled well over his face and carried a rolled umbrella. As the gig rolled past, the man seized the reins of the horse and thrust a pistol in Wilson's face.

The girls may have screamed but the highwayman was only after money. Wilson handed over a shilling, which was a pretty meagre reward for a crime that could result in the gallows, and the highwayman grabbed Wilson's watch, leaped over the wall and disappeared among the trees. Wilson drove on, probably a little shaken up but otherwise unharmed by his brief brush with the underworld. He reported the matter to the authorities, no doubt the girls told everybody else and for a while life carried on as normal. Then at the end of the month came the news that a man had been arrested on suspicion of the crime.

The man was Alexander Campbell, a twenty-year-old deserter from the 42nd Highlanders who now worked as a weaver in the nearby village of Kenmore. The robbery of Mr Wilson was not the only crime of which he was accused. Campbell had fallen out with his previous employer, lost his job and retaliated by stealing his employer's watch, which he pawned in Glasgow. His intention had been to raise money for a gun, but instead of buying one he travelled to Stirling and stole a pistol with a spring bayonet, a supply of lead balls and a cast for moulding more. Suitably armed, Campbell set on his new career of crime. As well as the robbery of the Reverend Wilson, he was also suspected of robbing a man on the road between Cumbernauld and Glasgow. The description and method of attack were very similar but it was a completely different type of crime that ended his brief career.

Campbell had come to McLellan's New Inn in Dunfermline in Fife on 14 October 1809, distinctively dressed in a long tartan coat and light-coloured pantaloons. He stayed overnight and when he left the next morning he carried away various articles that did not belong to him, including a pair of greatcoats and a saddlebag. Next morning one of the coats and the empty saddlebag were found in a plantation of new trees beside the nearby mansion of Hillhouse.

James McBean, a King's Messenger from Dunfermline, was ordered to hunt him down. It was not too hard to ask questions about a man who wore such a distinctive coat, so McBean followed the trail and caught Campbell on the road between Charlestown and Limekilns. Campbell came quietly and McBean brought him to Dunfermline Jail, tucked him in a nice dark cell and locked manacles around his legs. That should have been enough, but Campbell proved more resourceful than expected. He unfastened his legs from the manacles, removed the bar from the cell window and was about to lower himself to freedom when Thomas Ingles, the jailer, walked in and stopped him.

The case came to the High Court in December and Campbell was face-to-face with Wilson and the Barlass sisters. While Wilson was unable to identify Campbell because of the hat that had shielded his face, the sisters were adamant he was the man who had robbed the gig. Campbell had already tearfully admitted the theft from his former employer and the robbery on the Cumbernauld Road, so the jury had no difficulty in finding him guilty. Nevertheless, a string of witnesses testified to Campbell's weakness of mind and recommended mercy, so he escaped the gallows if not the long stretch in jail. Other robbers were more successful.

Robbing the Dunkeld Bank

Dunkeld is one of the most picturesque and historical towns in Scotland. It sits at the very gate of the Perthshire Highlands, with a

Village of Dunkeld

Thomas Telford built bridge over the River Tay and a cathedral that was built on the site of a Culdee church. It is the centre of a splendid area of tall trees and beautiful hills, yet crime could strike even such an idyllic place.

On Sunday, 13 October 1822 thieves struck at the Dunkeld branch of the Commercial Banking Company. They forced one of the windows, broke through the reinforced interior shutters, prised aside the iron cross guards and grabbed a box full of banknotes and gold, silver and copper coins. The thieves carried the box as far as the east end of the bridge, where they forced it open and fled with the contents. The chief suspects were Charles Brown, a chapman or peddler, and his wife, who both vanished shortly afterward. They were never caught. Other robberies were more violent.

Robbery with Violence in Inverness

Angus Fraser was a respectable man who worked as a porter, a man who carried bags and baggage from passengers at the Caledonian Coach Office in Inverness. When he was not at the coach office he often waited at the door of Bennet's Hotel in case a guest wanted him to carry his luggage.

On 14 September 1823 a gentleman named William Cameron travelled by coach from Rothiemurchus to Inverness with a large trunk including his clothes, personal papers and a number of documents and bills. When he arrived in Inverness it was a dull evening with no moonlight and only the oil-fed streetlights that reflected from the fast-flowing River Ness and gave a flickering yellow illumination to the streets. Cameron left the trunk at Bennet's Hotel and asked Fraser to carry it off to his lodgings in Church Street. Fraser added the trunk to the other bag he was already carrying and set off.

When he left the hotel, two men lurched from the lobby and offered to help, but he turned them down. Instead he handed the smaller item, the bag, to John Fraser, whom he knew, hoisted the weighty trunk onto his shoulders and set off. As he staggered toward Cameron's lodgings the two men again approached him and offered their services. Again Fraser turned them away and continued, with the trunk seeming to get heavier with every step he took. The very moment he arrived at Cameron's lodgings, somebody dragged the trunk from his shoulders. The force of the attack knocked him to the ground. He scrambled to his feet, but one of the men pinned his arms to his sides while the other disappeared with the trunk.

The man with the trunk shouted out, 'Come away, we have a spoil,' and handed the trunk over to a man that Angus Fraser recognised as being William McTaggart. Angus Fraser staggered as the man who held him released him. He recovered and saw his attacker make a grab for the bag that John Fraser carried. Angus Fraser lunged at the thief and called out 'Murder!', which was the generic shout for help at the time. On this occasion the cry worked as John Callander, the guard from the *Duke of Gordon* coach, rushed up to help. Between the two of them they managed to subdue and hold the attacker. He was identified as James Robertson and the man who stole the trunk was Robert Simpson. For a while there was no trace of either Simpson or the trunk, but Callander and Fraser searched around and found the trunk abandoned in a nearby lane later that night; the lock was broken open and the contents missing, except for a mess of scraps of paper.

Callander whistled up a man named David Mackay and asked him to help arrest Simpson, who was hiding in the house of a man named Bernard Woods. McTaggart was also arrested. He was a soldier of the 1st Foot, the Royal Scots, and until that day was believed to possess a good character.

The case came to the High Court in Edinburgh but the Lord Advocate said that there had not been enough violence in the crime for it to be called robbery. However there was little doubt as to the theft by Robertson and Simpson. He added that there may be some doubt as to the part McTaggart played. The defence did not try and deny that Robertson and Simpson had taken the trunk, but said it was just 'to torment the porter', in other words, a practical joke. The jury found Robertson and Simpson guilty of assault and theft but asked for mercy, while the case against McTaggart was found not proven. Despite the jury's plea the judge, Lord Gillies, ordered both to be executed in Inverness on 21 February. As Simpson left the court he declared his innocence: 'I saw the robbery and Angus Fraser observed me standing at the jail, but I had no hand in it, as I shall answer to God.'

Animal Theft

With the Highlands being a largely rural area, livestock was often targeted by thieves. In May 1833 Margaret Dunbar of Elgin was found guilty of horse stealing. She was a young woman in her twenties, but she had taken a fancy to a black mare that belonged to James Young, a farmer from Dallas, a few miles to the south. She tried to resist the temptation but her friends persuaded her that she could get away with it. Instead she was transported to Australia for seven years.

At the same court the same judge, Lord Moncrieff, sentenced a man named Gustavus Sutherland to nine months in jail for sheep stealing. That sentence seems benign compared to the spring Circuit court at Perth in 1820 when Alexander Reid was sentenced to death for the same crime.

Robbing a Deaf Man

George Boyne was the watchman on duty in George Street, Inverness, on Sunday, 24 May 1835. The day had passed as quietly as Inverness Sundays normally did, but around quarter past three he saw a deaf and dumb man named Alexander Whyte walking toward the vennel, otherwise known as Drum's Lane. Boyne thought nothing of it until about half an hour later when a woman ran up to him and reported that he was wanted in the house of Elspet Jack in the Vennel.

Boyne and another watchman named Roderick MacLean entered Elspet Jack's house. As well as Jack there were two other women, including Ann Brebner, a young man named Alexander Gibb and Alexander Whyte himself. As Boyne entered, Whyte was running around the house, obviously agitated.

Boyne asked, 'What's the to do?' and Jack told him that Whyte had stormed in 'raging about a pocketbook' but she knew nothing about it. Jack must have known Whyte well to understand the agitation of a man who could neither speak nor hear. She said that Whyte had seen some coppers lying beside the fireplace and tried to pick them up until Jack said they were hers and she had no more.

When Whyte saw that Boyne was a policeman, he pinioned his arms and pointed to Gibb. For a moment Boyne was nonplussed, but he realised that Whyte was indicating that Gibb had held him in that manner. Once he was sure Boyne understood, Whyte lifted a long knife from the kitchen table, and then loosened his breeches. Again, Boyne was unsure of the purpose of the pantomime, until Whyte pulled out his pocket and made a sawing motion with the knife. Boyne worked out that Whyte meant Gibb had used the knife to cut a hole in his pocket. When Whyte made a clasping movement with his hands and pointed to Elspet Jack, Boyne guessed that he meant Gibb had robbed him of a purse with a mouth that opened and closed and held money.

Boyne decided it was best to make further enquiries, so he ordered everybody present to the watch house and searched Jack's home more thoroughly. All he found was a straw hat and a few pennies and halfpennies until he scrabbled about in the straw of the bed, where there was a purse with five shillings in silver. He also found a pocketbook. When he was shown both items, Whyte indicated that the purse was his but showed no interest in the pocketbook.

The case came to the Circuit court at the end of September 1835, where a number of witnesses helped unveil the mystery of the stolen purse. The first witness was a woman named Catherine Teal, who saw Jack holding Whyte by the arm and forcing him up the stairs to her house. Whyte was obviously reluctant as he tried to hold onto the wall and the railings. Jean Allan lived in the same vennel; she heard 'a great struggling and crying' that lasted, she claimed, 'for about an hour'. People's perceptions of time could be elastic at such occasions. It was a woman who shared the same room who ran to fetch the watchman.

The court called upon a number of people who emphasised that Whyte understood the necessity to speak the truth; they said he knew the concept of right and wrong, and the punishment for people who lied when under oath. After that Whyte gave his oath and Robert Taylor, teacher at the deaf and dumb institution, acted as interpreter for him as he was questioned.

Whyte indicated that he was walking along the street sometime after three in the afternoon. A woman approached, took him by the arm and brought him to a house. He smoked for a while there, offered her some money and tried to leave. As he stood up, Jack grabbed the tails of his coat and hauled him backward. Gibb held him by the elbows from behind and Jack cut the pocket from his trousers and stole his purse and his money. He indicated that there had been five shillings in his purse and that Ann Brebner had not been involved in the robbery.

The jury had no difficulty in finding Brebner innocent and Gibb and Jack guilty, but when they asked for the judge to show mercy 'considering the peculiar circumstances of the case', Lord Moncrieff, the judge, voiced his confusion. He said the only peculiar circumstance was the robbery of a poor deaf and dumb man but promised to take the request into consideration. He thought eighteen months' imprisonment for Gibb and Jack was appropriate, and Lord Medwyn agreed and gave that sentence.

The Silver Snuffbox

For centuries St John's Town of Perth was a frontier town. It is situated on a crossing point of the River Tay and was an important port in the Middle Ages. It was a walled town, and with reason, for English armies besieged it more than once and the wild Highlanders were only a few miles away. In the nineteenth century the threat of siege had long gone, but the Highland hills still threw their shadows over the crowded streets. Sometimes the roads north and west were the scenes of crime.

Toward the end of December 1843 Colin Drummond welcomed two visitors into his inn, a few miles west of Perth on the Crieff road. They had a couple of drams of whisky, but when Drummond requested payment, they produced a silver snuffbox and asked if he would like to buy it. Drummond had a close look at the box and realised that the name engraved on it was that of a near neighbour. When the men asked if wanted it or not, Drummond said he had no need of it just then, but he knew a man who might want to buy it.

The men said they were quite happy to meet this possible buyer and waited patiently when a messenger ran off to fetch this third party. Naturally, the newcomer was the owner of the box; he grabbed it and immediately pocketed it. The two men demanded it back, claiming they had bought it honestly. The dispute became loud as tempers rose and there were threats of violence. Quite by chance, two Perth detectives – then called criminal officers – happened to be passing and they arrested the supposed thieves. They ended up in jail for theft.

A Dram for the Redcoats

The army had an ambiguous part in the Highlands. On the one hand, they were the redcoats who had taken part in the suppression of the Jacobites in the eighteenth century and who supported the sheriff officers and police in evictions as well as hunting for whisky smugglers. On the other hand, there was intense pride in the exploits of the Highland regiments in the various wars of the Empire and against France and Russia. However, the feelings of the soldiers themselves were rarely considered. For a man from a city to be stationed at one of the isolated outposts in the Highlands, subjected to inclement weather, lack of facilities and a difficult terrain, life must have been hard.

That was the situation in which a detachment of the 27th Foot, the Inniskillings, found themselves during the early months of 1847. The main force was stationed in Fort George, east of Inverness, but a unit of a sergeant, a lance corporal and six privates were ordered to garrison Fort Augustus, halfway down the Great Glen. This small detachment remained in Fort Augustus from March to September before being recalled to Fort George.

The Governor of the fort was Captain Spalding, and he had left the sergeant to take control of things while he indulged in more pleasant pastimes than his military duties. Once the soldiers had departed for the north he returned to Fort Augustus and invited round a friend. Captain Spalding was known for his hospitality, for he had laid in a supply of fine wines, ale and good quality whisky, all of which he kept in the powder magazine of the fort. It was quite secure there from predators, he believed, as it was under lock and key and, anyway, there was a garrison of soldiers.

Captain Spalding was pleased when the magazine door was still secure and he selected a number of bottles from the first rack without any problems. He was less pleased when he pulled out the first in the second row and found it had been emptied. So was the second bottle he extracted, and the third. By now Spalding was concerned. He checked his stock of beer: an entire hogshead had been emptied and carefully returned to its position. In a near panic he did a stock check and found he was short of fourteen dozen bottles of port, seven and a half dozen bottles of sherry, four dozen bottles of fifteen-year-old whisky and thirty-two gallons of ale.

The only people who could have stolen the drink were the garrison. As the sergeant was teetotal, attention shifted to the privates whose quarters had been immediately above the powder magazine. Two men, Privates John Short and George Thomson, were arrested and jailed.

Shop Theft

Shop assistants have always been overworked and underpaid. In the nineteenth century they could work twelve- or fourteen-hour days for six days a week. Occasionally one would try to augment his or her wages by removing items of stock without bothering about the tedious process of payment. One such was James Macbean. In 1849 he was employed as a porter in W& A Johnston, drapers of Inverness. Nobody will ever know the exact quantity of his employers' goods that he appropriated, but the thefts are thought to have started on 1 July 1849 and continued until 4 May 1850.

He was a prolific thief, but not a particularly clever one, for he went straight to the pawnshop and pledged the stolen items for cash. When the local policeman did his routine checks of the pawns, he found that Macbean was a very regular customer and did some background investigation. The result was inevitable. When the police searched Macbean's house they found forty-three pawn tickets, and he was sent to Australia for the next ten years.

Robbery at the Lecht

Even today the Lecht pass over the Cairngorm Hills from Braemar to Moray can be demanding. At around 2,000 feet above sea level, it is always one of the first to be closed with the winter snow and even in fog and heavy rain the steep, winding road can present difficulties. However, driving in a locked motor car on even the worst of days cannot compare to the rigours of walking the Lecht in the nineteenth century when there were other hazards apart from the weather.

On the evening of Wednesday, 18 July 1861, a young woman named Isobel Kennedy was walking from Tomintoul to her job as a servant in the hamlet of Bridgend in Strathdon. Her route took her over the steepest and loneliest part of the Lecht. Just as she began the descent from the summit a man emerged from the heather moor at the side and, without saying a word, attacked her.

Kennedy was a fit and strong woman. She defended herself vigorously but the man was bigger than her and vicious. He knocked her down and tried to rape her but she screamed and fought back, raking him with her nails and kicking furiously. He stepped back. She struggled up. He knocked her down again, kicked or punched her and stole her purse with its contents of a few coins and sundry receipts and bits and pieces. Kennedy continued to struggle even when the man robbed her and eventually he ran off, leaving her battered, bruised and penniless, but still defiant, on the lonely road of the Lecht. She managed to reach the nearest farmhouse, and the farmer took her home and alerted the resident policeman at Corgarff.

Constable Paterson was not used to serious crime so this was an opportunity to show his skills. He mounted his horse and urged it up the Lecht to search for the attacker. He saw nobody suspicious as he rode, so dropped into Tomintoul to ask the resident policeman for his assistance. The Tomintoul constable put his local knowledge to good use and suggested they call at a quiet mill farmhouse about five miles away, where a stranger was known to be. They stormed open the door and arrested a man who claimed to be searching for work on the railway. He gave his name as James McKenzie. A quick check with the records of the Aberdeenshire Police found out much more about this man. They knew him as Smith, not McKenzie, and told Paterson he had lately been in the Aberdeenshire Militia. More interestingly, just two years before he had been found guilty of a criminal assault on a young girl on Deeside.

The case came before the Perth Circuit Court in September. This time the attacker gave his name as Alexander Dodds and claimed to be eighteen years old. He was charged with assault with intent, and also with robbery. Dressed in a white moleskin jacket and standing at the bar with a glower on his face, Dodds pleaded guilty only to the robbery charge. Lord Neaves, the judge, told him that if he had pleaded guilty to both he would have a very long sentence. As it was, he was given six years' penal servitude.

Robbing the Post Office

Although the nineteenth-century Highlands were largely a rural area, there were pockets of urban areas where crime followed the same pattern as in towns in other parts of Scotland. As well as the usual backstreet assaults, drunken brawls and sneak thefts, there was a quota of white-collar crime. In September 1881 the post office in Inverness was the target of a robbery when a registered letter containing £900 was stolen, a colossal amount of money for the time.

Provost Fraser was the local agent for the Commercial Bank. On 21 September 1881 the agent of the Balmacarra branch of the bank asked him to forward £900, with £500 of it in five-pound notes and the remainder in one-pound notes. Fraser was not surprised as it was quite usual for him to send such amounts. He ordered his bank clerk to send the money and told the Balmacarra branch that the money was on its way. It was not long after that Alexander Falconer, the accountant of the Balmacarra branch, sent a telegram to Fraser, informing him that the money had not arrived. Naturally, there was consternation and William Allan, the bank's accountant, sent the details to the Procurator Fiscal.

Allan had ordered the bank teller, James Huntly Macdonald, to take the money from the secure box and make up the correct amount. Macdonald did so, putting the five-pound notes and the one-pound notes into separate bundles, and then William Middleton, an apprentice teller, bundled them into a single packet, sealed the packet and handed it to Allan to tie with a string. Middleton carried the packet to the post office and had it registered at about quarter to five.

There were two men on duty at the post office at the time, Robert Sim and John Proudfoot. Sim marked the packet with a blue pencil and placed it at the bottom of the window, which was the normal routine for registered letters. When questioned later he could not remember seeing any string or twine around the packet.

Sometime before seven that evening a clerk named John Gibson took the registered letters away to John Proudfoot in the sorting department. Proudfoot worked on the other side of a barrier behind the counter. Any registered packets not delivered that day should have been securely locked away in a glass-fronted locker at about half past nine at night. That night the key was left in the lock. The man who locked up had custody of the key. Roderick Reid, the chief clerk, had seen Proudfoot still working after eight at night, and wondered why, as Proudfoot had been looking forward to attending a concert by Sims Reeves, a popular operatic singer, after work. Proudfoot laughed and said, 'The charge is too heavy. I can't afford it.'

The Balmacarra packet should have been sent with the Skye mail on the train at nine in the morning. When Alexander Mackay opened the office next morning he noticed the registered locker was open and the key in the lock. Mackay was the sorting clerk who placed the registered letters on the train, but he swore blind he saw no registered packet for Balmacarra.

It seemed obvious that the registered packet had been stolen at some time in the post office in Inverness. The police arrested Proudfoot and he appeared at the Circuit court in Inverness in late March 1882, looking very smart and apparently unconcerned at the seriousness of the charges against him. He pleaded not guilty as his defence tried to show that there was virtually no security at Inverness Post Office. Mackay admitted openly that 'grave irregularities were frequently committed' at the post office. However, the evidence pointed to Proudfoot as the guilty party, and he ended up with seven years' penal servitude.

Squaddies on the Rampage

The Highlanders are justifiably proud of their soldiers. The Highland regiments of the British Army have earned a reputation for bravery and toughness second to none. However, sometimes there was an obverse side to the military. Highland regiments often contained a few bad apples whose behaviour could be less than angelic. For example, the Sutherland Highlanders who formed the famous Thin Red Line at Balaclava had rioted in Liverpool a few years beforehand and had the reputation of a troublesome and violent regiment.

Of course, not all soldiers were in love with their profession. In June 1877 three privates, Robert Fleming, John Cunningham and John Macalpine, all based at Fort George, decided they would be better in a different job. However, it would be impossible to desert while wearing the red tunic of a soldier, so the men decided to obtain some civilian clothing. A soldier's pay was so meagre that buying clothes was out of the question, which left theft as the only option. They left Fort George in the late afternoon of Saturday, 16 June and made their way to the manse at Petty. They noticed that a window was left open but waited until dark before they entered.

They pushed the window open as far as it could go and climbed into the house. There was a slight scare when one of the servants called out, 'Who's there?' but then there was silence and the three men had peace to search the house. They concentrated on the ground floor, as the inhabitants slept upstairs, but still managed to find a fine supply of clothes, three walking sticks and enough food to keep them going for some time. However, they were pursued by the police and caught a few days later. At the sheriff court on 11 August they were each given three months' hard labour.

Other squaddies were equally prone to break the law. In 1882 the Cameron Highlanders fought in the Egyptian campaign where the Highland brigade earned new laurels at the battle of Tel el-Kebir, but the conduct of some of the regiment at home led to trouble on the streets of Inverness. In November of that year a draft of reinforcements for the Camerons was stationed at Fort George.

On Saturday, 10 November 1882, a number of soldiers were given leave before going out east and they descended en masse to Inverness. Naturally, some decided to visit the public houses and accept the hospitality of the local civilians. When two of these men, Privates Murray and Lawson, left one particular pub, one of their drinking companions realised his watch and chain had been stolen and told the police. With so many soldiers roaming the town, the police were hard pressed to find the culprits but eventually arrested both men, who had separated. One of the soldiers came at once but the second fought back, so a third Cameron Highlander, Private Henderson, rushed to help his comrade, knocked a policeman to the ground, grabbed his baton and ran off with it.

All three men were eventually arrested, with Henderson picked up at Culloden, a few miles to the east of the town. He was fined £5 for his regimental loyalty while the other two were jailed.

Theft of a Shovel

Sometimes the authorities got it wrong and used the full power of the law to hammer down a very petty theft. Such a case occurred in November 1882 when Sheriff-Substitute Simpson faced John Mackintosh across the Inverness courtroom floor. Mackintosh was a labourer from Portree in Skye and he was charged with the theft of an old shovel on 27 July. The police accused first offender Mackintosh, arrested him and immediately thrust him into a cell in Portree Police Station. The case of the battered shovel was duly recorded, written down and the documents sent to Edinburgh. The Edinburgh authorities ordered a full jury trial at the Circuit court in Inverness.

After six weeks in the cells at Portree, Mackintosh was sent to Inverness to face the sheriff and fifteen good men and true of the jury. He had no sooner arrived than the Procurator Fiscal dropped the charge. Mackintosh was sent back to Portree, where he was again charged with the theft of the shovel. Together, Mackintosh's fares and upkeep in the cells had cost many times more than the value of the shovel.

Robbing the Tourists

It was all Sir Walter Scott's fault, of course, helped by Queen Victoria and Prince Albert. Where once the Highlands had been seen as a dismal place full of dark mountains and populated by cannon fodder for French and Imperial wars, by the time Sir Walter and Queen Victoria had finished with them they were a Mecca for tourists and a splendid place for sportsmen to decimate the local wildlife.

At the turn of the century books such as Sarah Murray's *A Companion and Useful Guide to the Beauties of Scotland* and Dorothy Wordsworth's *Recollections of a Tour Made in Scotland* were masterpieces of travel writing, but the reader still saw Highland Scotland as a wild and distant place. By the latter half of the century, transport improvements had ensured that spending a season in the Highlands was an accepted norm for the upper part of society, while many of the middle classes had also become interested in travelling north. A plethora of tourist hotels had sprung up for those with money to spend and time to spare. Money equates with temptation, and that often drags crime in its wake.

In early 1883 hotels in the Highlands were rocked by a succession of thefts and for a while it was believed that a gang of professional thieves were on the tourist trail. The first hotel to be hit was the Alexandra in Oban, where £35 was stolen at the end of July. The second was the Great Western Hotel in the same town, where £27 was stolen on 3 August. The thieves were then believed to have decamped to the Loch Awe Hotel, where they left with a diamond ring, and then moved to Braemar. At the Fife Arms in that royal place, a gentleman lost the huge sum of £200 on the night of 12 August, while a black lace shawl was also reported missing from the nearby Invercauld Hotel.

Three suspects were charged. There was forty-nine-year-old James Edward Lyon, who had fought as a Union Army lieutenant in the American Civil War. He claimed United States citizenship and demanded that the US Consul be informed when he was arrested. There was Eliza Thorpe, a twenty-year-old woman who acted as his wife, and there was forty-one-year-old unmarried and enigmatic Joseph Dowling, who claimed to be a club manager and travelled for the sake of his health. Although all three were charged with the theft in the Alexandra Hotel and the Fife Arms Hotel, only Thorpe and Lyon were accused of the other three offences.

Lyon and Thorpe had come to Edinburgh first, masquerading as husband and wife. They stayed at the Balmoral Hotel for a while, and caught the train for Oban in Argyll. Their first victim was Arthur Miller, an oil and lamp merchant from London who stayed at the Alexandra Hotel in July that year. He claimed to have left his wallet with £45 in Bank of England notes in his coat pocket overnight. Being a cautious man, he had kept a record of the numbers on his banknotes and could identify them. At that time Lyon and Thorpe were guests at the same hotel under the pseudonym of Captain and Mrs Lyon.

The second victim was Donald Beith, a Writer to the Signet. He had arrived at the Great Western Hotel in Oban on 31 July, coincidentally the same time as Lyon and Thorpe had booked in, again as Captain and Mrs Lyon. On the night of Friday, 3 August, Mr and Mrs Beith locked their bedroom door, and Beith left his trousers over the back of a chair with some money in the pocket. During the night Mrs Beith thought she heard somebody tapping on the door, and called out, 'Come in,' but nobody entered. A little while later Beith also heard a noise. When he lit a candle he saw their bedroom door was wide open. Mrs Beith woke and thought she heard somebody moving and talking in the room next door, but at that time there was nobody in their room. Beith closed the door but it was not until next morning that he discovered that the money he had in his pocket, around £27, was missing. Lyon and Thorpe stayed in the room next door. Dowling was also suspected of being in Oban at this time.

At this stage Lyon and Thorpe seemed scot-free, but they had already aroused suspicion. Mr McArthur, the proprietor of the Alexandra Hotel, had been in the business long enough to recognise a guest who was not genuine, and he contacted Inspector Campbell of the Oban Police. The inspector telegraphed the police in Edinburgh and Glasgow with a description of the supposed Captain and Mrs Lyon and a request that a detective be sent up to Oban, but at that time the city police took no action. However, Campbell was not a man to give up and he ordered one of his own men to follow the Lyons so he knew exactly what they were up to.

From Oban, Thorpe and Lyon moved to the Lochawe Hotel at Dalmally, another small tourist town in Argyll. They stayed there from Saturday, 4 August to Monday, 6 August. While they were there, a fellow guest, Mrs Thomson from Cheltenham, realised her diamond ring had disappeared. She claimed she had put the five-diamond ring on the dressing table on the Sunday evening but the next morning it was not there. She heard a noise during the night but saw nothing, and her door was still locked the next morning.

Duncan Fraser, who owned both the Lochawe and the Dalmally Hotels, saw Thorpe and Lyon in company with Dowling that weekend, and all three had left the same day, but not together. The Lyons were in so great a hurry that they left behind their luggage at the station, but later sent a wire asking that it be sent to Edinburgh's Waverley Station. Campbell again contacted the Edinburgh Police and asked that they look out for the couple.

In the meantime, the Lyons' next stop was the Braemar Hotel in Braemar, where a lace shawl was the first thing to vanish. Janet Nicol of West Hartlepool was the legal owner, and she had left it in the drawing room on Saturday evening, but realised it was missing on the Sunday morning. She was not the only visitor to have property stolen that weekend. William Marchant of Richmond took his family to the Fife Arms Hotel in Braemar on 12 August. He had brought £200 in Bank of England notes with him and stayed in room number 14. Dowling was in room number 16. On the Sunday night Marchant put his money in his coat pocket and hung the coat on the back of the bedroom door.

Suspicion fell on the quiet, solitary Joseph Dowling, who had left the hotel shortly after the theft was discovered. Originally Dowling's wife had been expected to join him at the hotel, but she had not turned up. Dowling had left for the Deeside village of Ballater on the half past ten coach. Inspector George Crae of the Aberdeenshire Police was waiting for him at the railway station at Ballater and arrested him there and then. There was already some doubt about Dowling. Mr Henderson, the Chief Constable of the Edinburgh Police, had seen Dowling acting suspiciously around Register House and discovered that he was a failed businessman who kept bad company in London. When Inspector Crae searched his prisoner he found a pocketbook that fitted the description of that lost by Miller. That gave the police some proof of Dowling's involvement and further enquiries revealed he had been seen talking to the self-styled Captain Lyon and his lady. The Aberdeen Police telegraphed their colleagues in the capital with their suspicions and when the police checked further they found the Lyons had stayed in the same hotel as Dowling in Edinburgh.

In Braemar the Lyons had ordered a carriage and pair and had also headed for Ballater, where they had caught the same train to Aberdeen that Dowling had intended to travel on. The Lyons continued to the Palace Hotel in Edinburgh, where they had previously stayed.

Although they had intimated their intention of remaining some time, when the proprietor put up a notice warning the guests that there had been a spate of thefts in hotels, the Lyons very quickly said they were going to leave.

To the police it appeared that the Lyons were about to abscond, so on 16 August 1883 Captain Henderson and Detective Inspector William McEwan came to the Palace Hotel. The police escorted the Lyons to a small room and sat them down. Henderson pointed out that they had been in or near every hotel where there had been a theft and said it was either an 'unfortunate coincidence' or they had been directly involved. Henderson said that Lyon should name somebody in Britain who could vouch for his 'respectability'. At this point Lyon claimed his US citizenship and demanded the right to see the US Consul. Although Lyon produced letters of credit from a bank in Boston, Massachusetts, the Edinburgh Police produced a telegram from the Aberdeen Police that stated that they had a warrant for the arrest of both Lyon and his wife. They were taken separately from the hotel to the police office.

When they were searched, Captain Lyon had two pairs of small curling tongs, or pincers, which could be used as a picklock, in his pocket. When these were tested, they were found to easily open the doors of the Braemar and Oban hotels. He also had some Bank of England notes. The numbers of the notes corresponded with the numbers Arthur Miller said had been stolen from him in Oban.

When Thorpe was questioned she admitted she was not Lyon's wife. The police searched her but she had little money in her possession. However, a man named George Calver claimed he had found a roll of seven Bank of England ten-pound notes lying on the ground in Bank Street at the head of the Mound. The police thought it possible that Thorpe could have disposed of the money on her way between the Palace Hotel and the police office in the High Street. However, Calver was a bit of an opportunist and rather than give the notes to the police, he handed them to a man named Albert, who reset them. Calver gained £35, exactly half the value.

The Lyons were taken to Oban to be interrogated by the local police about the hotel robbery. When Sergeant Donald Cameron of the Argyll Police searched through Thorpe's possessions, he found Janet Nicol's distinctive black shawl in a trunk of her clothing. It seemed that the evidence was mounting.

The case came to trial in the High Court in Edinburgh in November 1883. The suspects' stories did not quite match. Lyon claimed that Thorpe was his wife and he had given her any money she had. Lyon also said a bank in Piccadilly in London had issued the banknotes to him. Eliza Thorpe made no claim to marriage with Lyon, but said the two of them had been travelling together through Britain and the Continent for the past three years. Dowling merely said he was in no way connected to any hotel theft.

On summing up, the judge, Lord Young, pointed out that the charge of stealing the diamond ring had been withdrawn, and that although the pincers could be used as a picklock, the police had never tested them on Marchant's, Beith's or Thomson's doors. Lord Young also said that there was no physical evidence to say that Thorpe had been involved in any theft: the evidence that the shawl was found in her trunk he conveniently brushed aside. As far as Dowling was concerned, Lord Young agreed he had been in the Fife Arms Hotel, but there was no evidence at all to connect him to the robbery. The fact that he knew Lyon and Thorpe was not in dispute, but neither was it a criminal offence. Lyon and Thorpe had been guests in quite another hotel and there was no evidence to say they had ever entered the Fife Arms.

With the judge clearly advising in favour of Thorpe, the jury took only ten minutes to find her not guilty. She kissed Lyon soundly before she walked clear of the court. Lyon was found guilty of stealing £45 from the hotel in Oban and was sentenced to seven years' penal servitude, with the judge saying he 'had gone into the hotel as a thief, and a thief was about the meanest character that existed.' Dowling was found guilty of reset and given one year in jail, with hard labour. Lord Young regretted that he could not sentence him to more.

Robbing a Vagrant

Some robberies caught the public attention. Such a robbery occurred in February 1886 when a group of men and women stole £200 from the house of Charles Fraser at Ballifeary. The factor that made this robbery interesting was that Fraser was a vagrant. He had spent much of his life just wandering around the country begging. People had given him a penny here and there, and sometimes they had handed him a small packet of meal, which he had sold. He had kept the money he made, storing it as he wandered, and then putting it in the Royal Bank of Scotland. In 1885 he rented a house at Ballifeary from a carpenter named Neil Cameron.

Fraser was careful to keep the money in the bank, but one day he drank too much and the police were called. Cameron and a woman named Margaret Macrae told him that if he was arrested again the police might take all the money he had in his bank, so Fraser withdrew over £200. He counted it out on the night of 25 February and then retired to bed. After a few moments the bedroom door opened and Margaret Macrae, heavily disguised, entered. She persuaded Fraser to hand over his money. The woman subsequently vanished.

However, the police made enquiries and discovered there had been a conspiracy to rob Fraser: Cameron, Farquhar Macrae, Margaret Macrae and a husband and wife team of William and Christina Macrae.

As Margaret Macrae was an aged widow she was given two months in jail while the others got three months.

Sweeping Up the Loot

William Daly was a chimney sweep with a secondary occupation: he was also a thief, which netted him the resources to live the high life. On the night of 18 August 1888 he noticed that the back window of the Royal Ordnance Hotel in Inverness was open. The temptation was too much and he slipped in to see what he could find. Within a few moments he had pocketed five shillings and a bottle of brandy. He left undetected and happy. Two nights later he again saw the window was unlocked so slid it open and slipped inside. This time he found another unattended bottle of brandy and a box of biscuits, as well as a small bundle of documents he thought he may be able to sell at a later date. However, his propensity for food and drink proved his undoing on this occasion.

He found a table, spread a selection of cold meat and biscuits on it, opened a bottle of whisky to help wash things down and settled himself happily for a midnight feast. And that was how the police found him. He was given thirty days in jail to cure him of his delights in free hotel fare.

Housebreaking

Sometimes the thief just saw his opportunity and snatched at it, but at other times there were people who got into a habit of robbery. In November 1899 John Long was a labourer in Inverness but he had a second occupation of housebreaking. He was selective in his targets and concentrated on Falcon Square, where the Eastgate Shopping Centre now stands. Long was a fast worker, with eight robberies in the space of a few days. He preferred to rob offices and got away with a little over £10 in cash, as well as an eclectic selection of shoes, screwdrivers, keys, a pistol, a silver pocket flask and a number of old coins.

The Inverness Police knew Long of old as a thief and a robber, and were soon knocking at his door. He appeared before the sheriff court in early February 1899 and Sheriff Scott Moncrieff sentenced him to nine months with hard labour.

Highway Robbery in Shetland

On the evening of Saturday, 7 January 1899, William Laurensen, a member of the Royal Naval Reserve, was walking home to Delting. He was returning from a drill evening at Fort Charlotte and was pretty pleased, as he had just drawn his pay. He reached Girlata, about ten miles from Lerwick, and was on a lonely stretch of the road when three men loomed through the gloom. When he asked what they wanted, two of them attacked him.

Laurensen fought back. He smacked one of them over the head with his walking stick so hard that the stick broke and punched another, but the odds were too great against him. The man he hit with the stick pulled a knife and ripped open Laurensen's coat, then plunged his hand inside his pocket and stole £14. Once they had the money, all three men fled.

Once Laurensen recovered, he returned to Lerwick and reported the attack to the police.

Robbery and theft was as much part of life in the Highlands as anywhere else in the country.

4
Riots

Before the twentieth century, riots were common throughout the country. Most were targeted towards a specific purpose as people denied a voice showed their frustration in the only way available to them. There were a multitude of reasons to riot, from protests about bread shortages to expressions of political dissatisfaction. In the Highlands many of the riots occurred when people objected to the landlord attempting to remove them from their homes. The century opened with a targeted riot.

At the extreme south-west of the Highlands, Kintyre points its green finger toward Ireland. This peninsula has experienced more than its share of battle, famine and disease, and the opening of the nineteenth century saw it once again on the cusp of a disaster. In February 1801 there was hunger in the hinterland, so when ships carried grain away from the main town of Campbeltown, the locals decided to intervene. It was not so much a riot to destroy property, but a gathering of very concerned and hungry people trying to gain the means of subsistence by the only method they could. A number of people were arrested and ordered to appear before the Circuit court at Inveraray. When one of those involved, Duncan Sellers, failed to arrive he was outlawed, John Beith was given two months in Inveraray Tolbooth, Hugh Lamont six weeks and Mary Darroch one month in the same place.

That was not the only riot to take place in Campbeltown. In March 1813, when Britain was heavily involved in her life and death struggle with Bonaparte's Empire as well as sparring with the pugnacious Republic of the United States, the Royal Navy sent Midshipman James Hendry from Glasgow to Campbeltown to press as many seamen as he could. The Impress service was never popular and when they grabbed a number of seamen, the local population rose in protest. The mob gathered piles of stones and started a barrage against the gang, who retaliated with a volley of musketry. A fourteen-year-old girl named McLean was shot and killed, and Hendry had to stand trial at the High Court.

Soldiers on the Rampage

Throughout the nineteenth century the British Army had a large Irish contingent, partly because of the number of regiments based in and recruiting in Ireland, and partly because of the lack of employment in that country. The Irish made excellent soldiers but, in common with all other redcoats in the British Army, they had a tendency to alcoholic overindulgence. There were occasions when this heavy drinking resulted in trouble for the town in which they were stationed. One of the expected days for Irish soldiers to seek alcoholic solace was St Patrick's Day, 17 March, and in 1809 the town of Perth, at the southern fringe of the Highlands, was rocked by a sudden explosion of Irish soldiery.

There were two troops of Dragoons stationed in the town and the English and Scots soldiers joined the Irish trying to drain the pubs dry. Fighting drunk, they armed themselves with cudgels and roared into the streets, attacking anybody who happened to get in their way. Men, women, young or old, the Dragoons were not particular who they knocked down. They chased people into their houses, assaulted shopkeepers who were in the act of closing up for the night and generally made a nuisance of themselves.

However, the military were not the only people who rioted in the Highlands, often with genuine reason.

The Durness Riot

The Highland Clearances was one of the most tragic episodes in the history of Scotland. Tens of thousands of people were evicted from their homes, sometimes with months of notice, often without. As examples of the heartlessness of some Highland landowners, the Clearances still have the power to chill. However, there were some occasions when the victims fought back. The question today is: who were the criminals, the people who tried to defend their homes, or the landowners who sought profit at the expense of humanity?

In 1841 the women of the Ceannabeinne area of Durness in the far north-west of Sutherland defied the sheriff officers who tried to issue eviction notices. The township had fourteen houses containing fifty people and was a thriving community, but the landlord, James Anderson, wanted the people off his land. As so often during the Clearances, the sheriff officer came with the writ of eviction when all the men were absent, possibly cutting bent grass – marram grass – for thatching.

A woman climbed the hill Cnoc nan Uamhag and shouted a warning that James Campbell the sheriff officer was coming. The writ he carried ordered the people out of their homes within forty-eight hours. The women had other ideas. They grabbed hold of him, kindled a fire beside the road and made Campbell burn the writ, with one woman named McPherson allegedly holding his wrist so that he had no choice but to burn it himself.

The people knew that the authorities would not let matters rest there so a number took to the hills and lived rough in a cave for months. Superintendent Philip McKay of the Dornoch Police was the next man to visit the township, and it is possible that he wanted to persuade them to submit peacefully. Instead the men and women greeted him with a shower of stones and abuse that chased him back. To help him on his way, a piper played 'Caberfeidh' as a reminder that the men of this area had played more than their part in national and international wars.

McKay tried to whistle up support. He got a Messenger-at-Arms and three ancient veteran soldiers. The soldiers were sent ahead to reconnoitre, but when they reached Hope Ferry they realised the level of opposition and soon hurried back to Tongue and advised McKay not to go into the Durness area.

McKay was nothing if not persistent, and he signed up fourteen special police to back him. The whole attacking force gathered at Durine Inn at Durness on 17 September, all prepared to serve the eviction writs on the inhabitants. About 300 people from the scattered townships of the far north-west gathered in opposition. They formed up near the inn but did nothing aggressive at first. About forty-eight men tried to reason with Campbell the sheriff officer first, asking that the evictions not be carried out on the Sabbath, but Campbell was having none of it.

By that year the Highlanders knew that resistance was usually countered by the landlords calling up police or military reinforcements and ultimately failed. Even so, the Durness people were not prepared to do nothing and slink quietly away. At about ten at night a gathering of men attacked, burst into the inn, disarmed the police and sent them away.

Campbell, the sheriff officer happy to evict women and children from their homes, was not so happy when faced with men. He fled and hid amidst the rocks. McKay and the Procurator Fiscal tried to remain and tough it out, but the locals did not want such people in their neighbourhood and escorted them away from Durness. As so often before, an initial victory over an evicting landlord only postponed the inevitable. Sheriff Lumsden threatened to bring the 53rd Regiment from Edinburgh to force the evictions, but this did not happen. There was an official investigation, and some of the press backed the people of the threatened township, but in May 1842 Ceannabeinne was cleared of its people. However, the tenants at nearby Durine and Songomore were allowed to remain.

Today there is a trail and some interpretation boards at Ceannabeinne, telling something of the story of the Durness Riot, and the lonely wind soughs softly through the ruins of what was once a place filled with love and laughter.

There were many such justified riots as the people of the Highlands resisted mass evictions, but in other places in the Highlands rioting seemed to be a way of life.

Rioting Troubles

Beauly, February 1847. During the destitution years of the Hungry Forties there was a ship loaded to carry grain away from the town. Fearing starvation, the local people objected. When a number of carts arrived to carry away the grain, the people grabbed control of them and threw one over the edge of the quay. The drivers backed away quickly and called for help.

The authorities reacted by calling in the army, and seventy men of the 76th Foot marched over from Fort George. Faced with the massed muskets and glittering bayonets of the redcoats, any resistance faded away and five men and one woman were arrested and taken to Inverness Jail. The rest of the town could only look on in hungry despair as the grain ship sailed away.

There were also grain riots in Burghead and Elgin in February 1847. In early March the crowd at Fowlis prevented a shipment of grain leaving, for the famine struck the West Highlands. That same year in Invergordon a grain ship was ready to leave but a mob swarmed aboard during the night, unloaded the grain and hauled the carts from the pier to discourage any further attempts. As usual, the authorities called in the army. Other ports along the coast of Ross were similarly affected.

Following similar disturbances at Thurso that same year, a company of the 76th Foot marched into the town and took over the Masons Hall. The authorities called up 100 Special Constables to escort carts to the Shore to load grain. By that time the people had taken an open boat and moored it across the entrance to the river so that the grain ship could not leave. The Specials moved the boat away and marched beside the grain carts, as a crowd of women and boys gathered at the Braehead and voiced their displeasure. The prospect of possible starvation angered the crowd so they began to throw stones and abuse. The sheriff tried to talk them into submission but when they responded with hisses and more stones, he read the Riot Act and sent for the 76th. The soldiers fixed bayonets and slowly advanced on the crowd until they backed far enough away for the grain to be loaded. The people could only watch as the ship sailed away.

However, all these instances were one-offs and these towns soon reverted to their normal peaceful existence. But there was one northern town where riots seemed almost routine.

Riot Town

Situated nearly at the furthest extremity of north-east Scotland, Wick may seem an unlikely place for a riot, but within a period of thirty-two years Wick experienced four major riots, had the army called out and created questions in Parliament. That is not bad for an isolated town of just a few thousand souls.

The first riot was about politics.

At Inverness Circuit Court of April 1827 David Mackay, William Corbett and the shipbuilder William Bremner were accused of mobbing and rioting to obstruct the freeholders of Caithness from attending a meeting to elect a Member of Parliament. The elections were on 5 July 1826 and in those days before the 1832 Reform Act there was no idea of a secret ballot. Two candidates contested the

Caithness seat, George Sinclair and Captain James Sinclair. There had been rumours that there was to be a protest against those who chose to vote for the Honourable Captain Sinclair, and wild stories of taking those who supported him out to sea until after the election, but nobody expected anything to happen.

That morning, people packed the streets of Wick, some on their way to vote, but most just supporters or onlookers, as there was no concept of democracy at the time.

When Sheriff William Horne of Stirkoke, about three miles outside the town, left Murray's Inn to go to the courthouse to vote for Captain James Sinclair, a section of the crowd recognised him. 'There's Sheriff Horne,' somebody shouted. 'Seize him!' Horne yelled out, 'What's the meaning of this?' turned and fled back to the inn, where some of his friends had gathered. Somebody snatched at his watch chain, somebody else tried to knock off his hat.

He joined the other supporters of Sinclair and they tried to get to the courthouse to vote but the crowd prevented them, shouting loudly. There were about 3,000 people in the crowd and the knot of Sinclair supporters huddled together at the outer staircase of the inn, wielding sticks and whips and hoping for a chance to ease through. Instead, the mob grew more violent; some carried sticks and they threatened to attack James Sinclair's supporters, with Sheriff Horne being particularly singled out. The James Sinclair supporters retreated inside the inn and the mob remained outside, shouting and firing pistols.

About one in the afternoon the voters decided to force their way to the courthouse but the mob outside had increased in size and noise so the voters did not leave the inn. Instead they tried to send a message to the courthouse to delay the election; that failed as well. The sheriff officers grabbed a man from the crowd – that was probably William Corbett, who later appeared in court – but the arrest infuriated the crowd so the threats of violence increased and the prisoner was released.

About half past two Horne attempted again to get to the courthouse, with an escort of gentlemen and constables. This time the mob had decreased, and although they still shouted and waved flags supporting George Sinclair, Horne succeeded in getting through and casting his vote.

Apart from William Bremner, who was a shipbuilder and a respectable gentleman despite his alleged involvement in the riot, the rest they found guilty and sentenced to three months in jail in Tain. Wick was deemed too insecure to hold them. James Sinclair lost the vote; George was the Member of Parliament.

A Supposed Bodysnatcher

The second riot occurred in 1832 and was very much specific to the period. It was in that year that Asiatic cholera first appeared in Britain. People had watched its progress across Europe and waited for it with dread. Nobody knew how cholera spread and there were all sorts of theories, from it coming in dark clouds to the disease being a judgement from God. There was a call for a day of prayer, and some believed that it was a disease that would only affect the lower classes. The suddenness of a cholera attack and the horrible manner in which it killed its victims terrified the often still-superstitious population.

Cholera arrived in Wick in July 1832, bringing the usual quota of terrible sickness and a number of deaths. As nobody yet understood the cause of the disease, it was not surprising that people cast around for some logical explanation. Wick was at the centre of the herring industry and each summer thousands of fishermen packed the town while the fisher girls worked at the herring gutting and packing. However, the local people did not blame these strangers for the deaths. At that time Scotland was still raw from the murders of Burke and Hare in Edinburgh, who killed people and sold the bodies for medical research. Ill feeling against Dr Knox, who had bought the corpses from the body snatchers-come-killers, ran high in Edinburgh but was less strong in the north. Dr Allison, also from Edinburgh, ran the local hospital in Wick, and he seemed to have settled in nicely when an influx of fishermen from the Lothian ports of Fisherrow and Musselburgh arrived. These men recounted tales of resurrection men and murder.

Now that the men from Wick were faced with unexplained deaths from cholera, they may be excused for blaming an Edinburgh doctor who had recently come to live amongst them. The Lothian men wondered if the dead men had both been patients of Allison, and wild tales spread that the doctor hoped to send regular consignments of bodies south to Edinburgh to be dissected. The rumours spread and grew in the telling; soon some of the more credulous believed that Allison had poisoned the local drinking wells and would murder all his patients. The crowd that gathered outside the hospital, however, was not comprised of local men, but of fishermen from the Lothians and Fife. They roared their suspicions, shouted down Allison's attempts to plead his innocence and shouted out, 'Murder him! Off with the murderer!'

As the crowd grew, some men tried to attack the doctor, and when the chairman of the board of health stepped in he also became another target of the mob, which now was over 1,500 strong. They invaded the quarantine hospital and carried the contents off to the cholera hospital as Special Constables were hastily enrolled and sworn in. The Specials mounted patrols to guard the doctor and the chairman of the health board through the dark hours of the Highland night. Apart from some idle stone throwing that smashed a few windows, there was no damage done, and Dr Allison very sensibly tendered his resignation and fled Wick for the south in the morning mail coach.

That small episode led to a question being asked in Parliament with the Lord Advocate saying that measures were being taken to prevent any similar riots taking place. But Wick was to see more and worse.

Rioting Fishermen

The 1840s were bad years. A succession of bad summers meant poor crops and in the Highlands, where much of the land was marginal at best, that meant destitution or starvation. In the midst of this, merchants still exported grain from the east to the cities of the south. In some instances, the people in east coast ports took direct action to try and prevent grain ships leaving, while there were families starving in the north.

Castletown, on the northern coast near Wick, was one of those ports. *Fisher*, a Leith vessel, had come into Castletown to load up with grain. People from the surrounding district gathered together to try and prevent this food from being exported. George Traill, the local MP, together with Sheriff Greig, rushed to Castletown to try and prevent any violence. Although they tried to shout out what they considered reason to the crowd and ordered them back to their homes, it is unlikely that they were even heard above the general hubbub. Some of the crowd grabbed whatever weapons they could and made a rush to board the vessel and prevent her leaving. The mate drew a knife and tried to force them off, but somebody thumped him with a stick and he fell to the deck and lay there, still and bleeding.

Seeing the mate lying prone, the crowd thought he had been killed and promptly fled. That gave George Traill time to organise the less volatile people in the area to try and defend *Fisher* and called for reinforcements from Wick. He had the mate carried ashore to be looked after.

The next day a man toured the area, sounding a horn in the age-old way to gather the crowd. They marched across the Sands of Dunnet under a banner as the horn blared to the arc of the sky and echoed to the wind. Nevertheless, they did not attack anybody on the ship, but instead filled her hold with ballast so no grain could be loaded and they tried again to block her from leaving the harbour.

But of all the ports, perhaps Wick had the greatest uproar. There as well there was a vessel waiting at the quay at neighbouring Pulteneytown for the shipment of grain. On Friday, 24 February 1847, a piper stood on Bridge Street, summoning the people around him. A crowd gathered, growing all the time as they marched through Pulteneytown to the North Quay. They blocked access to the quay with a barricade of boats and, job done, marched back to Wick proper. They held a meeting at the Market Cross to decide on their next step before returning to the quay, where they filled the hold of the ship with rocks and stones to prevent grain being loaded.

Perhaps wisely, the authorities did not interfere, but late that night two sheriffs, Greig and Thomson, together with Mr Henderson, the Procurator Fiscal, ventured to the quay. By that time the crowds had dissipated and there were only a few stragglers hanging about.

The weekend passed quietly, but the forces of the law had not been idle. They had alerted the garrison at Fort George and on the Monday evening a body of 106 men from the 76th Regiment embarked on the Lighthouse Steamer *Pharos*. They crossed the Moray Firth but as there was a big sea running in Wick Bay, *Pharos* anchored off Ackergill, a couple of miles north where today a luxury hotel sits.

An officer braved the surf to come ashore and consult with Henderson, the Procurator Fiscal. The infantry remained on board, impotent and possibly seasick as they waited until there were small boats to take them ashore. However, the local fishermen refused to help. Henderson and the sheriffs scoured the local harbours for suitable boats, found two, crewed them from the local coastguard and some hands off *Pharos* and brought the men ashore in small groups.

The men of the 76th formed up on Ackergill beach with the waves crashing behind them and *Pharos* swinging to her anchor in the bay. Captain Evans Gordon led them on the march south to Wick, with fixed bayonets to overawe the civilian population who had dared to try and feed their families. Instead of being scared into submission, the population of Wick were probably irritated by the presence of armed men in their town. The soldiers halted in front of the courthouse and stayed the night in the Temperance Hall.

To augment the military, the sheriff called on the respectable men of the town to enrol as Special Constables. There were around 200 volunteers, complete with the long staffs that went with the job. On Wednesday afternoon the sheriff and magistrates led the combined force of military and Specials to the grain store in Pulteneytown. They acted as escort as a cart was loaded with grain and trundled slowly to the quay. A couple hundred local men watched as the heavily escorted cart arrived at the ship. The spectators may have smiled as the ship's master confessed he was not yet ready to load up, and the Specials began to get restless and demanded permission to go back to their occupations.

When the Specials melted away, Lieutenant Brett and twenty men of the 76th remained to guard the ship as night fell, but now the crowd gathered again. Men, women and children formed opposite and around the small party of soldiers. Around seven in the evening one of the 76th fired his musket as a signal for help, and the remainder of the company formed up and marched to the quay. Sheriff Thompson and his officers joined the crowd and read the Riot Act. This Act ordered any gathering of twelve or more people to disperse within the hour or the forces of the law could be turned on them. It is unlikely that many of the crowd actually heard the Act being read, and just as unlikely that those who did hear actually completely understood the implications. However, the sheriff may have been alarmed by the mob.

Splitting into small parties, the soldiers advanced on the crowd with bayonets levelled, injuring a few as they forced them back. Three of the crowd were arrested, the remainder withdrew and the majority of the soldiers marched back to their makeshift barracks. There seems to have been some resistance from the people as the soldiers retreated, or perhaps when the army was dispersing the crowd. There were various stone-throwing episodes and one woman attacked an officer with a stick. He slashed her with his sword.

The Provost, Josiah Rhind, was heavily involved on the side of law and order. He was in his mid-forties, was the agent for the Commercial Bank and had bought the local Sibster Estate. He and Sheriff Thompson were part of a group that were passing the academy where a portion of the crowd had reassembled. Immediately the crowd saw the military, or perhaps the provost; they began heaving stones down the brae towards them. There were some skilled stone-throwers among the crowd, for both the sheriff and the provost were struck in the first volley. That personal assault seems to have unbalanced the sheriff, for he ordered the soldiers to open fire and in the half-light of the Caithness evening a volley of musketry cracked out. There would be jets of red flame and thick white powder smoke in the streets, and cries rang out.

Two people were wounded, William Hougston, a foreman cooper who was so severely wounded in the wrist and hand that his fingers had to be amputated, and a girl named MacGregor, who had a flesh wound on her arm. Hougston had not been part of the crowd, but was passing by on his way home from work. Hougston and MacGregor were some 200 metres apart at the time, which suggests that the 76th were pretty poor shots if they used the volley fire that was normal at the time. Two other men were hit in the boots as they sat watching the fun; neither had taken part in the attack and neither were injured. Not surprisingly, the musketry caused panic throughout the town as mothers ran shrieking for their children, husbands for their wives and people ran to escape the army.

Duty done, most of the 76th returned to barracks, a small guard remained at the ship but the rest of the night passed quietly. On the following Thursday the electors, the respectable people of the community, met in the Town Hall and protested against 'the reckless step' taken by Sheriff Thompson when he called 'out the military when not the least symptoms of any outbreak were manifested'. They also said they would support the authorities, and they asked for the military to be withdrawn. Then they moved the barriers from the quay so the boat could be loaded with grain.

Again the disturbances in Wick caused questions to be asked in Parliament. The Lord Advocate said that the military had been 'distinguished by the greatest patience and humanity' and the provost and sheriff believed the grain ship would be scuttled in harbour and the crew thrown overboard. The Lord Advocate added 'that information turned out to be but too true' and the sheriff was a man of 'firmness and humanity'. Hansard, the official record of Parliament, reported that the House applauded and approved his words. Mr Hougston may not have agreed.

Of the two men arrested, Lord Moncrieff and Lord Cockburn sentenced one, John Nicholson, to ten years' transportation while the other, John Shearer, was sentenced to ten months in prison for being on the street after the Riot Act was read.

In France, where there were far more serious grain riots, over 400 people were arrested, but King Louis Philippe pardoned them all and blamed 'the badness of the times' rather than the individuals. Clemency from the Scottish authorities was rather less generous. However, in November Sir George Grey reduced Nicholson's sentence to two years in jail on the condition he pledged to keep out of trouble for two more years on his release.

Fishermen on the Rampage

Eleven years later Wick was again rocked by riots, which this time were occasioned perhaps by a culture clash and rivalry between people from the east coast and those from the Hebrides. Wick was an old established town with a Norse name, but it blossomed with the

Scottish herring boom of the nineteenth century. In 1828 there had been encounters in the town between Hebridean and local fishermen, but that paled into nothing beside the furore of 1859. By that year each summer brought thousands of fishermen to the town from many ports of the north. Many came from the Hebrides, and their Gaelic language and island culture were not always welcomed in Wick. At the end of July and beginning of August there were days of bad weather which kept the fishing fleet – mostly open boats – in harbour and the crews idle. Having thousands of men and boys hanging about a small town with nothing much to do, on top of local and cultural rivalries, is a recipe for trouble.

The figures are formidable. In the first week of August that year there were on average over a thousand boats out every day after herring, with six men and boys manning each boat.

The nearly inevitable outcome started over what was a trivial incident as two boys argued over a piece of fruit. One boy was from Lewis, the other from Pulteneytown. Even what fruit it was is disputed between the Hebridean and the Wick men; the Hebrideans claim it was an apple, while Iain Sutherland gives the Wick version in his pamphlet 'The War of the Orange'. It seems that the two young lads disputed the fruit in Market Square on the first Saturday in August, but as the Pulteneytown boy got the upper hand, a couple of Hebridean men joined in against him. Naturally, some Wick men backed their young lad and the argument turned into a free fight that wrecked the peddlers' stalls in Market Square and ended with the crowd surging toward Bridge Street.

The Hebrideans called the sequel the *Sabhaid Mhor*, the Big Fight. According to the Hebridean version, the fighting lasted days and there were stabbings as well as sundry other injuries, with men from both sides being thrown into the harbour. Shopkeepers locked their doors and put up shutters, people crossing the bridge were knocked down and the town was in general fear.

© Author's Collection

This bridge, built in 1877, occupies the site over which Hebrideans and east coast fishermen fought in 1859

The Hebridean version claims that the police arrested fourteen-year-old Malcolm MacLeod as well as a number of other men from Lewis, but did not arrest anybody from Wick. The Hebrideans were unhappy at this situation and one, Donald Mackenzie, whistled up the crew of his boat, unstopped the mast and used it to batter down the door of the local jail so the prisoners could escape. Hundreds, perhaps thousands, of Hebridean fishermen, some of them fresh from a Free Church service, mobbed the streets of Wick, hurled stones at the windows of the courthouse and generally caused mayhem.

The Wick authorities swore in around 150 Special Constables, who attacked the Hebrideans as they clustered around the courthouse. The Specials chased the Hebrideans across Bridge Street to the Pulteneytown side of the river, where the Hebrideans broke down a fence to make weapons. About eleven at night they charged back over the bridge and there was another full-scale fight with the Specials, with injuries on both sides before the Hebrideans returned back to Pulteneytown. Captain Macdonald, master of the revenue cutter *Princes Royal*, sailed to Wick from Ackergill Bay, armed fifteen of his crew and prepared to intervene on the side of the Specials, but the trouble died down overnight before he was required.

Some of the Specials used their batons with vicious force on anybody who looked like a Hebridean, including men with Bibles in their hands as they walked to church. In retaliation, the Lewis men targeted anybody who did not speak Gaelic, with the Specials being their favoured victims.

According to folklore, one man, Robert Macdonald, was celebrated for his strength. He was said to have broken up herring barrels to make staves as weapons for the Lewismen. Hebridean folklore, which is often as accurate as any history book, follows the adventures of this reputed strongman. When Macdonald heard the police were looking for him, he ran from Wick and tried to hitch a lift on a carriage and pair. The driver ignored him, so Macdonald leapt in, threw the driver and passenger out and drove the carriage to Poolewe on the west coast. He caught the ship to Stornoway but had to go into hiding when he heard the Island Police were also searching for him. He eventually went to sea and was drowned in the Thames.

The less sensational accounts of the riot say that of the thousands of Highlanders and Hebrideans in Wick, only about 150 were involved in the continuation of the riot, but 150 angry islanders would be a formidable foe. There were also rumours at the time that the Hebridean fishermen in Lybster would also cause trouble, but that proved unfounded. Men from Lewis were suspected of being the most prominent of the rioters.

Not surprisingly, many of the townsfolk locked themselves in their houses and did not venture into the streets while the bands of angry Hebrideans roamed around for the next few days, growling against the Specials. Some Wick men bought or borrowed pistols for their own protection. The sheriff requested military help and 100 men of the York Rifle Regiment sailed from Edinburgh in the steamer *Prince Consort*, augmented by the bluejackets of HMS *Jackal* and the crew of *Princess Royal*, with the Specials doubled to 300 men. It was not until the authorities called in both military and spiritual help in the person of the Reverend George Mackay of Tongue that the riot simmered to a close. Mackay must have been a brave man to venture into the war zone.

After a few days of seeming quiet, the trouble broke out again the following Saturday, with a nastier – even sadistic – twist. While Wick itself remained quiet, after nine that night a host of east coast fishermen had gone on the rampage in Pulteneytown armed with knives. Eleven of the islanders had been stabbed; one man had three wounds, including two in the scrotum, and others had their faces slashed. Many of the Hebridean boats were sitting in the harbour and crowds of youths and men stoned them as they lay windbound and helpless. The

Hebrideans retaliated, of course, and the whole town was a mess of fighting fishermen from the east and west coast.

When Sheriff Fordyce heard the news, he tried to get across to view events for himself, but battling bodies blocked the bridge. Injured east coast men, often drunk and usually bleeding, came back in a steady stream, and the sheriff knew he had to call for help. The steamer *Jackal* landed a body of soldiers, backed by bluejackets from *Princess Royal*, and while the police cleared the stone-throwers, the military restored order, if not tranquillity, to the streets.

While the original riots had led to indignation against the Hebrideans, the ugly stabbings had turned the sympathy around and now the decent people of Wick sympathised with the Gaels. On the Sunday the police arrested a fisherman named Reid, who they suspected of being involved in the stabbings. After that last vicious flurry the town seemed to be shocked into calmness. There were no more major riots in Wick.

However, Wick was not the only Highland town that experienced the wrath of rioting fishermen. That same year of 1859 there was trouble in Stornoway when three police – all the force the authorities could muster – had to cope alone. They wrestled a number of fishermen into custody and held them in their own houses until they could be more safely lodged in jail. In 1863 there were 205 arrests in Stornoway, mainly herring fishermen, so they were not a breed renowned for their quiet and orderly habits.

Rioting seemed to have died down as the nineteenth century wore on, but there were other crimes in the Highlands, and the law-abiding majority needed some force to protect them.

5

The Highland Police

As of 1 April 2013, Police Scotland is the national police force of Scotland. It consists of a number of divisions, including the Highlands and Islands, Argyll and West Dunbartonshire, and Tayside. All of these areas include parts of the old Highlands. This chapter will attempt to examine the growth of the police forces that covered the areas of the Highlands and Islands.

Police in the nineteenth-century Highlands had a difficult time. For a start, the terrain was against them, with tiny communities scattered across hundreds of square miles of wild country, so one officer had a huge area to police. Secondly, there was the nature of the crime, with whisky distilling and poaching occurring in some of the most remote areas, where a solitary bobby was unlikely to tread. Thirdly, there was the nature of the policeman's lot in supporting sheriff officers in evicting tenants across the land. Such actions did not make the police popular, and nineteenth-century policing depended on information and support provided by the public.

Assaulting the Police

The early police were often subject to assaults by disgruntled members of the public, but the authorities were aware of the problem. In October 1832 Hugh Lumsden of Pitcaple, Sheriff of Sutherland, held a criminal court at Dornoch. During the trial of a number of people for various assaults, Lumsden commented that the most serious had been an attack on 'officers of the law in Assynt'. He mentioned in melodramatic language that if there was any area where officers deserved protection it was Assynt, as there had recently been a nasty murder there of a peddler named Murdoch Grant. Lumsden continued saying that if it was not for the officers of the law 'the blood of the innocents might have been still streaming in the mountains of Assynt, calling aloud but in vain for vengeance'. Despite the poetic rhetoric, the message was clear.

A typical example of an attack on the law was in September 1833, when Colin Macgregor of Little Green, Inverness, was found guilty of assaulting a watchman in Inverness and sentenced to nine months at the Circuit court.

Even later in the century the police were often in danger from assault. For example, on Monday, 17 October 1878, the Inverness Police were escorting a prisoner from the police court to the prison when two men, Duncan Macdonald and James Bain, rushed them and tried to rescue the prisoner. The police resisted and there was a stern struggle. The two escorting policemen eventually won and took the prisoner to the jail in front of an excited crowd, then pursued Bain and Macdonald through the streets of Inverness. The two would-be rescuers ended up before Bailie Macdonald, who gave them three months with hard labour.

Early Forces

While the major cities and towns of Scotland formed their police forces early in the century, the forces of the rural Highlands were decades later. In the early nineteenth century each local authority was permitted but not required to create its own police force. The first official police force in the Highlands was that of Inverness-shire, which began patrolling on Hogmany 1840. Given the propensity for excessive drinking on that night they presumably experienced quite a baptism of fire. The force of nineteen men did not cover the town of Inverness itself until 1841, when it merged with the town police, only to split again in 1847 and finally reunite in 1968.

Ross-shire had two police forces, one for the west and one for the east side of a county that stretched from coast to stormy coast. The Wester Ross force was formed in 1850 and based at Dingwall, the old Viking capital only twelve miles from Inverness but some forty miles from the west coast, while the Easter Ross force was created a few years later, with its base at Tain. The Ross-shire Police was also responsible for the island of Lewis, with its strong and sometimes turbulent fishing population, while Inverness-shire had to try and police Skye, Harris and the other Outer Hebrides.

Sutherland, the old Southland of the Norse, was always a place with a mind of its own. In common with all other areas of the Highlands, at the beginning of the century there was no overall police force to care for this county of huge hills, vast distances and isolated communities, but many of the villages had a limited local force to watch for thieving and the occasional verbal or physical dispute.

Dornoch was one such independent-minded burgh with its own police force. By 1828 a man named James Stewart was the resident police officer, with a salary of £25 a year; he lasted until 1841, when Philip Mackay took his place. In 1844 John Sutherland, the Helmsdale sheriff officer, became police officer, with the princely wage of £15 a year. Two years later Golspie got its own policeman at £10 a year and in 1847 Philip Mackay at Dornoch was promoted, or at least titled as Superintendent, which was the normal rank for the chief constable.

In 1845 Sheriff Lumsden put forward a proposal for a police force for the whole of Sutherland, but there was no movement in this direction yet. The piecemeal, village-by-village policing continued. Bonar Bridge was next to have a constable in December 1846. In 1853 Scourie was given a police constable, making the Sutherland force five men under a superintendent. Their primary tasks were chasing vagrants out of their area, arresting drunks and stopping casual brawls, as well as transporting their prisoners to the jail at Dornoch. The parish of Tongue joined the policed areas in 1854 with a policeman at Farr, and in May 1857 a new superintendent, Peter Ewan, took over.

It was not until the 1840s that the Perthshire County Police was formed, with its headquarters at Marshall Place in Perth. The force of thirty-three men had to cover all of northern Perthshire, preventing poaching and illicit whisky making, as well as the common crimes of theft and assault. As seems common with all early Victorian police forces, many of the officers were heavy drinkers so there was a steady stream of dismissals over the first few months of the force's existence.

Argyllshire was another area of tiny communities with single officers, divided by wild hills and lochs. For instance, Hugh Livingstone policed Ballachulish in the 1840s, while Colin Campbell looked after Duror and John McGregor was based in Port Appin. He was the first of a line of dedicated family men who lived and worked in that area.

General Police Act

In 1857 the General Police Act made it law that each burgh and county should either have its own force or combine with a neighbour to create a unitary force. To organise and control the police, the position of

Her Majesty's Inspector of Constabulary was established with the authority and power to hold an annual inspection of each force and issue a report to the government. If the force was efficient then the government would pay for a quarter of the uniforms and wages, so there was pressure for good quality policing. This Act took effect from March 1858. The Act suggested that the county should provide uniforms and each officer should be paid a wage fitting to their responsibilities and rank in society and also that they should be decently housed. They were to be 'respectable', which was the buzzword of the nineteenth century.

Nineteenth-century society was multilayered but with one fundamental split between respectable and non-respectable. This split did not depend on money – a working man could be respectable – but on lifestyle. A respectable person would be hardworking, conscientious and sober and would preferably attend church. A policeman with all these qualities would not only be considered reliable, but he would also be seen as displaying the values of the Establishment to the people in his area.

Public support was invaluable in the policeman's job, for he depended on people giving him information about happenings when he was not present. However, in many parts of the Highlands it was years before the police were accepted. The policeman was often seen as a uniformed representative of the landlord class rather than a guardian against crime. That feeling was particularly strong in the crofting areas where it was part of the police duties to escort sheriff officers and other officials when they served eviction notices. Such a feeling was detrimental to police efficiency.

The Black Isle, that peninsula just north of Inverness, had no efficient police until the Cromartyshire Constabulary was founded in 1869. The independent-minded people of the Black Isle chose to ignore the demands of the 1857 Police Act. Twenty years after its foundation the Cromarty Police merged with the Ross Police to form the Ross and Cromarty Constabulary. The town of Dornoch, with its tiny population, did not have its own police force.

At the time of the 1857 Act, the Sutherland Police comprised the chief constable, with wages of £150 a year including house and horse, one sergeant and seven constables who were paid about £39 a year, plus uniform and footwear allowance. The county of Sutherland was divided into eight police districts, with one policeman for each. This miniscule force had to police a landmass of well over a million acres, with each man supplied with a uniform, a baton, a lantern, handcuffs, tape measure and a pair of compasses. They were banned from entering pubs when on duty, as would be expected.

Sheep Stealing

Sheep stealing was obviously a major worry as the 1859 Rules and Instructions were particular that the Sutherland Police watched for that crime. Sheep farms were not popular, particularly where they competed with crofting for land, and sheep were sometimes mutilated as well as stolen. In the 1830s there were threats against sheep farms on Skye posted on church doors. In 1841 the Reverend Norman MacLeod said that the hungry people of Skye stole sheep for food and mentioned the possibility of 'establishing a rural police throughout the island'.

Cases of sheep stealing occurred right through the century, with wildly varying sentences for those found guilty. For instance, in the Inverness Spring Circuit in 1852 there were two cases of sheep stealing, with one man sentenced to seven and one to fifteen years' transportation. At the Dingwall Sheriff Court of May 1883 Alexander Matheson, a Moray shepherd, was found guilty of stealing sheep from the hills above Lochcarron on the west coast. He was given only six months in jail, yet in September 1878 Alexander Clark was found guilty at the Inverness Circuit Court of stealing forty-eight sheep and lambs from a farm at Easter Duthie in Inverness-shire and was given seven years' penal servitude.

The police were also to watch for tinkers and 'thimblers, cardsharpers, and gamblers of all kinds, and do all in their power to prevent such parties from imposing upon or defrauding the public by unlawful games or deceptive procedure or acting'. Clearly, the police were expected to do a great deal of work with very limited resources.

Caithness, at the northern tip of the country, had the problem of a host of fishermen descending on the coastal towns during the herring season, with the clash of cultures between the Hebrideans and the Lowlanders sometimes leading to bloody confrontations. The force at Pulteneytown, beside Wick, was not always the most efficient in the country. Wick itself decided to have a separate force of two men, including a drummer, but that experiment did not work and after limping along for ten years in 1873 it merged with the Caithness force.

Having so many small forces spread over a huge area begs a simple question: how efficient were the men? One incident will serve to show the mettle of at least one of these Highland policemen.

Constable Roderick McKenzie

Although theft and robbery were much more prevalent in the larger towns and cities, the smaller communities of the Highlands also experienced their share of dishonesty. In the winter of 1862 and 1863 the northernmost counties were haunted by a wandering burglar. On 17 February this man struck the farm of Balinleod in Westerdale, a few miles south of Halkirk in Caithness. He broke open the door and stole a number of shirts and a silver watch.

The local policeman was Constable Roderick McKenzie. Perhaps he was pleased to have some real crime to show his skill. When he made enquiries about any strangers who had been seen in the area, he discovered that a man had begged food at the farm a few days before. The man had said he was a deserter from the army and had been working at casual jobs for a few weeks, but after the theft at Balinleod he had vanished. McKenzie decided to follow his trail. The man was believed to be heading westward to Sutherland so McKenzie whistled up two men to help him and followed the suspected thief. He called at the lonely cottages and small settlements throughout the next few days, moving slowly westward towards Strathnaver.

Once Strathnaver had held a large population, but the Clearances had been cruel to this part of Sutherland and houses were few and far between. McKenzie called at each until he found a stranger being given shelter in a shepherd's cottage. The man had the silver watch and shirts beside him and surrendered without resistance. He gave his name as Sinclair Sutherland, but in reality he was Donald Petrie, who was already wanted by the police for theft in various areas. He ended his thieving career with a spell in Wick Jail. This winter chase across some of the most remote terrain in the country proved the calibre of at least one man in the Highland police forces.

Improvements

As the century progressed, so experience taught the police what type of equipment was best suited to the occupation. By 1864 most rural forces had leather leggings as protection for the boots from the weather and the subsequent mud. That year the old rabbit skin top hats were also discarded in favour of helmets and greatcoats replaced the old swallowtail coats. By 1868 the police throughout Scotland were better regulated, with pay increased according to length of service, so a recruit earned seventeen shillings and six pence a week and an experienced man a guinea.

While the Caithness men had to be aware of tinkers and travellers, in Sutherland and Ross it was fishermen who continued to pose problems. In the 1860s the Sutherland Police were also responsible for the gold diggings at Kildonan. Unlike goldfields in other parts of the world, no grog shops were allowed at the diggings and there was virtually no crime from the male and female diggers. There was one Englishman imprisoned for stealing gold and a storekeeper imprisoned for selling beer without a licence. The licence fee for digging was £1 a month – for every forty square feet – four times higher than in the colonies, and paid to the Duke of Sutherland. The police regulated the licences and diggings.

Many parts of the Highlands had to cope with railway labourers, or 'navvies' as they were known from the original canal 'navigators', as well as poaching and the slow rise in tourism and the bitter evictions and land raids that were a feature of the century. The numbers of police gradually increased so that by 1882 Inverness-shire had forty-two men, excluding the separate force for Inverness city itself, while Sutherland had sixteen. Overall, the Highland police forces were facing the challenges of the century with adaptability and skill.

The evolution of the police could be seen as a small but important part of the nineteenth-century drive to a more efficient government that had more input in the lives of the people. However, the Scottish police were not only concerned with fighting crime, they were also part of the gradual improvement of social conditions as they regulated sanitation, dung heaps and street lighting, ran soup kitchens, controlled firefighting and coped with diseased animals. A policeman's lot could be very busy as they fought to control the uncontrollable with limited resources and lack of support. It was little wonder that many turned to drink as an alleviation of stress.

Sometimes the police could be over zealous. For example, in November 1896 the Inverness Police arrested a horse dealer named David McMillan on suspicion of stabbing a labourer named William Patillo. McMillan paid a bond of £50 to assure his attendance at court, but when he reported to the police station in Inverness they still clamped handcuffs on him and paraded him the fifty yards to the court in Inverness Castle. He was found not guilty of the stabbing and his solicitor and Sheriff Blair both made strong protests against the actions of the police.

Constable Donald Cameron

One busy Highland policeman was Donald Cameron from Port Appin in Argyll. He took over the policing in that area in 1899 and left some fascinating notes, including a case of assault in January 1900 against a carrier named Angus Cameron, who 'with his booted foot [did] strike' Murdoch Kerr 'one severe and violent kick on the left hip, whereby the said Murdoch was hurt and bruised'.

There was another assault in July that year when a railway gauger named Duncan Kennedy attacked a labourer named Neil McNeil and 'with his fists did strike him two or more violent blows on the face and did knock or throw him to the ground, and when lying there did repeatedly strike him on the face and head'. Kennedy was at it again later that month when he attacked Alexander McKay with his fists or a sharp implement.

There was also John McRae, who used 'abusive and disgusting language' to Margaret and Annie Davidson. Or William Leach, who drilled a hole in a beer barrel and drew out six quarts for his own use in January 1900.

Crime and Punishment

Petty assaults, petty theft and acts of petty vandalism were the day-to-day lot of the policeman in every part of the country. Sometimes they were involved in more interesting work, such as tracing a murderer or controlling a riot. While the police forces gradually evolved into unified and efficient forces, other measures of crime deterrence and prevention also altered.

In the early years of the century crimes could be punished in a variety of ways from fines to execution. The public hangman was not the most popular man and in the Inverness Circuit Court in spring 1811 James MacCurroch and John Lawson were charged with attacking him. Even so, executions were not as common in Scotland as they were elsewhere. In October 1832 Hugh Lumsden of Pitcaple, Sheriff of Sutherland, speaking at a criminal court at Dornoch, said that Scotland was fortunate in having a system of law where a Procurator Fiscal did not act 'in anger or irritation', while in England prosecutions were often left to the private party, and where men are often not 'public spirited enough to undertake the vindication of the law'. He further compared Scots justice to English, saying in England there were '300 capital crimes' but 'not more than fifty in Scotland, of which the greater part had been introduced by British statutes'. At the beginning of the century the lesser sentences included transportation and public whipping, as well as the more unusual punishment of being held in the jugs or jougs, a band of iron that fastened around the neck and held the offender secure for public display.

On 3 May 1800, Lachlan Grahame, who lived at North Knapdale in Argyll, was tried for distilling whisky at a Justice of the Peace court at Lochgilphead. The justices ordered him to swear his guilt or innocence and when they believed that he lied under oath they ordered him into Inveraray Jail until 6 June, and then to be placed in the 'juggs' on Sunday, 7 June in the parish church at North Knapdale. Grahame complained to the High Court in Edinburgh, reminding them that by the criminal law of Scotland no sentence of an inferior court could inflict corporal punishment unless a jury had convicted the offender. The Lords of the High Court agreed and Grahame was freed.

Transportation did not always inspire quite the feeling of dread it was intended to. For example, in the spring circuit court at Inverness in 1821, John Gunn, known as Miniart, was convicted of horse stealing and sentenced to fourteen years' transportation.

Using the name Hugh Mackay, Gunn had signed articles as a seaman on board the Peterhead whaling ship *Alpheus*. On his return, George Campbell, King's Messenger, boarded the ship and arrested him. As the court officers escorted him to the cells, he remarked that he was being carried free to a much better country and would get plenty of two-penny grog on the voyage.

Prisons

Most burghs also had their own jails, many of which were ancient and no longer secure. In the middle of the century in Inverness-shire alone there were local prisons at Fort William, Nairn, Tain, Wick, Portree in Skye, and Inverness. Of these, the jail at Inverness was arguably the most important. It was built in 1791 at a cost of £1,800. In the nineteenth century a new jail was erected on Castle Hill to cope with the increased population.

These small prisons dealt with local criminals, both petty and serious. The records of Dornoch Jail for a few months in 1824 will probably be typical of the type of criminal held in them. For example, on 9 June 1824 Gustavus Sutherland of Golspie was jailed for stealing hay from a haystack owned by Hugh McPherson of Drummuie Farm. On 12 July the whisky smuggler Angus Mackay of Blarach was jailed for six months or until he paid a fine of £20. On 18 August John Mackay of Rogart was also given six months or a £20 fine for illicit distilling. On 9 August Robert Murray was held pending trial for stealing a ewe and a lamb from Hugh Gordon. Sheep stealing and whisky distilling were possibly the most common offences, and on 20 February 1819 Isabel Gray was accused of sheep stealing from Cyderhall.

And so it continued, year after year. This was the reality of rural crime and punishment, the day-to-day mundane business of justice shorn of glamour or the excitement of major drama. For every high-

Police Headquarters in Inverness

profile murder there was a plethora of petty thefts and pointless assaults. However, as government increased its power, so justice also became centralised.

In 1877 the Prison Act transferred fifty-six locally run Scottish prisons to the authority of the Prison Commission for Scotland. Although this Act therefore relieved the smaller burghs of the responsibility and expense of housing convicts, it gave the government headaches in providing more prison accommodation. It also gave problems to Inverness when the resident, if reluctant, population of all the smaller jails were transferred to the red sandstone Inverness Castle that stood on the banks of the River Ness. The prison was naturally overcrowded, but in 1886 various improvements saw the addition of twelve new cells, so that male and female prisoners could be housed separately, while washing and laundry rooms were also added. With

Inverness improved, the small jails at Dingwall and Elgin were then closed down.

The extra twelve cells were not enough, however. Industrialisation came late to the Highlands, but new industries brought a different style of living, crime increased and as the number of prisoners mounted, many were sent south to the national penitentiary at Perth. Nevertheless, in 1903 a new prison was built in Inverness, with prisoners used as cheap labour. There were fifty-nine cells, including ten exclusively for women, and it proved adequate for a time.

Perth Prison, on the southern fringe of the Highlands, was huge by comparison. Completed in 1859 it had taken nineteen years to build and spread over twenty-five acres. There were 580 ordinary cells, 108 cells for females and sixteen punishment cells.

Police and prisons had altered through the century, and the Highlands were no longer isolated but were as much a part of the fabric of the country as Edinburgh or Aberdeen.

6
Nautical Crime

━━━━━━━━━━━━━━━━━━━━━━━━━━━━

With so much nautical activity around the nineteenth-century Highlands and Islands, it was not surprising that there also was crime. Fishing boats exploited Hebridean waters for herring and white fish, trading ships crossed and re-crossed the seas, passenger vessels raced to be first to the piers. Sometimes there was tragedy as the notorious Scottish weather caught a vessel off guard.

Looting the Wreck

In the summer of 1804 a West Indiaman was caught by a sudden squall off the West coast of Scotland. The wind drove her onto the rocks off Jura. No sooner had she struck than a horde of locals descended upon her, beat up the master and looted the cargo of everything that was portable. Despite the remoteness of the island, the forces of the law caught up with them and seven people were called to the Circuit court at Inveraray. They were John McFee, Archibald Ramsay, Archibald McDougall, Roderick Shaw, Alexander McKioch, Anne Campbell and Catherine Campbell. Shaw, McDougall and Anne

Campbell did not appear and were outlawed. The others were found not proven and released without charge.

There were other occasions when a wrecked ship was plundered, such as in January 1806 when a ship was wrecked on the island of Sanda off Kintyre and some men from the area plundered it. The western seaboard of Scotland held many hazards for sailors.

Racing for the Pier

The nineteenth century saw massive changes to the economy of the Highlands. One was the advent of crowds of summer visitors by land and sea. Tourism brought many benefits to the Highlands, but it also brought its dangers as the small ports of the west coast were visited by pleasure steamers. In one case on 5 August 1867 two steamers, both carrying a large number of passengers, ran into each other off Dunoon pier. Both masters were charged with 'recklessly failing to direct, manage or steer the vessel which each of them was then in charge'. The two vessels were *Eagle* and *Levan*, both registered in Glasgow. Ronald McTaggart was the acting master of *Eagle*, taking her on a voyage from the Broomielaw in Glasgow to Rothesay, while John McLachlan was acting master of *Levan*, sailing in the opposite direction. *Eagle* had around eighty passengers on board and *Levan* had fifty, so between them the two masters were responsible for 130 lives, plus the crews of their respective vessels.

Both ships were approaching the pier at Dunoon at the same time, but in an age where competition and speed were important, neither slowed down. *Eagle* was nearly twice as long as the pier and Captain McTaggart was standing on the paddle box supervising, but there were no ropes thrown out to attach the vessel to the pier. The master of *Levan* was also on the paddle box of his ship, which had started to slow near the Castle Rock, about fifty yards from the pier, where she intended to berth.

Fishing boat of the type used at the turn of the nineteenth and twentieth centuries

Eagle had been at full speed all the way from Kirn, and Captain McTaggart did not order her engineer, Robert Nairn, to slow down until they were nearly at the pier. Perhaps because McTaggart wanted to be first, *Eagle* had altered her normal course and steered between *Levan* and the pier. It was usual for her to come up to the east corner of the pier, but on this occasion she approached from the west, the side from which *Levan* was also approaching. *Levan* was at her usual time and on her normal approach route. She had slowed down around the Castle Rock and was reversing into her berthing place. While approaching Dunoon from Kirn during flood tide, the correct procedure for paddle steamers was to take the bow in first, creep past the pier and reverse in. *Eagle* had passed the pier and her paddles were stopped, as if she was about to reverse into her berthing space.

The rule was that when two or more steamers were approaching the pier, the vessel that was closest when they blew off steam had the right to berth first. *Levan* was then closer than *Eagle* when she blew off steam and was backing into position. The two vessels came into contact, with the side of *Eagle* close to the foremast thumping into *Levan*'s stem.

A number of passengers were injured, nine of them seriously. John Kay, a Glasgow shoemaker, was badly shocked; Mary Bowie, a widow, was extensively bruised; Isabella Edgar damaged her spine; Agnes Henderson banged her head and her back; and her daughter Elizabeth, one year old, was ruptured; while others were more or less bruised and battered. The stem of *Levan* was damaged in the collision, while *Eagle* lost a good amount of her bulwarks, and then *Levan* backed away.

However, David Kidd, the deck hand who was steering *Eagle* when the collision took place, remembered events differently. He said that *Eagle* had followed her usual route from Kirn to Dunoon and was closer to the pier than *Levan* was. He was sure that *Levan* was coming on at speed and if she had not struck *Eagle*, she would have gone through the pier itself. He thought *Eagle*'s engines were stopped first, and *Levan*'s engines afterward. Hugh Stewart, another seaman on *Eagle*, agreed with that version of events and said it was the force of the collision that made *Eagle*'s bow face toward the quay.

Dugald Livingstone was a seaman on board *Levan* when the ships collided and was equally adamant that his vessel was closer to the quay. He said *Levan*'s engines were slowed at the Castle Rock, but *Eagle* was moving faster. Captain McTaggart of *Eagle* was seen to signal to the master of *Levan* to slow down. George Taylor, a Glasgow police inspector and a passenger on *Levan*, also thought *Eagle* was closer to the pier. He saw the master of *Levan* arrive on the bridge about a minute before the collision, saw him give three raps, which was the signal to slow, and heard him shout out, 'How the hell have you not stopped her before this?' Another passenger on *Levan*, James Currie, thought the master said, 'My God, Jock, you've done in now. Why the hell didn't you stop the boat in time?'

Alexander Cameron was the pier manager at Dunoon and thought that *Eagle* was travelling too fast. She was the larger vessel and was trying to race to the pier. Cameron believed *Eagle* was moving faster than *Levan*. Other witnesses, such as the corn merchant James Forrester, believed *Levan* had more way on her than *Eagle* had. The masters of both ships pleaded not guilty.

Lord Deas heard the case at Inveraray Sheriff Court in April 1868, and the jury found both masters guilty of culpable neglect but recommended mercy, particularly for McLachlan. Lord Deas gave them each a month in jail.

Murder on *Heather Bell*

In the nineteenth century, Scottish fishermen were not known for their quiet demeanour and often appeared in the police courts during the great herring booms. It was a tough, relentless life, with men working long hours in often terrible conditions in open boats. Sometimes tensions flared into harsh words and even violence, sometimes the men drank too much and that exasperated small disputes. Such a case occurred in June 1874 when the smack *Heather Bell* was fishing in the Sound of Mull. As with so many squabbles involving drink, the truth is hard to unravel behind a maze of lies and barely remembered instances. The following is the case made up mainly from the point of view of William McDonald, a seaman on board.

Heather Bell was a typical Scottish fishing smack. She was a small, oar-and-sail-powered vessel with a crew of four: elderly William Scott; his son, James Scott; James Smith of Banff; and William McDonald of Gardenstown on the south coast of the Moray Firth. *Heather Bell* was at the Lewis fishing but called in at Tobermory in the island of Mull on 26 June. As was common among some fishing crews, the men found a pub and sampled the local whisky. After a few drams, James Smith and William Scott began to quarrel about the workings of the boat. The argument petered into nothing but dirty looks and all seemed forgotten as the four men returned on board.

Heather Bell and a lugger named *William and James* left Tobermory at around eight that evening, but the drink was still working on James Scott and he left the deck to go below to the forecastle for a sleep. William Scott was steering, while McDonald and James Smith were working the sails. A flick of the halyard caught McDonald on the face and drew blood. With a following wind and fine weather, *Heather Bell* made good time out of Tobermory, but Smith and William Scott again began to argue, this time about the way the boat was steered. William Scott advised Smith to go and get a sleep, but Smith refused and instead demanded that he take over the helm. What began as a simple, if drink-fuelled, argument escalated into violence when Smith punched Scott on the side of the head.

McDonald looked astern from his work at the sails. 'What kind of work is that you are at?' he asked.

By way of reply, Smith grabbed hold of Scott's shoulder and legs and threw him over the port side of the boat into the sea. As Scott splashed overboard, Smith shouted, 'Let the old devil go!'

McDonald ran below to wake James Scott, but he was deep in the sleep of the drunk so McDonald returned quickly on deck. He saw old William Scott floating astern, quite nearby, and let go the peak halyards to wear *Heather Bell* round, and then put up the now unattended helm to close with the man in the sea. William Scott sunk quietly, without a cry for help, and it is possible the fall had rendered him unconscious. Smith had left the helm, possibly to go below and rouse James Scott. He re-emerged about half an hour later and helped McDonald reset the sails, but they did not discuss the loss of William Scott.

With the sails reset Smith returned below, leaving McDonald alone on deck for some hours as *Heather Bell* sailed idly in the Sound of Mull. McDonald sat on a barrel and cried at the loss of his companion. Around four next morning, when dawn coloured the eastern sky, Smith came back up on deck, took the helm for a few moments and returned to the forecastle. At about eight o'clock, James Scott came on deck, still unaware of the death of his father. When Smith told him that his father had gone on board *William and James*, Scott searched for a bottle of whisky he had brought on board and when he could not find it he supposed that his father had taken it onto the lugger for a drinking spree.

Unable to tell the truth, and afraid how James Scott would react, McDonald said he did not know, but Smith later found the whisky and handed it to James Scott. Only when *Heather Bell* approached the buoys that marked the entrance to the Caledonian Canal did Smith say that McDonald should relate what happened. It appeared that McDonald was quite a weak character, but so indeed was Smith to kill an old man and hide the truth from the son.

When *Heather Bell* berthed at Corpach, McDonald told James Scott that his father had fallen overboard, emphasising that it had been an accident. They told the young man that his father had been sitting on the bulwark aft but overbalanced and fell overboard. James Scott wondered about the blood on McDonald's face, but did not believe the halyard had caused it. He thought that McDonald had argued with his father and knocked him overboard in a fight. He told the same tale to the local policeman but told the possible truth to the Procurator Fiscal in Fort William. When Smith was charged with William Scott's murder, James Scott told the court that his father had mentioned quarrelling with McDonald, rather than Smith, and said that his father intended 'waiting his own time to get things settled'.

With so much contradictory evidence and the probability that nobody even remembered the truth, yet alone being able to relate it, the court found Smith not guilty and the death of William Scott was never solved.

Ducking the Artist

William McTaggart was a Kintyre man, born at Aros Farm near Machrihanish, on the west coast of the peninsula. His parents were Gaelic-speaking crofters, and his mother descended from the poet Duncan MacDougall. When he was sixteen, McTaggart moved to Edinburgh and studied to be an artist, an occupation at which he excelled. He is remembered as one of Scotland's finest landscape painters. One of his paintings, 'Through Wind and Rain', hangs in the McManus Galleries in Dundee, and shows a small fishing boat under a lugsail in a choppy sea. It was in a small boat very similar to the one in the painting that McTaggart became involved in a criminal case in August 1884.

Although he became famous and lived in Charlotte Square in Edinburgh, McTaggart never forgot his roots and returned to Kintyre every year. On 11 August 1889 he was fishing in Campbeltown Loch with his wife, Marjorie Henderson, their two sons and a tailor friend called Thomas Young. It was a perfect west coast summer day with the sea flat calm and few clouds to mar the blue of the sky. For an artist who specialised in the play of light and shade on maritime subjects, it would be a dream of a day.

They watched as the steamer *Meteor* came out of the harbour. McTaggart's boat was at anchor near the entrance to the loch, but as there was plenty space at their side and a fishing boat about thirty yards away, they felt no alarm when the steamer steered towards them; *Meteor* would obviously alter course soon. They continued to fish until they realised *Meteor* was getting very close and had not altered course to avoid them. When she was about 120 yards away, McTaggart and Young stood in the boat, waved their arms and shouted to the steamer to 'Clear off!' The people in the boat could see two men standing at the gunwale of the steamer, working at the hatchway, so were quite sure that they had been observed. However, rather than sheer away, when *Meteor* was about sixty yards away she altered course so she came directly onto McTaggart's boat. McTaggart continued to shout, especially when he saw a third man join the two in the bow of the steamer, but there was no response. The bow of the steamer smashed into the port side of their boat about a foot from their stem. The small boat was sliced in two, the occupants thrown into the loch and the steamer passed right over the top of them.

It was only then that the crew of *Meteor* seemed to realise that they were not alone. David Japp, the engineer, was content with his position on board. He respected the master, who he thought was a quiet, reliable and steady man. He was down below before the accident but had come on deck in time to see the mate standing at the mast. He felt the shock of collision but did not hear anybody in the boat calling to them. As soon as they hit the small boat, the mate ordered 'full speed astern' and Japp glanced over the side and saw the people in the water.

He shouted and asked the master to stop engines, got permission and returned to the engine room.

The steamer's boat picked up McTaggart's party and brought them on board. McTaggart approached the master, Archibald Grassam, and the mate, James Boyle, and asked who owned the ship. Grassam told him the owner's name. McTaggart, dripping wet and concerned about his family, asked Grassam why he had come all the way from Leith just to ram Edinburgh people in a small boat in Campbeltown Loch. Grassam only said that he did not have a lookout posted.

Duncan McLean, who had been in the fishing boat nearby, thought he saw a man run forward to the bow of *Meteor* just before the collision, and heard somebody shout out, 'You're over them! Lower your boat and stop the steamer as quick as you can!' He thought the steamer stopped within sixty yards. He also thought the steamer was riding light in the water so the bows were high and the steersman would be unable to see the small boat low down in front of him. Peter McCallum, another professional Campbeltown fisherman, said there were three men on *Meteor* and nobody posted as lookout. He thought her a dangerous vessel because of that.

The case came to court in September of that year. Archibald Grassam was given three months in jail and the mate, James Boyle, two months.

Tiree's Whisky Galore

Tiree sits square in the centre of the Inner Hebrides, an island of surprising fertility and thriving population. However, in common with its neighbours, it was often plagued by bad weather, and shipwrecks around the coast were frequent in the nineteenth century. One such was *Cairnsmuir*, a 1,123-ton schooner-rigged Leith steamer who was sailing from Hamburg to Glasgow and then onward to China. She went north about round Scotland, and on Monday, 6 July 1885, while negotiating the Inner Hebrides, she ran into dense fog. At quarter to three in the morning she ran aground on the reef known as Bogha Mór, off Tiree's Rudha Craignish Point on the tricky west coast. *Cairnsmuir* had struck amidships, and water was gushing into her engine room.

Captain John Scorgie tried to reverse her engines, but the sea flooded the engine room, and as the weather worsened into a full gale, the crew headed for the boats and came ashore. Shipwrecked seamen are not known for their taciturnity and soon let the islanders know that there was spirits and wine in the cargo. Naturally interested, the men of Tiree began searching what cargo had been washed ashore, emptied the crates and carried them away.

When the local coast officers of Customs and the Lloyd's agent visited Tiree to assess the wreck, they found hordes of local men busily looting. The officials tried to chase the looters away but were subjected to what they called 'gross abuse'. The islanders had men constantly on watch for any cases being washed ashore, which were then pounced on. The contents of any bottle was emptied into more durable containers, which were buried somewhere beneath the sand, safe from prying official eyes. The officials saw one case bobbing on the sea and estimated it would come ashore on the bay next door.

As they walked round, keeping an eye on their prize, a man named Kennedy stripped naked and plunged into the water. He wrestled the case through the breakers back to the beach when the officials challenged him. However, a large group of men arrived to back up Kennedy, and the officials backed away.

At a court of enquiry in Edinburgh on 31 July 1885, Captain Scorgie was blamed for the accident and lost his master's certificate, but it was restored on appeal. The islanders retained the secrets of where they concealed this bounty from the sea.

The Scuttler

In 1883 troubles gripped Tiree. The islanders were making newspaper headlines with their opposition to the Duke of Argyll, the landowner, but simultaneously there was another drama unfolding. Even as the islanders watched for the arrival of the Royal Marines to support the Duke, two policemen slipped quietly through the quiet townships and arrested John Malcolm Brown, the son of a crofter. They took him back to Oban on the steamship *Trojan*. Brown had not been involved in the rioting in the island but was accused of scuttling a ship.

Brown had been the part owner and mate of the 99-ton sailing ship *St Athens*, also possibly owned by his father, Archibald Brown. It was suspected that the schooner was in the father's name to save creditors from grabbing her. *St Athens* was a schooner coaster and in April that year she had loaded a cargo of china clay at Sutton Pool, Plymouth, in the south of England and headed for Runcorn, in the Mersey. China clay was often considered a heavy and dangerous cargo. Until that time *St Athens* was in good condition and Captain Walker had ascertained that she did not take in water.

On the twelfth of the month, *St Athens* was sailing on a calm sea in fine weather. Brown and an able seaman named John Lamond were on deck, sawing a piece of wood, which they took down below. When somebody shouted that *St Athens* was taking in water, James Walker, the master, hurried below and saw chips of wood floating on the water, and also saw Brown's mattress in the *lazarette*, the compartment where stores were held. He mentioned the facts to Brown, who said, 'Oh, let her go. She's no use to me.' Walker suspected that Brown had lain on the mattress and bored through the hull of the vessel in order that his father could claim the insurance of £750.

Brown appeared at the High Court in Edinburgh in November. The prosecution claimed he had bored several holes in the hull and concealed them with plugs. According to the prosecution, when the schooner reached a point twenty-nine miles north of the Longships Lighthouse near Lands End, Brown had removed the plugs to allow the water in. Brown pleaded not guilty.

Captain Walker told the jury that when he learned of the leak he ordered the hands to the pumps, but only one pump was operable, as the handle for the second was missing. The handle was later found under the floor of the cabin. The crew abandoned and eventually arrived in Kingston in Ireland.

Oban man James McDougall was a member of the crew. He claimed that Brown had mentioned that he might scuttle the ship to save her from creditors and offered him a bribe to help, but McDougall refused. He also claimed that Brown had offered him a bribe of £40 and a gold watch to scuttle the ship on an earlier voyage and had boasted he would buy a new vessel with the insurance. He offered McDougall the post as master if he helped. McDougall had turned down the offer but was so unsure of Brown that he did not undress at night in case Brown sank the ship. The schooner was insured with a number of insurance companies, including the Union Association of Underwriters in Dundee, the Dundee Shipping Association, the Banffshire Mutual Marine Insurance Association, the Union Freight Insurance Association of Dundee and the Dundee Shipping Freight Insurance Association. Charles Levison, the ship's carpenter, also claimed that Brown offered him £70 and a good position on a steamer he would allegedly buy with the insurance if he helped scuttle *St Athens*. He also asked how to bore a hole in a ship's hull: Levison suggested using an auger.

The defence were not quite mute. They called James Finlay of Lossiemouth, a previous master who declared that *St Athens* had sprung a leak on her last voyage with him and he had difficulty in keeping her afloat. However, the jury had no difficulty in finding Brown guilty and the judge, Lord McLaren, sentenced him to five years' penal servitude. Lord McLaren said the term would have been longer if he considered that any lives had been put at risk.

Fishing Disputes

Fishermen sometimes fell foul of laws that may have seemed designed specifically to prevent them from making an honest living. Such a case occurred in April 1885 when Alex McKay, Kenneth Cumming, Donald Smith and Donald Duff, four fishermen from Portmahomack, took seventy baskets of mussels from a scalp at Ardjachie Point off Easter Ross. Mussels were commonly used as bait for fishermen who long-lined for white fish. The fishwives would shell them and painstakingly attach them one by one to the hundreds of hooks on the line.

Unfortunately in this case the fishermen had dredged mussels from a scalp they apparently had no right to. Major Rose of Tarlogie claimed that he owned that scalp. When the case came to the sheriff court at Tain, the fishermen vocally challenged the major's claim. They said, loudly, 'Whose scalps are they?' and 'They belong to the Lord God Almighty.'

Not used to such a hubbub in his courtroom, Sheriff Hill threatened to clear the court of the spectators, who were mainly local fishermen and their supporters, come to lend moral support to the men from Portmahomack. None of the men denied taking mussels from the Tarlogie scalps but their agent, Mr Macrae of Dingwall, complained that Major Rose's claim to the scalps was 'more in keeping with the laws enacted two or three hundred years ago than the more humane laws during Her Majesty's reign'. He said the fishermen had 'as good a right to fish for mussels as for fish'. However, the sheriff ruled that the major owned the mussel beds and the fishermen had been trespassing, and he fined them £1 each or ten days in jail. Not surprisingly, the audience in the courtroom received the sentences with loud displeasure.

There was a not dissimilar case in July 1889 when two fishermen, Malcolm Kennedy and Lachlan Currie, both of Bowmore in Islay, were fishing nearly a mile offshore. They were in their boats and used nets to catch salmon and grilse at Gartnatra, in Islay. Major Lovat Ayshford Wise, the tenant of Islay House since April 1887, who controlled the shooting and fishing of the area, prosecuted them with the full approval of Charles Morrison, the proprietor. The case came to Inveraray Sheriff Court on 11 October that year. Wise was seeking a forfeit of the fishermen's boats as well as a fine of between ten shillings and £5. However, there were some complications in the case.

In July some men working for Wise had seized nets and gear belonging to the same two fishermen, but in Lochindaal, Islay. The local men had fished Lochindaal for centuries without hindrance and Wise's minions had acted without any warrants, so the seizures were illegal. The fishermen had taken an action against Wise, so this case appeared to be a pre-emptive strike by Wise to forestall a case against him. It appeared that the local gamekeepers had informed Wise that there was considerable salmon poaching in the area and he had asked them to try and stop it. He had asked his keepers to seize any nets that could be used for catching salmon, as when he was in England he seized rabbit nets belonging to poachers. When Malcolm Kennedy called at Islay House and asked for his nets to be returned, Wise had refused. Kennedy had handed him a copy of the Fisheries Act and said the nets were shot legally and Wise had no right to them. In response, Wise said, 'You may think yourself very lucky I did not prosecute you.'

When the case came before the sheriff court at Inveraray, Wise claimed he had exclusive rights to fish for any kind of fish within certain limits of the shore but he was only interested in salmon and trout. He admitted his ignorance of the kind of nets habitually used in Islay but insisted that they were suitable for poaching. Malcolm Kennedy repeated that the nets were a mile beyond the low water mark and said when they were seized they held only dog fish.

John Frost, the head gamekeeper of Islay House, stated that on 23 July he was out looking for poachers' nets at Lochindaal. There was a line of five nets together, which was the formation normally used when poaching salmon. They were not much use, according to Frost, for catching mullet, which were the only other fish in Lochindaal. Not only that, but Frost also produced a letter that Kennedy was alleged to have written. It said:

> *I admit to have set two nets within two hundred yards of the head of the loch but never in the channel. If Major Wise will give me a reasonable wage to look after loch and river, I will guarantee you that none of them will set their nets there … as the saying is you can watch a thief but you cannot watch a liar. You will oblige me by consulting Major Wise and if my offer is not reasonable he will do me a favour by buying these two nets. I would rather burn them than sell them to any of the Bowmore loafers.*

There was evidence from other fishermen. Donald McFee and George McDiarmid agreed that the nets were salmon nets, while John McArthur said that nets like that were in common usage all along the west coast. John McNab of Inveraray said that salmon nets had a wider mesh. Sheriff Campion said he believed the nets had been set to catch salmon and fined both men ten shillings, while the nets were forfeit.

In April 1899 four fishermen from Cromarty appeared at Dingwall Sheriff Court charged with illegally trawling for white fish in the shallow water and with their nets on the seabed. This type of action was presumed to damage the spawning ground of fish. The men – Andrew Finlayson, known as Pinder; Hugh Maclennan, known as Bochan; Don Maclennan, known as Doal; and John Skinner, known as Johnder – objected strongly when the water bailiffs challenged them. They lifted sticks and attacked the bailiffs so that three of them were injured. They were found guilty and fined two guineas with an alternative of seven days in jail.

The French Connection

Smuggling was not confined to whisky distilling in the remote glens. There was also smuggling into the country by sea. In 1878 the French lugger *Amelia* was caught off the coast of Sutherland. On 10 July the crew – five men and a boy – were charged at a Justice of the Peace Court at Thurso. The same captain had been tried at the same court three years previously. The captain was charged with smuggling fifteen and a half casks of spirits, three contained gin and the remainder brandy, with an average of eleven gallons in every cask. Each of the adult crew was fined £100, while the vessel was seized by the coastguard and the crew taken to Thurso Jail.

French vessels were also sometimes involved in fishing disputes when they strayed inside British territorial waters. In May 1883 the masters of three French fishing boats, *Julen, Maillard* and *Bourgoin*, were arrested in Scalloway Bay by revenue officers for illegal fishing, tried in Lerwick and fined between £1 and £3. One of the crew was also fined for smuggling.

False Registration Numbers

Fishing disputes were quite common in that period, but different methods of fishing creating anger. At about dawn on Sunday, 21 July 1895, an Aberdeen steam trawler, *Commodore*, Captain Adam Sutherland, fished near the island of Eunay Beg in East Loch Roag. This was a sea loch of Lewis in the Western Isles and therefore inside the three-mile limit where trawling was banned. Every fishing vessel had to have its name and identification number prominently displayed, but Captain Sutherland tried to hide the identity of his vessel by placing covers over the bow and stern. However, a number of local fishermen were watching him and as he was trawling away their livelihood they kept a close eye on him until about five in the evening.

When *Commodore* anchored in the loch, the Lewis fishermen sailed out, clambered on board and spoke to members of her crew. The local fishermen reported that Captain Adam had placed black canvas with the false number 'A. 77' over *Commodore*'s proper identification number. They also saw that the canvas cover on the port side had been taken away and the number 'GN. 31' was underneath. The fishermen asked the crew why they concealed their identity and one said they 'sometimes did that sort of thing'.

The case came to the sheriff court in Stornoway in October that year and *Commodore*'s crew denied they had ever trawled in Loch Roag or that their numbers had been concealed. However, they freely admitted that they had been anchored there.

Sheriff Campbell found the charge of covering the official number not proven but decided they were guilty of trawling. The maximum penalty allowed was a £100 fine. The sheriff fined Sutherland £50 or thirty days. Sutherland chose to go to jail.

There were many disputes between trawlers and the authorities. That same October another Aberdeen trawler was captured by HMS *Jackal* while illegally fishing in Lybster Bay off Caithness. The trawler was taken into Aberdeen and her starboard gear was seized by the authorities.

The sea was as prone to crime as was the land.

7

A Maelstrom of Murder

Murder is the monarch of crimes. It continues to fascinate many years after the event, and is discussed long after the protagonists have gone. Given their relatively small population, the nineteenth-century Highlands and Islands had more than their share of murders, some of which were soon forgotten, but others which were talking points the length and breadth of the country and still have the ability to intrigue today.

Death of a Soldier

The nineteenth century began with war as Britain faced the military muscle of Revolutionary France. Most eighteenth-century wars had been fought by professionals with the only civilians directly involved being seamen, merchants or those unfortunate enough to be on the path of marching armies, but this was different. The vibrant French Republic had put a whole nation in arms and Britain strained to match her. The Royal Navy expanded to protect the trade routes and convoy the army to various trouble spots around the globe. For a while Britain became an armed camp as new regiments were formed for the regular army and men were encouraged to join the militia and yeomanry. Inevitably, with so many armed men trained to violence, there was some friction with the civilian population. Sometimes, however, the soldiers were the victims and not the perpetrators of aggression.

On 2 June 1812 Captain Charles Munro, late of the 42nd Highlanders, the famous Black Watch, was in George Thomson's shop and smithy in Chapeltown. A ship's carpenter named Robert Ferguson was already there, and the two argued. When Ferguson called Munro a 'damned bugger' and added more insulting comments, Munro reacted by grabbing Ferguson by the collar and pushing him outside the smithy. The bystanders watched, shrugged and continued with their own lives. It had been a minor incident and they thought it was closed and forgotten.

Ferguson, however, was not finished yet. To be dismissed with such contempt rankled. He was outside for only a few moments before he returned, reached inside his pocket and produced a knife, with which he attacked Munro. There was no warning and little chance for Munro to defend himself. The officer backed off and cracked the knuckles of Ferguson's knife hand with his cane. Faced with a man with a knife, Munro could only stand with his back to the wall, but Ferguson got under the swing of his arm and thrust the knife through Munro's coat and into his side. The wound was small but so deep and dangerous that the intestines seeped out. Munro shouted, 'I'm gone. Take hold of the man,' and with one hand trying to hold in his intestines, he followed Ferguson as he retreated back outside.

Badly hurt, Munro shouted out, 'Why don't you seize the murderer?', which may have been the signal that caused Ferguson to run, but somebody grabbed him, threw him to the ground and grabbed the knife.

As a neighbour, Mrs Thomson, helped Munro into her house, the wounded man said, 'I did not think the man would do this to me. God knows I would not do this to him. We had but a few words and I only put my hands to the back of his neck to throw him out for insolent language.'

When it was realised how badly Munro was hurt, a man hurried to Dr George McDonald in Cromarty. The doctor came over, opened the wound and replaced the intestines inside Munro, who said he 'wished he had fallen on the field of battle'. However, twenty-eight hours after being stabbed, Munro died.

At his trial, Ferguson claimed self-defence, and a witness named John Home said that Munro was a 'warm-hearted man, although rather rash when anything vexed him'.

Lord Hermand was the judge and he sentenced Ferguson to be hanged on 30 October, and his body given to the anatomists. The execution was delayed for two weeks due to an election, but whether this was a kindness or a cruelty to Ferguson is hard to tell. He was hanged instead on 13 November and met his end with considerable bravery.

Murder or Not Murder: That Is the Question

Not all cases were cut and dried, with simple solutions. Often there was considerable doubt about the innocence or guilt of the accused parties. Although all the evidence seemed to indicate a murder, there remained just enough doubt for the jury to hesitate to declare somebody guilty. The Caithness murder case of 1830 was a case in point, where initial damning evidence given by witnesses was later thrown into dispute.

The killing had taken place years earlier, on 2 December 1825 in Wick. James Small was mate of the vessel *Rose*, which was then berthed at Pulteneytown, a fishing village that was then separate from Wick. On the morning of 3 December he was found dead, lying on his back on the ground behind the quay. His face was black, as if he had been strangled, there was a deep gash on his forehead and his hands were clenched into fists.

As the police pondered the dead body, a man by the name of Farquharson approached them and claimed to know what had happened. He said that he had been with Small and three men, William Durrand, George Jamieson and George Henderson. All had come to Durrand's house about five in the Saturday evening. They had been drinking and were quite convivial for most of the night, until around midnight when the drink took control. All the men began to argue and then to fight. The crucial point came when Durrand leaped on Small and gripped him by the neck. They had struggled for a while, and then Durrand grabbed hold of a bottle and smacked Small over the forehead. Small had slumped to the ground, already dead.

The police took notes, and then a woman named Emily Sutherland also claimed to have seen what happened that night. She said she was Durrand's servant and agreed with Farquhar's account of the death of Small. Indeed, she agreed in the smallest details.

The authorities thought they had enough evidence to prosecute and took Durrand, Henderson and Jamieson to the Circuit court in September 1830. Farquharson and Sutherland both gave evidence and for a short while the case seemed proved, but then the defence set to work. The defence brought forward a string of witnesses who stated categorically that Emily Sutherland had not been a maid in the Durrand's house at the time Small's body was discovered, while Farquharson was himself a criminal whose word could not be trusted. Furthermore, the two witnesses had spoken together at length to create a similar story of what happened, as Sutherland had been over a mile from the house on the night in question.

The jury found the accused not guilty. The murder was not solved.

The Man with Two Names

Domestic disputes are as common to the Highlands as to any other part of the world, and in the nineteenth century they all too often ended in violence or even murder. Sometimes there was doubt about the facts of the case, but few murders seemed as confused as the killing of Jean Brechin in 1835. She was married to John Adam, but their relationship was not the most conventional and the marriage did not last long.

John Adam was a man with a shady past, which he recorded for posterity. It is unlikely to be entirely accurate, but the gist reveals exactly what sort of man he was. Adam was born in 1804, the son of a kirk elder, and at the age of fourteen he fell heir to the tenancy of the twenty-acre farm of Craigieloch, near Forfar. He was not a good farmer, fell into difficulties and soon found himself labouring on the farms of others instead. He had other talents, though: he had a smooth tongue and a consuming interest in women. Indeed, he apparently seduced two women in his local parish. That was bad enough, but he had recently joined the Kirk, which made things worse, and both girls were the daughters of kirk elders, which was a terrible breach of trust. Worst of all, one girl was deaf and dumb and was Adam's own cousin.

Not surprisingly, Adam was hauled before the Kirk Session, severely censured and kicked out of the congregation. He moved from the parish and found a job as a farm labourer at a place called Carrisbank Farm. It was here he first met Jean Brechin. He was immediately attracted to her, but she sensed he was a bad man and turned him down flat. Either as a direct result or because of unrelated matters, Adam left the area and moved to Aberdeen.

Adam became involved with Deism, which was an anti-Christian group who believed in nature and reason. He bought Thomas Paine's *Age of Reason* and turned completely away from the Kirk but continued his alternative religion of womanising. Before long, even the horizons of Aberdeen were too small for him and he moved to Lanarkshire, where he met yet another woman and this time proposed marriage. That idea fell through and eventually he enlisted in the 2nd Dragoon Guards, then based in Glasgow.

He went south with the regiment and met an eighteen-year-old girl named Dorothy Elliot, with whom he eloped. They did not marry but lived together as man and wife. Adam was back in Scotland by 1834, having deserted from the army. They moved north to Dingwall, posing as Mr and Mrs Anderson, with their supposed marriage funded by money that may have been stolen, and Adam found work in a quarry. In the natural course of events, Dorothy became pregnant and Adam realised their money would not stretch to properly caring for their child. He decided on raising cash and at the same time paying off an old score. His rejection by Jean Brechin still rankled and now she had money and was still unmarried. Spinning a yarn to his supposed wife, Adam travelled south to her home in Montrose. He wooed Jean Brechin with his old charm and married her on 11 March 1835 and the couple moved north. Adam neglected to mention his other wife in Dingwall.

Before she married Adam, Brechin had run a shop in Montrose, but now she gave it up, sold most of her furniture and put all her trust in her charming new husband. The remnant of her possessions she put in a wagon and Adam sent it ahead, but to Dorothy Elliot. The newlyweds caught the coach to Aberdeen and then to Inverness. The couple had taken up lodgings with Hector and Janet Mackintosh of Chapel Street, Inverness, but rather than use their own name, they claimed to be Mr and Mrs Anderson. They had told Jean Mackintosh that their furniture was following them by carrier. Adam had not informed Elizabeth of his plan but had invented an elderly aunt who had died and left him around £100 in money and all her furniture.

After three weeks and three days in lodgings, Adam and Brechin told the Mackintoshes that they were going to their new house between

Beauly and Dingwall. Hector Mackintosh thought that was slightly strange, as Adam had previously claimed their house was at Brahan, between Dingwall and Strathpeffer. Whatever their destination, they left after five in the evening of Friday, 3 April, saying they would cross the Beauly Firth by the ferry, travel a few miles and find somewhere to stay the night. The supposed Mr Anderson carried an umbrella but left his stick behind, while his wife carried a basket that contained a partly completed pair of stocking she was knitting.

Roderick McGregor was the Kessock ferryman when Adam and Brechin crossed by the ferry to the north bank of the firth at about six in the evening. He remembered them. Robert Thomson also recalled Adam. Thomson was a carrier and Adam had hired him to take a load of furniture to his house in Dingwall. However, the strange thing was that Adam had claimed to be John Anderson at the time, and said that his wife was already living in Dingwall. The furniture, apparently, had been left to Anderson by a deceased aunt. Thomson met Anderson's wife in Dingwall; she was around twenty years old, and the couple did not act as if they were newlyweds. John Urquhart would have confirmed that. He was a sawyer in Dingwall and said that Adam rented a house from him for a year. Adam lived with his wife, who was named Dorothy Elliot, and was certainly not Jean Brechin.

Adam travelled south around Martinmas for three weeks or so, apparently to visit a relative in Montrose. He returned to Montrose in the spring as well, again for about twenty days. Shortly after that, a cartload of furniture arrived. Sharper-eyed than her husband, or perhaps more interested, Christian Urquhart noticed that there was more than furniture that arrived. She saw a woman's silk shawl and gown, as well as two women's caps and a basket that contained one knitted stocking and one that was still being knitted.

Robert Gordon was another man who knew Adam. Gordon was the teller of the National Bank in Dingwall and on 13 March 1835 he saw that Adam had deposited £100 in British Linen Company notes in the bank. He had again used the name of John Anderson. He drew the money back out on 13 April.

A few days after Adam and Brechin crossed the Kessock Ferry, a girl named Jane Stewart was working alongside her aunts, Peggy Stewart and Betty Gray, and a man named John Campbell. They were employed in a plantation amidst moorland at Millbuie, opposite Inverness. Young Jane entered a ruined cottage and saw a glove lying on the ground. She lifted it and noticed a piece of gauze 'coming out of the ground'. Within a few moments she also saw a shoe. She thought this was strange so told Peggy Stewart, who lifted the shoe and realised it still contained the foot. The two women ran to William Forbes, a cottar who worked at nearby Merkenich of Kilcoy, for help. He dug up around the shoe and found the feet and head of a woman, with a large, blood-stained rock over her face. Forbes sent for the authorities, and John Jones, a Dingwall surgeon, together with the Procurator Fiscal, were present as the rest of the body was dug up. The woman was lying on her back in the corner of the building, and had been buried under sand and turf. Jones inspected the remains and found that there had been at least two savage blows to the head, which had fractured the skull, while both sides of the jawbone were smashed. There were also a number of other injuries. He thought a large stone had been the murder weapon, probably the one weighing around 28lb that was found with the body. That corner section of the wall had also collapsed around her.

It was obvious that there had been a murder, but there seemed no motive until questions were asked. The prime suspect was John Adam, and the motive seemed to be theft. He was arrested and appeared before the circuit court at Inverness on 18 September 1835. Adam was bald but handsome, with side-whiskers and a set expression on his face.

When James Beattie, agent for the British Linen Company Bank at Montrose, appeared, he said that Jean Brechin often put money into a deposit account. He also said that an unknown man produced the receipt and withdrew the money on 9 March. David Hill was the agent for the Montrose branch of the National Bank. He also said that Jean Brechin put in sums of money, but he was able to identify John Adam as the man who made the withdrawals.

The court then heard John Adam's own story, or rather stories. He had given three versions, at three different times. In his first and second statement, Adam claimed that his name was John Anderson. He said he had never been to Montrose in his life and did not know Jean Brechin. In his third statement he admitted his name was indeed John Adam and he came from Lintrathen, Forfarshire. In 1831 he enlisted in the Dragoon Guards, but deserted in 1834 when they were at Derbyshire. Around that time, he met Dorothy Elliot and they acted as man and wife, although they never formally married.

Adam stated he had met Jean Brechin in Montrose last Martinmas (11 November), and added he was hoping she would repay a loan he had made to her before he joined the army. Brechin, according to Adam, refused to part with a penny unless he agreed to marry her. As Adam wanted his money back, he returned to Montrose at the end of February, married Brechin at Laurencekirk and withdrew her money from the banks. After they were married, they travelled together to Inverness. They parted company when he took the ferry at Kessock and he had never seen her again. It was not quite a plausible tale.

The Procurator Fiscal had Adam brought to the corpse of his wife and made him lay a hand on it. It is possible this event was part of the old Scottish superstition of trial by touch, when the dead body was supposed to bleed when its murderer laid a hand on it, but more likely the Fiscal was merely hoping to scare Adam into a confession. Adam touched Brechin and swore he had never seen her before in his life.

The defence pointed out that Brechin had never been seen alive on the north side of the Kessock Ferry, and argued that it was possible she had been killed by the wall falling on top of her. The jury were having none of it and found Adam guilty of murder.

When Lord Moncrieff donned the black cap, Adam knew he was condemned. Moncrieff's statement may have been rhetoric, but the words, to an audience brought up with strict religion, must have struck home to many of them. 'John Adam,' Lord Moncrieff said, 'Unhappy and miserable man! The jury have unanimously found you guilty . . . in a dark hour of your existence, the Prince of Darkness took advantage of you and in a bloody action almost unparalleled in enormity, has sealed your guilt.'

John Adam, alias John Anderson, was condemned to be hanged 'at the usual place of execution in Inverness on Friday, 16 October next.'

'You have condemned an innocent man,' Adam claimed. 'I am condemned at the bar of man, but I will not be condemned at the bar of God!' He wrote a single letter, to Dorothy Elliot, who visited him in his cell. He also made what could be a true confession to a cellmate. He finally admitted he had strangled his wife by pressing his thumbs below her ears and on his subsequent flight to Dingwall he had seen a ghostly figure.

He was hanged at Longman's Grave at the south shore of the Beauly Firth, with the scaffold giving him a view to the Black Isle and Millbuie Ridge, where his wife was murdered. It was said he turned his back on the view and faced Inverness instead.

Murder in North Uist

The Outer Isles are places of pristine seas and unsurpassing beauty. However, they have a dark history of violence and bloodshed, of raid and feud. Even in the nineteenth century when the days of the clans were long gone, there were ugly reminders of the passions that lingered beneath the surface.

On Thursday, 26 June 1856, a visitor found an old woman named Margaret MacLean lying dead in her bed in her isolated cottage in Claddach Kyles Paible in North Uist, fifteen miles inland from Lochmaddy. Nobody was quite sure of MacLean's age, but she was presumed to be over seventy but less than eighty. A pauper who lived alone in a black house of dry stone and turf, she followed a solitary life, so there was no real concern when she was seen on Monday, 20 June and then not seen for a few days. As her door was padlocked, any casual passers-by would believe she was away somewhere, possibly visiting a distant friend or relation.

As the days passed with no sign of her, the neighbours in the clachan began to wonder, and on the Thursday they forced open the door and found Margaret MacLean lying dead. There were marks on her neck and throat that suggested she had been strangled, while the house had been stripped of everything portable.

The neighbours tried to think of any strangers they had seen recently, but there were none. However, some people had seen a woman called Catherine Beaton loitering around the cottage on the previous Saturday. They knew it had been Saturday because it was the same day that a steamer from Glasgow had called, and with the slow pace of life in Uist, such things marked the passage of time.

Catherine Beaton was a bad character for the island. She already knew the inside of Inverness Prison, where she had been incarcerated for theft on more than one occasion, so the locals were quick to accuse her of the murder. When Beaton's house was searched, some of MacLean's possessions were found inside and she was arrested and escorted to the jail at Lochmaddy.

The case came to the Circuit court in Inverness in September and lasted fourteen hours and continued into the following day. Without any proof, the jury could not convict Beaton of murder, but theft seemed quite obvious and the judge gave her six years' penal servitude.

Murder in Assynt

Second sight may be scoffed at, or may be accepted as a fact. In the twenty-first century people may be more sceptical than they were in the nineteenth, but at that time in the Highlands, many people lived with what was sometimes thought of as more of a curse than a blessing. In the case of the Assynt murder, second sight was accepted as part of life.

Murdoch Grant was one of many peddlers who wandered the highways and byways of Scotland. In March 1830 he was in Assynt in western Sutherland, looking for custom. When he was not working as a peddler, he lived at Strathbeg, at Lochbroom, a man known and well liked by his neighbours. At a time when shops were few and far between outside the towns, peddlers such as Grant provided a necessary service to the scattered communities they served. He was a distinctive and popular man in his tartan coat and waistcoat, his loose trousers and his bonnet, so when Grant disappeared that spring his absence was noted and commented upon. It was four weeks later that somebody noticed a body floating in Loch Torr na h Eigen, but news spread fast in rural Scotland and half the neighbourhood gathered as men waded into the loch to pull the corpse ashore.

After so long immersed in water the body was misshapen but the clothes helped identify it as Murdoch Grant, but there was speculation if he had been killed, or had simply fallen into the loch and drowned. It was a classic case of 'did he fall or was he pushed?' Somebody pointed out that his pack was missing, and as peddlers never travelled without their pack, thoughts turned to murder and robbery. The Reverend Gordon, the local minister, was among the crowd. He considered himself a friend of Grant and he immediately suspected murder and robbery. Grant's head was severely battered, and some people thought there was evidence of a fight on the heather nearby, although that could have been entirely unconnected with the death. Overall, people could not understand how Grant could have fallen into the loch himself, and his pack was clearly missing. He had carried a mixture of banknotes and pack goods to the value of around £40, which was a great deal of money in 1830. He had so much money at the one time because he had been gathering up debts that were due to him.

With the community in doubt what to do, they turned to probably the best-educated man in the community for advice. Hugh McLeod was the local schoolmaster, the son of Roderick McLeod, the tenant of Lynmeanarch. He was a familiar and trusted figure. McLeod gave his opinion that Grant must have simply tripped, banged his head and drowned. Yet despite McLeod's assertion, some people continued to suspect foul play and searched for the murderer.

With no policeman or other figure of authority in the area, the local people used an ancient Scottish method of finding the killer. 'Ordeal by touch' was hallowed by tradition. Any suspect had merely to touch the body, which was supposed to bleed if handled by the murderer. Of course, the idea was flawed, as the corpse would not issue blood, but there was also some sense there, for if people believed strongly enough in the efficacy of the method, the murderer would be loath to prove his guilt in such a public manner.

One by one the inhabitants of the locality touched the body of Murdoch Grant, and one by one they proved their innocence, to the satisfaction of themselves and their neighbours. But one man refused to put himself to the test. Hugh McLeod was having no part of such a silly superstition and refused to touch the body. He was far too educated and sophisticated for such beliefs. Rather than doubt his innocence, his neighbours began to scoff at their own credulousness.

The crofters and cotters – a cotter was a landless man – asked McLeod to inform the authorities about the discovery of Grant. He took on the task quite willingly, told the magistrates that poor Murdoch had fallen and drowned in the loch, and returned home. Murdoch's body was returned to Loch Broom and given a Christian burial.

However, despite the officials' acceptance of the accidental nature of the peddler's death, Alexander Grant, Murdoch's brother, was not so easily convinced.

Alexander Grant was convinced that Murdoch had been murdered. He pressed the authorities to disinter the body, pushing forward his reasons until they did so. The doctor who examined the mouldering corpse tended to agree with Alexander Grant; the indentations on the skull were not like those from a fall, but very like those inflicted with a weapon of some kind. He also said that 'Murdoch Grant was dead before he was committed to the water, because, had he, when alive, been thrown into the loch, it is most probable that a quantity of water would have been found in the stomach which ... was perfectly empty.'

Alexander Grant was obviously a determined man. He began a thorough search around the loch for his brother's missing pack and money. Neither was to be found. It was now that the second sight came into play. Kenneth Fraser was a local man, also known as Kenneth the Dreamer. He claimed he had dreamed of the murder and saw Murdoch's pack under a cairn. Now the Highlands are littered with cairns, the piles of loose stones that are used as way markers, or to signify the burial of somebody important, or for other often forgotten reasons, but Fraser's description of the cairn was so precise that many of the local population recognised it. They looked beneath the cairn but there was no pack. Instead, there were a scattering of Murdoch's possessions. No dead man could have put them there, so the theory of murder and robbery looked more accurate.

In the meantime, Hugh McLeod was spending more money than he had ever earned, especially since he had given up his teaching position. Despite pleading poverty not long before, McLeod had changed a £5 note, and could not explain from where he got such a sum. The finger of suspicion pointed at him, and the authorities questioned him for a few days at the village of Lochinver, and then escorted him to Dornoch Jail. James Stewart, a King's Messenger, had been present when Grant's body was fished from the loch. Now he searched McLeod and his home at Lynmenmnich. He took Grant's stockings from McLeod's legs and found Grant's tartan trousers in McLeod's house, as well as a hammer, which could well have matched the indentations on Grant's skull. When blood was found on McLeod's coat, the ex-teacher claimed it came from a bird he had shot. Nobody was convinced.

While he waited within the jail, McLeod experienced his own second sight. He had a dream in which his father came to him. His father was standing beside a coffin in a graveyard and told Hugh he only had another year before he would fill the coffin. Not surprisingly, McLeod worried as he lingered in Dornoch Jail. The days merged into weeks and months, and his trial was postponed. It was 26 September 1830 before he appeared before the court. He pleaded not guilty, but there were a number of witnesses who gave evidence against him. These included the Widow Mackay of Drumbeg, who had knitted Grant's stockings and identified the pair McLeod had been wearing at her work. There was also a young girl named Isobell Kerr, who had met McLeod on the hillside. McLeod had said to her, 'You need not be saying that you saw me,' which was taken as evidence he had not wished to be seen there on the day of the murder.

However, it may have been the evidence of Kenneth Fraser that drove the final nail into McLeod's gallows tree. Fraser was a tailor as well as a seer, and in April 1830 he had gone for a drink with McLeod. McLeod had £1 and 11 shillings, which he claimed to have earned working as a schoolteacher at Lochcarron. He also asked Fraser to say nothing about the money, or the red pocketbook in which he carried it. They spent a couple of days drinking amiably, with McLeod footing all the bills. Fraser also told the court about his dream where he had seen the pack lying under a cairn:

I was at home when I had the dream in the month of February. It was said to me in my dream, by a voice like a man's, that the pack was lying in such a place. I got a sight of the place just as if I had been awake: I never saw the place before. The voice said in Gaelic, 'The pack of the merchant is lying in a cairn of stones near their house.'

The voice did not name the McLeods, but Fraser was shown the house, illuminated by the sun and with a burn passing McLeod's house. Fraser had no other knowledge of the pack except from his dream.

The court heard that McLeod had been penniless before 19 March, so he had been even refused credit for a gill of whisky. However, after that date he flashed a £5 note around and a number of notes of smaller denominations. He had not given any plausible account to explain from where he obtained this money.

McLeod still maintained his innocence, but the judge and jury disagreed, and he was sentenced to hang. He was taken below, still arguing his innocence. 'The Lord Almighty knows I am innocent,' he said. 'I did not think in this country one would be condemned on mere opinion.'

As the time for his execution approached, McLeod must have realised there was no escape and worried about the state of his immortal soul. He confessed to the murder and explained how he had gone about it. Hugh McLeod wanted more from life than a cottar's income. He rose to become a teacher at Loch Broom, but he had expensive tastes and wanted more. In March 1830 he met Murdoch Grant in Drumbeg and gave the pedlar an offer nobody could refuse: he said he would purchase everything Grant had. Grant agreed, and the next day the men met near Loch Torr na h Eigen. As they walked past the loch, McLeod forced a quarrel with Grant and produced a hammer that he had borrowed from his father. He thumped Grant on the head, chest and in the ribs, robbed him, hit him some more to make sure he was dead and tumbled the body into the loch. He also threw the hammer in the water. As usual in Scotland, there were plenty of stones nearby to keep the body submerged, but Grant glared balefully from under the clear water of the loch. With Grant disposed of, McLeod rifled his pack for whatever was worth having and hid the remainder in one of the many lochans that were nearby.

He was hanged at Inverness on 24 October 1830, one of only a handful of men executed there in the nineteenth century. He was just twenty-two years old.

Mass Murder in Benbecula

In the nineteenth century murders were rare events in the Hebrides, but in 1857 there was a triple murder, and it occurred on one of the quietest of all the islands. At a time when Scotland was still discussing the Madeleine Smith poisoning case in Glasgow, this new tragedy should have filled column inches in the newspapers and occupied people over the breakfast table, but instead it was given minimum attention and was quickly forgotten. Yet it was a story of drama and tragedy that rocked the little communities at the time.

On 9 July, Mr Briscoe, Inspector for the Board of Supervision, and Mr Macdonald, the local banker and Inspector of the Poor, arrived on the island of Benbecula, the central island of the trio of North Uist, Benbecula and South Uist, in the Western Isles. Briscoe was coming to visit an elderly pauper named Mary Macphee. On the road to the village of Nunton, the men met Macphee's niece and asked after the old lady, and also about her brother, who was known to be unstable. The girl said that both were fine, and she took them to her aunt's house.

The house appeared empty but as they were about to leave, Briscoe thought Mrs Macphee was asleep on the bed. He checked and found her dead, with her throat slashed, her face ripped and her skull battered. There was also a pair of handcuffs on the ground, smeared with blood. Not surprisingly, the niece screamed, which attracted the neighbours. Led by Briscoe and Macdonald, the whole concourse crossed to nearby Linecate, where the middle-aged relatives of Mary Macphee lived with their unstable twenty-four-year-old son, Angus Macphee.

The house was in darkness but a short search found the hideously butchered bodies of both the occupants. Briscoe gave a quick warning to the crowd that had gathered outside the door, telling them that Angus Macphee must have gone mad and would be roaming the island. He told them to carry weapons in case Macphee attacked them next, and to guard the fords that led to North Uist, the next island north. With the local people alerted and possibly terrified, Briscoe sent a messenger to Lochmaddy, the chief town of the three islands, to inform the sheriff of the murders. However, the messenger refused to go. It simply was not safe with a mad murderer on the loose.

The story gradually came out. In the spring of that year Angus Macphee, a powerfully built man of twenty-four, had moved back in with his parents in Linecate near the township of Nunton in Benbecula. Linecate was a fairly typical old-style Hebridean house, long and simple with the living quarters at one end and the byre for the cattle at the other. The parents noticed that Angus was acting slightly strangely, but they dismissed the thought and carried on with the routine of the croft. The situation continued for some months, with Angus having bouts of unusual behaviour followed by periods when he was absolutely normal. When it became obvious that Angus could go over the edge at any time, the local people asked the Nunton blacksmith to forge a pair of handcuffs to keep him, and them, safe.

On the day of the murders, Angus walked to the home of his aunt Mary Macphee, who lived just a few yards away. There must have been some sort of argument and perhaps Mary Macphee tried to put the handcuffs on him. It was known that being confined exasperated him and now he cut her throat, slashed her face to ribbons and pummelled her head with the iron cuffs. With that business completed, he returned home and murdered his mother, Catherine Macinnes, in the same fashion. His father, also Angus, was outside at the time, employed with the potatoes, so Angus stood at the door of his house and shouted for his father to come in and get a pipe of tobacco. When the father walked over, Angus grabbed hold of him and ran his knife across his throat, then smashed his head with the handcuffs until it was a bloody pulp. Satisfied he had done a good job, Angus bundled his father under his bed, closed the door and ran to the hills.

During the course of the afternoon, he met a pensioner named Munro and invited him home for a smoke. Munro and Angus Macphee had never got on, so the invitation rang false. Munro turned him down, which possibly saved his life, and Angus returned to the hills. Sometime during the night, he came back down, opened the floodgates of the local water mill and ran off again. Unattended, the mill wheel ran unfettered until friction set one of the beams alight and the building caught fire. Luckily, it was extinguished without loss of life or serious damage. Meanwhile, Angus continued his career, tapping on the window of another house in time to the peals of a clock and loitering near a house where Dr McLean from Uist was staying the night.

That night the good people of Benbecula kept their doors and windows locked and it is unlikely many slept peacefully. Men would keep weapons close to hand. Next morning they searched the island, keeping together for protection. They found Angus sitting on a rock in an island within one of the many lochs that festoon Benbecula. He was holding a sharpened spade and the rumour spread that he intended to murder the blacksmith who had made his handcuffs. A crowd gathered on the shores of the loch and tried to persuade him to give himself up. Angus agreed, and said there was 'no point in opposing so many'. He threw his spade into the loch and surrendered. Only then did two men wade through the water to secure him.

The sheriff met the crowd as they escorted Angus across the fords and all the way to the jail in Lochmaddy in North Uist. Once there, the remainder of Angus's story came out. Months ago he had been working as a farm servant in South Uist but fell out with his master and left that job. It was then that his unstable nature came to the fore, so the local priests stepped in. Their solution to his mental problems was to tie him up and feed him on bread and water, arguably the worst possible thing to do. Naturally, Angus resented this treatment and in the only retaliation he could, he named the priests John Murder and James Kill. Shortly afterwards, Angus returned home to Benbecula.

At his trial later that year, the influence of the priests again surfaced when Angus said that he was the Christ and he had killed his relatives by Divine Command. Even more ominously, he said he had intended to kill some others. The judge and jury found him insane and confined him to a lunatic asylum.

The Tinkers

Love them, romanticise them, fear them or loathe them, tinkers were part of life in the Highlands. Tinkers were wanderers, 'gaun-aboot-folk' in vernacular Lowland Scots, or *ceardannan* – craftsmen – in Gaelic. They were distinct from the Gypsies, who arrived in the late-fifteenth or early-sixteenth century from abroad, and they usually spoke Gaelic or *Beialrearich* or *Buerla Reagaird* – a complex language of their own that encompasses elements of Gaelic, Scots and perhaps even Romany. Today the term 'tinker' is more used as abuse, and this group of people are Travelling People.

By the nineteenth century they did not have a good reputation among the more settled peoples of Scotland, although they may have been in the country for countless generations. The 1859 *Book of Rules and Instructions for the Sutherland Police* specifically advised the police that:

There are 'gangs' or 'tribes' of tinkers who live principally in Caithness-shire, but make periodic tours through different parts of Scotland. A gang of these people, with horses and carts, after passing through Argyle and Perthshire a few months ago, were detected by the police in Forfarshire, where they were carrying on their depredations; in the carts were found some of their plunder from Perthshire and elsewhere; two of them were convicted of various acts of theft; and they are known at Aberdeen and Wick as 'habit and repute' common thieves. Another gang from Caithness-shire has lately been passed out of the same county by the police.

Colonel Kinloch, the man responsible for inspecting the Scottish police forces after the 1857 Police Act, estimated there were 62,278 vagrants, including tinkers, in 1862, with 2,560 police in Scotland to control them. Kinloch believed these vagrants were responsible for most rural crime. In 1865 the Trespass Act put some pressure on these people. They were believed to have helped spread disease such as cattle plague by their habit of sleeping in barns. Some of the Sutherland vagrant families were rumoured to have immigrated to North America.

There was another side to the story. According to Isabel Grant, arguably the finest of all Highland folklorists, the original Highland tinkers were wandering craftsmen, metalworkers and silversmiths who created much of the beautiful artwork of the Gaelic people. They were noted for their honesty and skill, with some being registered as silversmiths and having their own hallmark. Some also made horn spoons and may also have made the seventeenth-century powder horns that can be admired in museums the length and breadth of the country. Others bought sheets of tin to create the tin wear that gave them their name, or made baskets, drinking beakers, horn tumblers or bagpipes and fished for freshwater pearls. They were nomads, roaming the byways of Scotland, living in large birch-framed tents known as 'ghiellies', and some claimed to be descended from clans that had lost their lands. There is also a legend that they were descendants of the Picts, the indigenous peoples of the country even before the Gaels arrived. They moved in family groups of which the best known were the Stewarts, McPhies and MacDonalds.

Mostly these people were an asset to the Highlands, but as the centuries passed and urbanisation spread, with its plethora of town-based industries, there was less demand for the tinkers' crafts, and the position of the tinkers was undermined. Rather than welcome them for their news, skills and entertainment, the people came to believe that they were drunkards and thieves. In September one family of travelling tinkers came to the notice of the authorities for the worst possible reason.

In September 1874 the circuit judges Lord Ardmillan and Lord Neaves stayed the night at the Royal George Hotel in Perth before travelling on to the Circuit court. As always, there was pomp and ceremony at the opening of the court, with a colourful show by the band of First Perthshire Rifle Volunteers, together with a body of police in their smartest uniforms and the sheriffs and magistrates of the district marching or riding alongside the judges. People watched them pass and wondered at their power.

Although every case that came before the court was of intense interest to the people who were charged, the most intriguing case to the public was a killing in Crieff, which the press imaginatively dubbed the Crieff Murder. There were two accused, George McCallum and Mary McCallum, son and mother. When they first arrived in court they wore prison dress, to which the Advocate Depute, Mr Muirhead, objected, as it might have made identification difficult by the witnesses. The accused changed and returned in their own clothes, with Mary McCallum, a woman of seventy who looked ten years younger, dressed in what looked like dirty rags with a white mutch and a shawl. George McCallum had long unwashed brown hair, thick eyebrows above deep-set eyes, a long nose and ragged beard, he looked a wild man, but with a surprisingly weak face.

George and Mary McCallum were both tinkers and as such they were not quite in the mainstream of respectability. They were jointly charged with the murder of a mason named Peter Sharp on the Back Road of Crieff, known as the Duchlage. The prosecution alleged that the McCallums had stabbed him in the abdomen with a knife on the night of Sunday, 7 or the early morning of Monday, 8 March 1874. After the killing, they were accused of robbing the body of a bottle of whisky, a silver watch and a gold Albert chain, and a leather purse with some money inside. There were a great many witnesses to the actions of the McCallums that night, but not all their stories matched.

A local labourer named Donald McGregor thought he was first to discover the body. He was walking through Cornton Place just before seven on the Monday morning when he saw a man sitting with his back against the wall near the door of a weaver named Thomas Roy. The man looked very still. McGregor looked closer and saw the man was sitting in a spreading pool of blood. He was sure the man was dead, but he did not recognise him.

He knocked on Roy's door and cried out, 'Are you sleeping?'

'No,' Roy shouted from inside.

'There's a man at your door,' McGregor said, 'and there's something wrong with him.'

Roy came to the door. After a brief look, Roy said the dead man was named Peter Sharp. McGregor noticed that Sharp had neither watch nor watch chain, and there was a lower button missing from his waistcoat, while his hat was lying about ten yards away. McGregor also noticed he had blood on his own boots and trousers, as well as on the step at Roy's front door.

Roy and McGregor borrowed a wheelbarrow from a plasterer named William Forbes. They bundled Sharp inside and immediately noticed a gash in his trousers around the groin, and saw a line of blood spots that terminated at Roy's door. Roy and his daughter Janet hurried to tell Inspector Stevenson, the local policeman. Roy asked Stevenson if he should fetch a doctor but the Inspector said Sharp was past help.

Thomas Roy had not slept well the previous night. When he had arrived home from work he had to knock on his door to gain entrance, which was unusual, as his wife never locked the door. However when she explained there were tinkers about he understood, because tinkers had a bad reputation, earned or otherwise, for petty thefts from houses. Shortly afterward, Roy went to bed but sometime during the night he heard a thump, which he took to be somebody banging against his front door. He lay for a few moments until he heard voices outside his house. When he got up to investigate he heard somebody groaning and then a heavy tread on the ground outside. He heard a voice say either 'I know you, Peter' or 'Do you know me, Peter.' There was silence for a while, and then Roy heard light footsteps and the murmur of two voices and maybe the name 'Mike.'

Roy's wife was also listening to the noise outside, but when it faded away Janet said he had better get to bed. It was only a few hours afterward that McGregor hammered on his door.

With the police alerted and Sharp trundled away on a barrow, Roy sent his son to tell Sharp's family the news.

Janet Roy remembered events slightly differently. She had gone to bed about half past eleven the previous night and shortly afterward she heard somebody run past the house and thought someone gave the front door a shake. She put her candle away from the window and heard a very weak voice call, 'Are you in? Are you sleeping?'

When her mother asked her what was happening, Janet Roy looked cautiously out of the window. She thought she heard a woman say, 'Bell' and she heard somebody moaning softly.

There was another voice. 'I ken you fine. Come awa' hame.'

Janet Roy looked out the window and saw two policemen walk past the house. She went back to bed until McGregor woke them up next morning.

The police traced the background and movements of Peter Sharp. He was an unmarried, good-natured man approaching his twenty-seventh birthday. On the evening of 7 March he had dressed a little less smartly than usual and had gone out. He wore his soft 'Fenian' hat and silver watch with a gold Albert chain and carried perhaps sixteen shillings in change. His parents bid him goodbye and next morning they were informed he had taken an ill turn. Shortly afterward their son's body was wheeled in to their house.

Sharp had been seen in the town at about eleven when he had a quiet drink at Mrs Sinclair's pub at the Cross with a scavenger named John Tracey. Sharp bought a half mutchkin – small bottle – of whisky at Mrs Sinclair's and parted from Tracey. Peter McGregor, a joiner, saw him lying outside Roy's door at about half past eleven at night, thought he was drunk and propped him against Roy's door. He asked, 'Do you know me, Peter?' There was no response.

Peter McGregor returned home, passing two couples, neither of whom he knew. He told his wife that he should go back and put Sharp into a more comfortable position, but his wife said that there would be plenty people passing by on a Saturday evening who would take care of him. It was the next morning before Peter McGregor realised there was blood on his trousers and his shoes.

The police who Janet Roy had seen were Inspector Stevenson and Constable McHardy. They saw Peter Sharp propped against the wall but thought he was drunk and passed on. That was at about five past twelve.

There were four suspects for the murder. Two were the tinkers, George and Mary McCallum, the third was a local photographer named Kidd and the fourth a hairdresser named John Hardy. Kidd had recently left the woman with whom he had been living, and the police scooped him up, mainly because his house was on the route that Sharp would have taken. He and Hardy were soon released and all the attention turned to the tinker McCallums.

Inspector Stevenson had seen the McCallums near the murder scene that fatal night. He ordered them and another pair of tinkers out of the town and thought no more about it, as they were well known around Crieff. After the murder Stevenson began to collect evidence about their behaviour that night. They had been drinking at the Star Hotel in East High Street, where the landlady, Jane McCulloch, served a number of tinkers, including George McCallum, who had a damaged hand and said he was going to see a doctor about it. Ann Gordon also saw George McCallum with a sore hand as she bought half a tartan shawl from a female tinker. There was quite a large family of McCallums, with John McCallum, the father; a wife; two sons; and two daughters.

James Morrison, a Crieff plumber, was also out on the Saturday night. He was with one of his friends when they bumped into a band of tinkers on Commissioner Street; there was a man, a boy and two females. The woman begged tobacco from them and asked for money, which they refused, and walked away quickly before the tinkers 'annoyed them'. The woman took the tobacco but rather than light her pipe, she began to dance and sing. Morrison thought she had had too much to drink but was not yet drunk. One of the tinkers shouted, 'Are you away that way,' as Morrison and his friend left.

Thomas Thomson also saw the band of tinkers that night. He was a mason who doubled up as the local lamplighter, but that Saturday night he was later than normal in putting on the lights. He saw the tinkers in Manse Road and then again in Commissioner Street, one man with three women.

Duncan Reid and his girl, Mary McRory, had a more dramatic tale to tell. They were walking along Manse Road when they heard a shout of 'Murder' and then again 'Murder,' with the second call much fainter than the first. They thought the cries came from Duchlage Road. A few moments later they saw a man in a dark coat and light trousers running across a piece of ground that was known as the Pecks. Reid knew and had worked with George McCallum and thought he was a peaceful man.

James Stobie lived near Thomas Roy in Duchlage Road. Mary McCallum came to his house at about ten on the Saturday night to get a light for her pipe; she was not sober. He heard heavier footsteps pass. Alexander Roy of Commissioner Street heard somebody moaning that night and when he investigated he found the elderly woman McCallum lying on the ground; Janet Roy, Alexander's wife, made her a cup of tea and the woman remained lying on the ground all night. Janet Roy said the woman mentioned she had a fright the previous night and when she heard about the murder she said, 'It would be my good daughter that stabbed the man.'

Mary Gorrie of Commissioner Street heard a slightly different tale from the tinker. According to Gorrie, when she heard about the murder she threw her hands up and said, 'It's my husband that's murdered and my good daughter that has done it. She has long threatened to do it and she's done it now.'

The house of Peter Stewart overlooked the Pecks. About twenty to seven on Sunday morning he saw a man that looked like George McCallum crossing the Pecks. He went into the shed in the Pecks later that day and found the door unlocked and a broken gin bottle on the floor. He thought there had been a man sleeping on the floor there as well.

The Honourable Elenora Gordon Cumming was staying in Glenearn House in Crieff; she saw a bunch of tinkers, including a man with a bandaged hand who she thought was looking at a watch with his left hand. A young farmer's boy named William Wedderspoon saw the tinkers as he took milk to Glenearn House and thought he saw a watch chain from the trouser pocket of a tinker with a bandaged hand.

In common with most people in Crieff, young Wedderspoon did not want to pass the tinkers and altered his route to avoid them.

On that same Sunday morning after the murder, George McCallum was in the shop of Grace McLean, with money which he told her he had not had the previous day.

Mary McCallum entered Ann Crerar's house on the Sunday. Mary McCallum told her that a man had been murdered on the back road and 'his siller and watch were taken off him ... I will never forget his cries.' James Robertson lived in the same house and Mary McCallum, or Reid, told him about the murder and added, 'God have mercy on my soul, for I can't get the cries of the murdered man out of my ears. We had a scuffle and followed him on his blood. His last words were, "God have mercy on my soul." John Grant, a criminal officer from Perth, found fragments of a bottle in the shed, while John Thomson, a mason, found a button about ten yards from Roy's door, beside a line of blood spots.

Although the evidence was contradictory and confused, the police believed the McCallums were involved. That same Sunday morning constable John McHardy stopped the tinker band and searched through their possessions. He found three knives and arrested two men: George McCallum and his father. He ignored Mary McCallum at that time. When McHardy arrested the men, Mary McCallum said, 'Just go with the man and let them see you had nothing to do with it.'

The tinkers were taken to Perth Prison and strip-searched, but James Stewart, the warden who searched them, did not find another knife. However, Stewart said that there was a button missing on George McCallum's coat and the other buttons matched the one found beside the blood at Roy's door.

When the case came to the Perth Circuit Court the police said there was no trace of Sharp's blood on any of the knives found on McCallum. Andrew McCallum, the son of Mary McCallum and brother of George McCallum, was questioned in court. He did not know how old he was but he said the 'whole lot of us were in Crieff' and agreed that George McCallum often had a knife. The gamekeeper Duncan McAra confirmed that he had seen George McCallum with a knife. A very young tinker girl normally named Mary McCallum, although her real name was Ann Neilson, described what she saw happen. She was George McCallum's step-daughter and mentioned them all being on the Back Road when 'a strange man that had drink in a kettle came up to us' and gave George McCallum and Mary McCallum 'a good drop' of it. 'After the man gave my father and my granny the drink, my father stabbed the man and went away with the knife.' When the man was stabbed he cried, 'Oh me! What am I tae dae!'

The young Mary McCallum also said, 'My granny, after the man was stabbed, took the bottle from him and gave it to my father. I saw my granny take nothing from the man. When the strange man was with us he had a watch and chain. My father took it out of the man's pocket and went away with it to a garden with stones and made a mark where the watch was put.' The little girl had already shown Inspector Stevenson the site of the murder and mentioned her stepfather saying, 'Eh, there's blood; I'll be putten in jail and I'll be killed. Come away up and see the blood.' Inspector Stevenson could not find the watch or the murder weapon, although he searched the gardens and other places where they might have been hidden.

In his statement, George McCallum said he was twenty-four years old and they had all been very drunk on the evening of the murder. He said he remembered the police moving them along but denied any quarrel or any murder and claimed to have been mainly in the High Street. He said he returned to Crieff the next day to search for his mother. In a later declaration, George McCallum admitted they had been at the place where the man was killed. He said they met a man who was very drunk. His mother, Mary McCallum senior, took a half-mutchkin of whisky from him and the man 'bullyragged' to get it back, at which point his mother stole the man's watch from his left waistcoat pocket and stabbed the man, saying, 'You son of a bitch, I'll make you pay for it.' George McCallum then claimed that he ran away and spent the night in a shed.

A little later, George McCallum made yet another statement where he said that when the man and his mother had quarrelled he had tried to split them up but the man had pushed him to the ground and returned to his mother's company. In this declaration, he said that his mother had got the knife before the fatal argument. In a fourth declaration, he said that all his former words were true, except that his mother had taken threepence from the murdered man's waistcoat pocket and told him to go and buy whisky. He also said his mother had thrown the knife and watch into the Earn from the bridge at Crieff and had said that if he ever told anybody where she had thrown the knife and watch she would stab him 'as surely as she had stabbed the man', and emphasised her words by banging him on the back of the head with a large stone, at the same time calling him a 'bitch's son'.

Mary McCallum junior gave her own version of events. She said she was over seventy years of age and admitted that the whole family was in Crieff on the Saturday night and were drunk, with herself being 'real drunk'. She spent the night in a close near the east toll. In the morning she walked to the Cross and to the murder site. She asked a police sergeant if he had seen 'any of her people' but he just told her to move on, so she left the town. On her way to Gilmoretown, she met her son and her husband, both were under arrest. She denied any knowledge of, or participation in, the murder.

The evidence left no doubt that Sharp had been on the Back Road and had been stabbed there. The tinkers had been seen there. The button, the sound of heavy footsteps, and the fight over the whisky, all of this pointed to George McCallum, but was all circumstantial.

George McCallum was found guilty of the murder of Sharp while the jury unanimously found his mother not guilty. The jury also voted fourteen to one to ask the judge for mercy for George McCallum. Lord

Ardmillan sentenced him to be fed on bread and water until Saturday, 3 October, and then to be hanged to death.

The Crieff murder brought some public attention to the tinkers. The press seemed unanimous in their disapproval of what the *Dundee Courier* of 16 September 1874 called 'these miserable outcasts of society' who lived lives of 'gross licentiousness and drunkenness'. The *Courier* suggested that the church should attempt missionary work because 'nowhere in the wide world is there any gross heathenishness than is lived by these miserable men and women'. In the case of the McCallums, the *Courier* perhaps had a point.

The Killing in Grantown-on-Spey

Grantown-on-Spey is a pretty place in Speyside, a planned village with a broad main street and access to the northern slopes of the Cairngorm Mountains. It is an unlikely setting for serious crime, but in July 1878 the population was agog when a prominent farmer was involved in a murder.

Andrew Grainger coupled farming Fettes in Easter Ross, with a secondary occupation as a railway contractor. Perhaps it was the pressure of holding down two jobs, but on occasions, Grainger had a tendency to drink too much. In the middle of July he hit the bottle quite seriously and by 17 July he was in an alcoholic haze. That day he left home for Inverness, intending to go to Ballinluig, near Pitlochry, where his wife was visiting her sick mother. When he was in the railway station he shied away from the crowds in case somebody robbed him, and asked a passing acquaintance to buy his ticket for him.

When the train reached Forres, Grainger slipped off, bought a bottle of whisky and boarded again, entering a compartment already occupied by a Dr Scott. Grainger sat down, took a knife from his pocket and thrust it up the sleeve of his coat. Not surprisingly, Scott

Grantown on Spey

was a little alarmed, particularly as Grainger seemed very excited. The alcohol must have been working through Grainger's system because as the train pulled into the tiny stop at Dunphail, he jumped out of the compartment and ran up the full length of the train until he came to the engine.

The driver knew Grainger so, rather than be alarmed, he welcomed his company as he started the train for the remainder of the journey south. However, Grainger had other ideas, and as soon as the train began to pick up speed he moved to the back of the tender that was immediately behind the engine. As the driver followed after, Grainger tried to jump off. The driver grabbed hold of him in time and Grainger yelled out, 'Murder!'

The driver stopped the train; two of the passengers came forward to see what all the fuss was about. They held Grainger secure until they reached Grantown, where he was taken off and locked in the station master's office. For a while Grainger was quiet, but eventually he asked to see a doctor. The station master sent him to a hotel, but as soon as the doctor took his pulse, Grainger wrenched free and stormed from the room. The doctor was naturally concerned and asked the hotel manager to post somebody to watch him. Grainger booked a room for himself and no doubt everybody sighed with relief, hoping he would sleep off whatever was bothering him.

They were wrong. About three hours later, the cry of 'Murder' resounded through the hotel, and again 'Murder.' Rather than go and investigate, the hotel manager called for the police and Constable James Fraser came to investigate. He entered Grainger's room but before he could do anything Grainger slipped the knife down his sleeve and stabbed him low in the belly, hard and fast. More police arrived and arrested Grainger. Fraser died two days later.

The police took Grainger to a cell in the police station but he was unable to understand why he was there or what he had done for a number of days afterwards. His case was heard at the Circuit court in Inverness in September and a large crowd waited outside the courtroom to watch him be taken in. He pleaded temporary insanity due to delirium tremens. After a case that lasted nine hours, the jury accepted that and found him not guilty of murder, but guilty of culpable homicide.

8

The Land Wars

Throughout the nineteenth century, the Highlands and Islands seethed with unrest over the question of land, or, as the crofters put it, Landlordism. Put very simply, the indigenous population needed land for crofting, but the landlord class held the land for sheep farming and later for sporting estates. These rival requirements were not compatible in an area where fertile land was in short supply. The result was a steady trickle of forced evictions or alteration of use by the landlords, and bitter resentment by the dispossessed. There was resistance to the Clearances, but it was not until the 1880s that the crofters and cottars really began to fight back in a campaign that brought the military to the glens and caught the attention of the wider British public. There had always been some retaliation, but it was sporadic and usually futile.

Their renewed resistance made the national newspapers, often raising support from the public that had been lacking in previous decades. These Land Wars appeared to be a threat to the establishment, while some may have feared a revival of the old Jacobite spirit. To the men and women involved, it was more a matter of economic necessity.

They Must Be Taught Submission

In the summer of 1854 Major Robertson of Kindeace near Invergordon cleared some tenants from his lands. That was not unusual in the nineteenth century, and neither was the resistance from the tenants and their friends. When the sheriff officers and police arrived to evict the tenants, Peter and Ann Ross were among the people who tried to resist.

The police arrested the Rosses and in September they appeared before the Lord Justice Clerk at Inverness Circuit Court. His Lordship was very much of the same class as Major Robertson. He had been staying locally for some time, shooting on the Sutherland estate of his son, William Hope. The Rosses were charged with mobbing, rioting and breach of the peace. They pleaded guilty to the latter only.

The Lord Justice Clerk said he saw little distinction between the two charges and continued with his opinion of the Rosses' attempt to retain their homes. He spoke of their lawlessness: 'The course of the law must have its effect with all in order to protect all persons, high and low, and all must submit whatever their feelings or rank or perverted feelings of right and wrong. What is it that these parties can propose to themselves? Do they think that they are above the law? Is the feeling of the respectable and well-educated peasantry of Scotland not to be served upon them? It is quite essential that such a spirit as that which these panels expressed is to be repressed. They must be taught submission in the very first instance and that the slightest resistance must lead to exemplary punishment.' Peter Ross was given eighteen months with hard labour, and Ann was given twelve months.

In that same court, the Lord Justice Clerk sentenced James Sutherland, waiter at the Commercial Hotel Inverness, to eight months. He had fired a gun in Invergordon and killed a woman. The charge was culpable homicide.

Human life was less important than submission to the laws of landed property. A generation later, attitudes had hardened and altered.

Battle of the Braes

One of the areas where the crofters fought back was the Braes, about nine miles south of Portree in the Island of Skye. There were three small townships here: Gedintailor, Balmeanach and Peinchorran. All had Loch Sligachan to the south, a sliding range of low brown-green hills on the west, and the sound of Raasay on the east. Basically, the Braes was an isolated peninsula, a unique community with a single narrow road for entrance and exit.

Crofting was a precarious way of life that usually depended on a secondary income for the crofters to make ends meet. A croft is a small parcel of land that is rented from a landowner. It usually has a few acres of arable land for crops, and the crofter also has the traditional right to graze animals on communal land, usually also owned by the same landowner. There were seldom any written rights to this grazing land, and often the crofters depended on tradition that stretched back into the unknown past.

Until around 1815 the crofters, particularly of the Outer Hebrides, augmented their money by kelp – seaweed – farming, although the landowners soaked up most of the profits. The kelp was burned and the ash used in glass and soap production. The gathering was pure hard labour, but a few years after the end of the Napoleonic Wars in 1815, the bottom fell out of that industry when deposits of sulphate of potash were found in Germany. A decade later the industry was only a memory and the bad times returned with a vengeance; MacLean of Coll cleared the entire population of the island of Coll to America in 1828 in the first of a new wave of forced evictions, and two years later the shoals of herring deserted the Hebrides. Men looked for alternative work. Many turned to the east coast fishing, others looked for agricultural work in the Lowlands, but if either of these failed, then the crofters faced destitution. Crofting was the backbone of much of the Hebridean economy and every scrap of land was needed.

The crofters of the Braes were in a longstanding dispute with their landlord, Lord MacDonald, over grazing rights. The crofters had used the slopes of Ben Lee, one hill of the range that stretched between the Braes and Glenvarrigil, as common pasture for grazing their livestock, but in 1865 MacDonald gave the lease to a sheep farmer. In late 1881, the crofters drew up a petition requesting the return of their traditional land. The timing was crucial; the lease to the sheep farmer was about to expire and there was a new spirit of defiance among the Hebridean and Highland crofting communities. In part, that was due to desperation, as times were hard, but there was a new political edge as well. There was great agitation over land rights in Ireland, and some of the Braes crofters had been employed in Irish fishing boats, where they no doubt learned of the successful tactics employed there, such as boycotting and withholding of rents. Many crofters were also part-time fishermen and when a storm sank many fishing boats the men were forced to rely only on their crofts, so the availability of land became even more crucial.

The crofters took the petition to Portree and handed it to Alexander MacDonald, the factor. As so often, the landowner's man refused to compromise and resorted to the old methods and excuses. Alexander MacDonald agreed that the crofters had used the hill pasture prior to 1865, but said it was 'on sufferance' and they had no legal claim to the grazings. The crofters claimed long centuries of usage as their right and disputed the factor's words. Rather than surrender, the crofters marched in a body to the factor's office, again demanded access to the grazing on Ben Lee, adding that unless their rights were returned, 'Their rents would not be paid.'

Alexander MacDonald was every bit as determined to win as the crofters were, and searched for methods of retaliation. His first was to accuse the crofters of intimidation to raise support for their protests, but when that failed he turned to the traditional method of landlord control. On 7 April 1882 a sheriff officer named Angus Martin arrived with a notice of ejection for a dozen of the crofting families. However, the crofters were not in the mood to back down. Two boys were on watch; they saw Martin coming and waved flags to gather support. Soon around 150 crofters surrounded Martin. Some of the men grabbed hold of him and either burned the eviction document themselves or forced Martin to burn it. There was a song written about the incident:

A Sheriff from the factor came
and he came down our way,
From Lord MacDonald he was sent
to clear us out from Skye.

By attacking the sheriff officer and removing the writs of eviction, the crofters had committed the crime of 'deforcement'. Until that t ime they had merely been in dispute with their landlord. Now they had broken the law and were criminals. The crofters knew that matters would not end there, so they prepared for the factor's next move. They set sentries to watch the single road into their community, lit their pipes, tended their land, and waited.

Martin reported to his headquarters in Inverness and Sheriff William Ivory requested help from the police. The Inverness force was too small to spare any men to cope with what seemed a major disturbance, so Ivory asked the Superintendent of Police in Glasgow if some men could be sent to Skye. The Superintendent agreed and sent fifty police officers.

The sheriff officer gathered together his fifty-strong escort and returned to Skye. When they neared the Braes, the sheriff officer slipped to the back so he could direct their pounce. In the dark pre-dawn a cold, wet and rainy 19 April, they took the crofters by surprise, arrested their suspects and were hastily retreating

Idyllic views of the Kinloch gold fields in Sutherland

before the Braes crofters were properly awake. However, once the warning was given, the crofters dashed out of their houses and fell on the rearguard of the police with sticks and stones and yells of wild rage. There were around 100 people involved in the attack on the police, from grey-bearded men who remembered the old days when clearance was commonplace, to women, and young children who knew nothing of the political disputes of the past. There was a bloody clash; sticks and stones against the truncheons and discipline of the stalwart policemen, with broken heads among the crofters, men and women. Seven women were reported as being injured.

The police, however, did not escape injuries either, and had to baton charge the crowd to escape, taking ten or so limping casualties with them. They made a fighting retreat to Portree with their prisoners. A poet described the incident slightly differently:

A wet and dismal morning dawned
As from Portree they rode;
the men of Braes were up in time
and met them on the road.

Today there is a plaque marking the spot, with an inscription in Gaelic and English that reads: 'Near this cairn on 19 April 1882 ended the battle fought by the people of Braes on behalf of the crofters of Gaeldom.'

The Battle of the Braes was the opening round in a long campaign for better crofters' rights throughout the Highlands and Islands. It encouraged resistance to other examples of landlord abuse and brought the attention of the press to living conditions in the far reaches of the country. For the arrested men it meant a trial in Inverness, but there were other strings to the factors' bows other than straightforward eviction. Caithness Archive Centre holds a petition that was sent by fifteen residents of Portree to Sheriff Ivory some time after the battle. The petition asked that a force of police should be stationed in the village as the 'much agitated' Braes crofters had threatened 'to come to Portree in a body and destroy or burn several houses'. The police were to remain in the village 'until the present excitement abates'.

Sheriff Ivory wanted more than a mere increase in the number of police. In September 1882 he requested 100 troops to be sent to Skye to deal with the crofters, for there had been mutinous growling in other parts of the island as well.

Once more MacDonald's anger broke.
'Invade the Isle of Skye!
Two thousand soldiers, boats and guns
The people must comply!'

By the end of that year the Inverness-shire Police had more than doubled their numbers from forty-four to ninety-four, but the crofters still continued their campaign for better rights. The five men from Braes appeared at court in Inverness and were fined between £1 and £2 and 10 shillings. They returned to Braes in time to help drive the cattle onto Ben Lee, in defiance of Lord MacDonald, his factor, the sheriff officers, the Glasgow Police and Uncle Tom Cobley and all.

The factor obtained a Court of Session order to take their cattle elsewhere, but when Alexander MacDonald, the messenger at arms and his escort arrived with the document, the womenfolk of Braes sent him packing. The men were at the east coast fishing at the time.

The poet put it in simpler terms:

> 'Oh, if we send one million men'
> In London they declared,
> 'We'll never clear the Isle of Skye.
> The people are not scared.'

The people were certainly determined and resistance continued. On 23 October the messenger at arms, this time backed by a ground officer – an assistant factor – named Norman Beaton, again tried to deliver his Court of Session order. MacDonald asked the crofters to fetch the 'principal tenants' who he thought were hiding in the hills, but the crofters refused to comply and again forced the factor's men to retreat.

The People Are Mightier Than a Lord

The Battle of the Braes was only the foretaste of unrest that spread all across the Highlands. There was further trouble in Glendale, near Dunvegan, at the north-west of Skye and at nearby Husabost. At Husabost the landowner, Dr Nicol Martin, demanded ten days' annual unpaid labour from his tenants, with a fine for those who disobeyed. Donald MacDonald, the factor on the Glendale estate, ordered the crofters to stop collecting driftwood and said they could not own dogs. There was a meeting to discuss resistance and men began to fight back.

At Glendale the crofters, led by a man named John MacPherson of Milovaig, drove their animals onto disputed land and they were, if anything, even more militant. There were reports of crofters preparing to repel the police with scythe blades tied to poles. A shepherd at Glendale was attacked and driven away. When the police tried to establish a permanent presence in the area, a lookout saw them approaching and blew his horn to gather the crofters in support. Around 500 crofters knocked the police to the ground and drove them to Dunvegan. The crofters armed themselves with scythes, sticks and whatever else they could find, marched on Dunvegan and cleared the area of the police, sheriff officers and any other symbol of eviction and oppression. Because of these and other demonstrations elsewhere in the Highlands, in 1883 the government set up a commission, the Napier Commission, to investigate crofters' grievances.

The Napier Commission was a start, but it was weak. It was a step forward, but only a small one. However, clearing the forces of authority in Skye was an impressive victory for a class of tenants which had been subjected to oppression and eviction for over a century. With the factor and the majesty of the police set at defiance, Lord MacDonald and the Sheriff of Inverness were left seemingly impotent, but there were further developments in Skye.

In autumn 1884 the crofters of Kilmuir and Glendale areas moved their stock into a number of sheep farms. By that time the crofters were well organised and a group calling itself HLLRA (Highland Land Law Reform Association) had united all the scattered communities under a single banner. The HLLRA was also known as the Highland Land League and their slogan was: 'The people are mightier than a lord.' As usual in such cases, there were a few men who went too far and intimidated crofters who did not want to join, with hayricks of those who refused being burned and livestock mutilated. Rightly or wrongly, the authorities believed that the crofters of Kilmuir were particularly guilty of intimidation and sent a superintendent and ten constables to restore order to the area. The crofters drove them off with stones and sticks and hard words.

The situation worsened as rumours grew: the police on Skye were said to be armed with revolvers; the crofters at Kilmuir were waiting with rifles. Anything could happen, from a massacre of civilians by frightened police to a full-scale battle. There were stories of some Glendale crofters advocating the use of real violence in the Irish manner unless their situation was taken seriously.

The troubles were not confined to Skye. Tiree and South Uist also witnessed the crofters seizing back land they had previously occupied, while crofters on Barra, North Uist and Lewis had similar designs. Throughout the Hebrides, crofters cut the wire fences of sheep farms, withheld their rent and occasionally burned the hayrick or mutilated the livestock of a man who failed to support the Land Leaguers. Most newspapers supported the landlords; *The Scotsman* called the actions of the Land Leaguers 'terrorism'.

Instead of sending nervous police into the hotbed of volatile and angry crofters, the authorities sent for the marines. In November 1884, in accordance with British gunboat diplomacy in other parts of the world a Royal Navy gunboat, *Jackal*, a troopship with 300 Royal Marines and one of MacBrayne's steamers, *Lochiel*, arrived off the island. *Lochiel* did not have her original crew, who had refused to sail against the crofters, but it seemed the authorities were determined to finally squash the land disputes on Skye.

Sheriff Ivory ordered that 250 redcoated Royal Marines should parade around Trotternish, the area of Skye most disaffected. They did so, carrying packs, rifles, bayonets and ammunition. The crofters had no ill will toward the Royal Marines, so they gathered to enjoy this free military tattoo. The marines were, however, used to back up the sheriff officers when they arrested various crofters. The Marines remained for months; the crofters still withheld their rents and when the election came in late 1885, large numbers of the crofters voted for the HLLRA.

Troubles at Uig

In May 1885 there was trouble at Uig in Lewis. The pattern was the same: the crofters had taken possession of land they needed. A sheriff officer and a party of his men entered the area to hand over warrants to remove their livestock. The crofters refused to accept the warrants and instead de-forced the sheriff officers.

On 5 March 1886 eight of the crofters accused of de-forcements appeared before the Inverness Circuit Court. They were all young men and appeared quiet and respectable in court: Peter Macdonald was a baker, Donald Smith was a blacksmith, Angus McLeod and Allan Morrison were crofters, Norman McIver and Murdoch MacLeod, William Macdonald and Donald MacLennan were fishermen. They were charged with assault and breach of the peace, but pleaded guilty only to the latter.

Sheriff Black said that the local minister was doing a good job in trying to preach the crofters into keeping the law, and there had not been much agitation in Uig for some time. He fined each man twenty shillings with the alternative of fifteen days in prison. His very next case was similar, as he faced a number of women who were charged with mobbing and rioting. They had banded together to prevent the tacksman James Mackenzie from grazing his stock on lands the crofters claimed at Linshadder, Uig. Sheriff Black fined them five shillings each.

When the elections came in 1886, four of the Highland Land Leaguers were elected, so becoming the first members of Parliament from the working classes and perhaps the first native speakers of Scottish Gaelic. For once, crimes had resulted in a positive outcome. But while the people of Skye and Lewis were fighting authority, Tiree was also facing its own difficulties.

Trouble in Tiree

Today there is an indefinable atmosphere of peace in the Inner Hebrides, something that relaxes the visitor as soon as he or she looks across from the western coast of the mainland to the scattered skerries and mountains that seem to rise straight from the sea. Visitors come year after year to breathe fresh air and some choose to remain and live in a safe and secure environment. However, that was not always the case. Throughout the Dark and Middle Ages these islands were the homeland of some of the most warlike clans in Scotland.

The island names are evocative: Rhum, Skye, Mull, Eigg, Raasay, Tiree. They carry the music of the Gael and the crash of winter seas. Of them all, Tiree is among the most beautiful and the most welcoming, yet in the 1880s this small island was so troublesome that the British government had to resort to sending in the Royal Navy and Royal Marines to subdue its population. The police just could not cope.

Tiree is around ten miles long and perhaps five miles at its widest; it sits twenty-two miles west of Ardnamurchan and very close to its neighbour of Coll, yet when the weather is bad it could be cut off for days or weeks at a time, so wild could the sea get. Unlike other Hebridean islands, Tiree is both fertile and low-lying. The highest point is only 462 feet above the surrounding sea, a pimple of a hill. There is little doubt that in the nineteenth century the population of Tiree was too large for the island to accommodate unless there were major economic changes. In 1846 there were around 4,500 people living on the island. Soon after, the landowner, the Duke of Argyll, sent a new factor to the island.

Folklore remembers him as *am Baillidh Mor*, the Big Factor, but his real name was Colonel John Campbell and he set about reducing the island's population. This he did by rent increases and forced evictions, even of blind men, heavily pregnant women and the elderly. The great famine of the later 1840s also encouraged people to emigrate so the population dropped to around 2,700 by the 1880s. That was another bad decade, with an agricultural depression that lowered farming income. Destitution haunted even the fertile fields of Tiree, but the landlord did not lower the rents, as had happened in Skye. All across the Hebrides, crofters faced starvation, but rather than succumb or emigrate, they began to retaliate.

In 1883 the crofters of Tiree asked the Duke of Argyll for a rent reduction and the return of common pastureland on Ben Hynish that had been taken from them some years before. In 1848 the rents had been raised to pay for some drainage works undertaken by the factor, but that work had been long paid for and the islanders asked that the rent return to its previous level. On 7 August 1883 a Royal Commission under Lord Napier was held on the island to listen to the islanders' grievances, which included security of tenure and compensation for improvements to the crofts. However, the ground officer declared that the estate did not grant leases on land with an annual rental of less than £100, so there were no secure tenures for the crofters. The Napier Commission did nothing to ease the plight of the Tiree crofters.

With their hardships increasing, many of the crofters began a rent strike and spoke of re-occupying disputed grazing land on Ben Hynish and Ben Hough. Criminal acts began, with the cutting of wire fences surrounding the sheep farms that had spread over land long used for communal grazing. The crofters, mainly members of the 136-strong Tiree branch of the Highland Land League, also organised a land raid on the farm of Greenhill. This sheep farm had been empty for a number of years but the Duke of Argyll had recently let it to a Jura man named Lachlan MacNeill. There were rumours of underhand dealings, and stories that the Duke had offered MacNeill the farm cheap if he informed on his fellow Land League crofters. The Land League very quickly revoked his membership and gave him and his brother verbal abuse. There were rumours of personal violence on the pattern of the Irish Land League, but they came to nothing.

In July 1885, 300 crofters occupied Greenhill Farm, removed the property of the new tenant and brought in their cattle. Once ensconced on the land, they began to divide the land between themselves and the landless cottars. When news came to the Duke of Argyll, he served writs to the squatters, and on 21 July 1886 the steamer *Nigel* sailed from Oban with what the newspapers grandly named the 'Tiree Expeditionary Force', forty policemen and a Messenger-at-Arms to enforce the Duke's Law. They landed from small boats in the wide Gott Bay in the south-east of Tiree with the legal documents. Guided by a local joiner named McKinnon, the sheriff officers on horseback or in gigs led the Expeditionary Force inland. At Ballyphuil they pushed five summonses under the crofters' doors in the sneaking hope there would be no resistance, but they were wrong.

The crofters had assumed the group of dark-clad men was a funeral party, but one of their number realised what was happening and blew a horn as a signal for them to gather together. Other horns echoed in the breezy peace of the Hebridean air, gathering the crofters together as men had once gathered to face the Norse, or on the call of their chief. There were over 200 determined men with sticks that formed around these new invaders. At first they thought the police had come to destroy the houses in the time-honoured manner of Authority during previous Clearances, and they demanded answers.

Colin Mackay, Chief Constable of Argyll, explained that the police were there to escort the sheriff officers, who were serving interdicts. When the crowd asked what that meant, he explained it was a document that instructed the crofters to remove their cattle from

Greenhill. There was no intention to evict anybody. Not impressed, the crofters surrounded the police so they could go no further. They took hold of the bridles of the carriage horses, turned them around and sent the sheriff officers back toward the coast.

Many of the crofters shouted comments such as: 'Never come back on such an errand as this,' and there were threats to throw the gigs and their occupants 'over a precipice'. One crofter named Hector McDonald attempted to punch a horse. McDonald also told the crowd to 'Go for the man with the papers now,' meaning the Messenger-at-Arms. A man named McKinnon called out, 'Stone the bastards!'

The crowd cheered when one driver flicked his reins and headed back towards the coast. Unable or unwilling to do anything against such numbers, the police returned on the road to Scarinish. Not surprisingly, they were quite keen to enter the local inn and mull over what had happened. However, the crofters were not yet satisfied. They followed the police to the inn and demanded that they leave the island, and then marched in a body to Island House. The crofters told Mr McDiarmid, the factor, and Mr Wylie, the chamberlain, why they had taken over the farm and said they wanted the Land Court to decide a fair rent.

That night the crofters kept watch over Greenhill Farm and over the police at Scarinish, in case they tried a sudden raid, but the dark hours passed peacefully. In the meantime, as the inn could not hold all the police, some had to spend the night in a barn. Some of the more militant of the crofters demanded that the police hand over McKinnon, the joiner who had acted as their guide and who remained with them inside, or they would pull the barn down among their heads.

With the weather turning foul, the steamer *Nigel* had run to Tobermory, leaving the police stranded in Tiree and at the mercy of the crofters. Despite that temporary hitch, the police were allowed to leave unmolested. Nobody had been injured and only the pride of the police and sheriff officers was hurt. Perhaps not surprisingly, the newspapers supported the establishment and the *Glasgow Herald* of 23 July 1886 said, 'This foolish rebellious spirit should be repressed.'

Round one had gone to the rebellious spirit of the Tiree crofters, but the Campbells of Argyll had not created and held their duchy over the centuries without being equally tenacious. The Duke spluttered that the island was 'under the rule of savagery' and demanded that something should be done about it. This was the period of gunboat diplomacy in the British Empire, with any challenge to imperial rule being met by force. The government intervened by sending two Portsmouth-based Royal Naval ships backed by Royal Marines from Plymouth, plus the ubiquitous police. The crew of HMS *Assistance* were called from leave and so urgent was the case considered that some were left behind as the ship sailed for Tiree. This show of force was welcomed in many quarters, but in a meeting in Liverpool. Angus Sutherland, MP for Sutherland, condemned 'the military expedition to aid the Duke of Argyll in depopulating Tiree, an act of military despotism'.

While the Navy gathered its ships to vanquish the unarmed crofters of Tiree, a Cumberland-based Irishman named Kennedy offered to draw up a statement of the islanders' grievances. He suggested that Charles Parnell of the Irish Land League would present the document to Parliament. When the crofters heard that the Marines were coming, they used the time-honoured method of blowing a horn to gather the men together to decide on their response. They decided that fighting professional and well-armed Royal Marines with sticks and stones would be pointless but still sent sentries to the hills and vantage points to watch for their arrival. Instead, the crofters boycotted those people who supported the Duke, including the island's single hotel. As the hotel was not licensed to sell drinks, this may not have been a major problem for residents or the hotel owner.

There were the usual rumours, such as the story that the blacksmiths' forges on the island were busy with islanders making spears to fight the Navy head-on, that women planned to roll great rocks down the mountains onto the Marines, and that there was a stockpile of sufficient firearms to start a small war, but none of these were true. The islanders got on with their lives while they waited for the Navy to arrive.

On 31 July 1886 the turret ship – a ship with a revolving gun turret – HMS *Ajax*, and the troopship HMS *Assistance* with the police boat *Nigel*, landed fifty police and 250 Royal Marines on Tiree. *Nigel* had shipped a special large open boat as a landing craft for the police. About a dozen crofters stood at the landing place at Scarinish but said little as the red-jacketed Marines marched ashore. The crofters had driven their animals from Greenhill Farm but now returned a token score of them. *Ajax* left Tiree on 5 August, as there was a heavy mist and the sea rose into a dangerous swell; her anchorage was insecure. She waited in Tobermory Bay on Mull.

Having already decided not to resist the landings, the crofters did nothing as the Royal Marines plodded ashore. Colonel Heriot, who commanded the Marines, was a man of tact and sense. Where he could have used a heavy-handed approach that would have led to resentment and perhaps fostered retaliation, Heriot instead encouraged his Marines to fraternise with the islanders, who responded with hospitality and free refreshments. All the same, the Marines acted as military escort to the Messenger-at-Arms, as around twenty police toured the island serving eviction notices to those crofters who had dared stand against the Duke's authority. Most of the men who were served reacted in a polite manner, but one named John Kennedy reacted with '*cagair mhor*', or 'great evil', and the mother of one man summonsed threw the document back out of her house.

There was some trouble at Kilkenneth. *The Scotsman* had run a story against the crofters, claiming that stones had been thrown, shots fired and had named three women as witches. When a reporter from the *Scotsman* arrived at Kilkenneth, he was subject to verbal abuse and an old woman said, 'My prayer is that when he dies he may open his eyes in hell' and, 'If you were hanging on the gallows I would stone you to death.' The reporter was probably quite relieved to withdraw physically unscathed.

The Hebridean weather was on the sides of the landless cottars; pelting rain drenched the police who were serving writs. On their initial march to the township of Balemartin, the Messenger-at-Arms, the police and the Marines experienced the conditions in which the Tiree crofters had to live and work. When Mr McDiarmid, the factor, told McNeill that Greenhill Farm was empty, he moved in without a single protest; indeed, his neighbours provided horses and carts to help carry his household possessions into his new home. The Land League crofters said they would not disturb him as their action had already had the desired result of calling attention to their situation.

When the Marines first landed the crofters were friendly, supplying them with free milk and food, smiling and talking to them. The islanders had no quarrel with the redcoats. The Marines, 250-strong and with twenty rounds apiece, marched in quarter column to support the police, who arrested the unarmed crofters. The rain continued so that the redcoats were soon sodden. As the military marched, the crofters blew horns as a warning of their approach and people began to gather to watch. In all, eight crofters were arrested, with one, Alexander McLean, proving elusive. He was not hiding but had been working elsewhere on the island. The police and armed Marines searched his sweetheart's house and when he was not found, ten Marines and four policemen were left there in case he should come. The colonel gave the Marines orders: 'Any man can defend himself, but don't fire.' When Donald Sinclair, local head of the Land League, was arrested a body of women shouted, 'God bless you, Donald.' A crofter named Donald McKinnon protested at being arrested and showed some resistance. 'May God help you, Donald,' one old woman shouted.

'You are going away very innocently.' Handcuffed and dripping in the rain, the men were marched away under the escort of armed Marines.

After the arrests and the display of force, the attitudes of the islanders altered. The free milk and food was no longer available and the crofters even refused to sell the Marines or police anything.

The arrested crofters were tried at the High Court in Edinburgh. They were Alexander McLean, Colin Henderson, Hector McDonald, John Sinclair, John McFadyen, Gilbert McDonald, George Campbell and Donald McKinnon. Lord Mure presided over a court that was crowded with well-wishers and the press, while a Gaelic translator was there to ensure the men understood the proceedings. Five of the arrested men were given a hefty six months in Calton Jail, the others four months – that was a far longer sentence than was expected. When the crofters and the Highland Land League protested about the severity of the sentences on first offenders that had hurt nobody, Arthur Balfour, the Scottish Secretary, did not deign to reply until November, when he said it was not his duty to interfere.

In the meantime, the crofters' cattle were removed from Greenhill Farm and a token force of an inspector and ten men left on the island. By the beginning of September the island appeared quiet. McNeill was back in Greenhill Farm and the police spent their time searching vainly for illicit whisky stills. The estimated thirty to fifty shebeeners of the island frustrated every attempt by the bored police to try and unearth their stock of peat reek. The crofters watched their efforts with a wry smile, knowing the whisky was buried together with the distilling equipment under sand banks. The islanders needed their shebeens as since 1855 a ground officer had banned the use of whisky to anybody on a croft whose lease was less than £30 a year. As crofters and police played hide-and-seek, the gentlemen of the island joined the Marines and Navy in nightly sing-alongs and displays of the sailor's hornpipe. As would be expected of British redcoats, the Marines had no difficulty in locating the shebeens and often returned to camp slightly worse for wear from the islanders' whisky.

When the Marines eventually returned south after their sodden weeks in Tiree some claimed that they had found the expedition very trying. As well as the rain that put many on the sick list, there were the midges, which had free play when they were camped out in their bell tents.

The Napier Commission of 1883 had made a tentative start on crofting reform, but in 1886 pressure from the Highland Land League paid off. Gladstone passed the Crofters Act that gave security of tenure to crofters and fairer rents, with crofts now allowed to be handed to a successor, rather than being disposed of at the landowner's whim. A Crofter's Commission oversaw the Act and in 1887 they cut the rents on Tiree. For the cottars, however, the landless and most impoverished people, nothing was done.

There were other troubles to come, but the first battles had been won and the groundwork laid.

9

Troubled Relationships

As in any age, nineteenth-century marriages and families faced difficulties. Most often the troubles would be resolved within the family, but sometimes there were less legal reactions. One such was bigamy.

Bigamy

Bigamy is rarely encountered today, but in the nineteenth century it was a crime that frequently came to the courts. Whether this was because of the problems of communication or, more likely, the difficulty of obtaining a divorce is hard to judge, but each case was its own tragedy. One case that occurred in Inverness in October 1814 is probably fairly typical.

The man in question was John McDonald, a tailor in Perth. In 1804 he married Grace Blair in a normal Church of Scotland ceremony. The pair lived together in seeming harmony for a number of years, but in February 1814 McDonald approached Mr Condie, a Writer to the Signet in Perth, and asked if it was legal for him to marry another woman. Mr Condie replied that it was illegal when his first wife was still alive, unless they got a divorce. It was then that the reality of McDonald's marriage became apparent.

Rather than married bliss, the couple were trapped in their own form of hell. Arguments were as common as Highland rain and McDonald's friend George Knox spent a great deal of time and energy attempting to reconcile the irreconcilable. Even so, when McDonald informed Knox that he intended to marry again, Knox was astonished, particularly when McDonald seemed to lack any conscience about the act.

McDonald's next choice of wife was Barbara Leslie, but only two days after the Reverend Duncan McIntyre had performed the service, he discovered that McDonald was still married to Grace Blair. It was unfortunate that Barbara Leslie was already carrying McDonald's child, but that could not influence the decision of the court in finding McDonald guilty. He was sentenced to six months in jail.

Sometimes the two wives of a bigamist could meet in the court, as happened in the spring Circuit court at Inverness in 1860. The bigamist was named Donald McMillan and both his wives were present at his trial. The older of the two women was a Borderer from Coldstream in Berwickshire, the younger was from Ross-shire. When McMillan admitted his guilt, the young woman broke down and was weeping in court. Immediately as she did, the Coldstream woman came over to her, patted her shoulder and offered a handkerchief and sympathy.

'Are you Donald's other wife?'

'I believe I am,' the Ross-shire woman said between sobs.

The Coldstream woman nodded. 'How many bairns do you have to him?' she asked.

When the Ross-shire woman said she had mothered two children, but one had died, her fellow wife gave her sixpence. 'And I wish you luck of him,' she added, 'gin he kick you as aft as he has done me, I fear you'll be tired enough of him.'

Military men had arguably more opportunities for bigamy than those who had more settled occupations. In 1890 Frederick Chadwick was a lance-sergeant in the Royal Irish Rifles, based in Fort George, a few miles along the coast of the Moray Firth from Inverness. Chadwick had not always been in the Royal Irish; he had originally enlisted in the Seaforth Highlanders but had deserted and then signed up for the Royal Irish. In November 1884 he married Amelia Grace Thomson, a domestic servant at the fort. Unfortunately, he neglected to tell Amelia that he was already married to Ann. The judge sent him to jail for a year to brood on his matrimonial misadventures.

However, women could also be guilty of bigamy, and in the Inverness Circuit Court in April 1836, Catherine Fraser, although married to Donald Grant of Culcabock, admitted she had a second husband tucked away for her spare time. The court sent her to prison for a year.

The final bigamist in this short depiction is another woman, Catherine Finlayson or Mactaggart, who came from Lochcarron. In January 1897 she was charged with bigamy at Inverness Sheriff Court. She got her second surname when she married Private Mactaggart in Edinburgh in 1885. Despite the initial romance, their relationship rapidly soured and they lived an unhappy life in Sheffield. Mrs Mactaggart left her soldier husband and returned to the north of Scotland, where she met a merchant called David Pollock.

Perhaps she genuinely believed that her first husband was dead when she married Pollock, but not long after Mactaggart turned up at the railway station at Kyleakin. He asked Pollock for money, with the threat that if he was refused he would tell the world about the bigamy. When Pollock refused to give in to the threats, Mactaggart informed the police and Catherine Mactaggart found herself in front of the court. Sheriff Blair gave her only fourteen days, as she had suffered a terrible marriage with what was obviously an obnoxious man. Other marriages, however, were even worse.

Assaulting the Wife

Murdoch Macdonald was not happy in his marriage. In 1881 he lived with his wife in Inverness, but their relationship was punctuated by quarrels and ill feeling and late that year they began to argue seriously. Macdonald lost his temper and thumped her, somebody called the police and Macdonald appeared before the police court. The magistrate bound him over to keep the peace and keep his hands to himself in future.

The warning seemed to be enough, and for the best part of a year Macdonald behaved himself, except for the odd grouse and grumble. Then in early December 1882 he fell out with his wife again. Perhaps he remembered the police warning for rather than assault her he stormed out of the house and moved in with his brother in Union Road, about a mile from his own house. He remained there for a couple of days, brooding over his situation, and in the early morning of the eleventh he decided to do something about it. At about half past two in the morning he left his brother's house and walked across town to his own house and let himself in.

His wife heard him enter and knew by the sound of his footsteps that he was not in the best of moods. She got out of bed just as Macdonald entered the room. Mrs Macdonald was not alone, for there was a sixteen-year-old maidservant with her, and both noticed that Macdonald carried an open razor in his hand. Macdonald began to shout at his wife, she retaliated, and then Macdonald grabbed her by the hair of her head. She tried to fight back and push him away, but he drew the blade of the razor across her face, from the corner of her mouth to her ear. Both Mrs Macdonald and the maid screamed, and Macdonald fled from the house.

He did not go far but threw himself into the River Ness in an attempt to commit suicide, but either he thought better of it, the water was too cold or he lost his nerve, for he struggled back onto land. He tried again a second and a third time but failing each time he returned home to see if his wife was badly injured.

In the meantime, the women's cries had woken the neighbours, who came in to see Mrs Macdonald with her face ripped open and the blood pouring down. They sent for the police and a doctor. Both arrived within the hour to find that Macdonald was sitting by the fire, sodden and shivering. Dr Macdonald stitched and bandaged Mrs Macdonald and the police arrested her husband, who was eventually jailed. Mrs Macdonald may have been unfortunate in her choice of a husband, but other husbands were equally unfortunate in their choice of a wife.

Assaulting the Husband

In the Inverness Burgh Police Court on 31 Aug 1895, Elizabeth Robertson was charged with assaulting her husband. James Robertson, known as 'Glasgow Jamie', was a labourer. He was sixty years old and worked on the bridge then being built over the Ness at Waterloo. Elizabeth was a good ten years younger than James and liked her drink. When the drink took over, she started an argument with James, smashed an earthenware plate and slashed him across the neck with the jagged edge. James fell down with the blood pulsing out. He was rushed to the infirmary and for a while there were thoughts Elizabeth may have been charged with murder.

Death of a Wife

When a man and a woman commit themselves to marriage, they enter a private world, the rules and workings of which are known only to themselves. A matrimonial curtain descends between the couple and the outside world. There are many benefits to this seclusion, but in the rough, rowdy and often violent world of the nineteenth century there were often spouses who abused both their position and their wives or husbands. Sometimes the violence was verbal, sometimes physical and far too often it ended in a sordid murder by somebody who should have supplied nothing but love and loyalty.

The Loch Nevis death of 1830 was one such. Archibald Maclellan was the tenant of Kylesmorar in the parish of Glenelg, on the wild west coast of Lochaber. He was married to Catherine Gillies, but their marriage was not the most traditional. The couple must have had some serious disputes, for ever since 1828, Catherine had lived as a wanderer, roaming the land and occasionally returning to visit her husband at his farm. When they were together, Catherine revealed her poor state of mental health and Maclellan would slap her into obedience. In the long absences of his wife, Maclellan sought the company of another woman, who shared the name of Catherine.

In June 1830 both the Maclellans were on one of their sporadic times together. They had a number of arguments, which appears to have been their way of communicating, or at least passing the time. It was surprising that Catherine had arrived at Kylesmorar, for Maclellan had made a number of threats against her during the past year or so. They argued again on 22 June and Maclellan grabbed her and thrust her head into a nearby burn.

Even after that assault, Catherine remained with Maclellan. What exactly happened next is not certain, but the local people thought they knew. Their version of it ran like this: On the morning of 25 June Catherine Maclellan walked alone by the shores of Loch Nevis. Maclellan followed her, either to talk to her, to renew their argument or purely by coincidence. Either way, the couple seemed to have a dispute and Maclellan lifted one of the many sharp, heavy stones that littered the side of the loch and cracked her over the head, on the neck and on the body. When Catherine slumped to the ground, Maclellan jumped on her, grabbed her by the throat and strangled her. She was either dead or unconscious when he dragged her onto a rock that protruded into the loch and threw her into the water.

Catherine must have floated ashore, because not long after, her body was found on the shore of the loch. She had a woollen cloth around her body and her face and neck were marked, cut and bruised. Searchers also found scraps of a woman's dress on a rock overlooking the sea. To clinch their theory of a murder, they found a depression in the ground from which a rock had been torn and a stone that fitted the hole.

One of the men who found the body walked across to Maclellan's house. 'It is not agreeable, what I have seen', he said quietly, speaking in Gaelic, of course.

Maclellan tried to act innocent. 'What is the meaning of this?'

'There has something wrong been done.'

The local authorities were alerted and Maclellan was arrested. In September that year he appeared before the Circuit court at Inverness, but the jury disagreed with the verdict of the neighbours. In his summing up, Lord Meadowbank pointed out that the doctor who examined the body was not certain that the marks on Catherine's neck were the result of Maclellan's hands, and the other marks could have been caused when she fell off a rock. Maclellan walked free.

It was much more common for matrimonial disputes to end in simple violence, but even that could end in a summons to appear in court. In July 1850 John Williamson, a Caithness farmer, attacked his wife, beat her up and broke her arm. He was arrested and ordered to come to the Inverness Sheriff Court in September. When he failed to appear, he was outlawed.

Death of an Uncle

Murder by poison was a favourite method in the nineteenth century. The trials of Madeleine Smith and Dr Pritchard in Glasgow were only two of the high-profile cases that shocked and possibly delighted the respectable people of the country, but in 1859 the Highlands had their own case of suspected poisoning.

David Ross and his uncle Walter Ross lived together in the same house in Invergordon. On 16 April 1859 Walter Ross died and the police suspected that he had been poisoned over a long period, with David putting small quantities of arsenic in his tea, whisky and food. The motive for the suspected murder was property. Walter Ross had found himself a woman and was talking of marriage, and if so, then the house he lived in would have gone to his new wife and not to David.

When Walter was still hale and hearty, David told a sheriff officer named William that his uncle was due to be married. Kennedy commented that the house would go to the new wife then. David Ross smiled and said, 'Although my uncle may wish to do that, I have in my pocket what would hinder him.' At that time the words meant nothing to Kennedy, but he remembered them later, after Walter Ross died and there were whispers of poisoning.

On Thursday, 14 August 1859, both uncle and nephew visited John Ross, the local surgeon and doctor, as Walter Ross was unwell. Dr Ross recommended carbonate of soda and tartaric acid and sent them away. He visited the house on the Saturday and found Walter Ross lying in bed on his back, unconscious. Dr Ross was very surprised when Walter died about half an hour later.

Dr Ross and Dr Vass of Tain both examined the body, and they decided that he had died from 'excessive discharges from the stomach and bowels' but neither could say the origin of the trouble. They consulted with Dr McLagan of Edinburgh, who said, 'All the organs from the body of Walter Ross ... were impregnated with arsenic; that the contents of the stomach contained a barely appreciable trace of this poison but that there was present in them an insoluble compound of mercury.' He thought that 'a dose of calomel had been administered to Walter Ross shortly before death'. He concluded that Walter Ross 'must have received a considerable dose of arsenic ... there can be no doubt that he died from poisoning by arsenic'.

Naturally, suspicion fell on the nephew, and the police made enquiries. John Fraser, a chemist in Tain, said that David Ross had bought arsenic, claiming that it was for rats, although the next door neighbour, William Sutherland, was adamant there were no rats around at all. McGregor, the veterinary surgeon, said that David Ross had bought some powder to cure a sick horse. McGregor had warned that the powder could be very harmful if taken by a human.

Even more damning was a statement by David's sweetheart, Georgina Mackay. She claimed that David Ross had told her that his uncle had not long to live and that if she agreed to marry him he would 'give me his hand that his uncle would not live long'. Georgina had asked what made him think that and David gave a mysterious answer: 'There is none that knows that but one,' and added, 'Never you mind that. If you give me your hand, I'll let you know that.'

Perhaps the words scared Georgina, for she turned down David's offer of marriage and walked away from the relationship and the chance of a share in Walter's house. That fell to another woman, who coincidentally was also named Georgina, and he married her shortly after.

When the case came to trial at the Inverness Circuit Court, David denied that he had ever possessed arsenic in Invergordon. He made two contradictory statements. His first statement was that 'I never had any poison in my possession at any time to my knowledge' but his second claimed 'I bought three or four ounces of arsenic from a druggist in Tain in February last, for the purpose of killing some cats that were annoying me in my workshop and a dog that used to frighten me . . . and some rats which were in the back wing of my uncle's house. But I lost that packet on my way from Tain to Invergordon.' David also mentioned the white powder he had purchased from the vet, saying that he had bought it for his uncle's horse. This powder was kept on the top shelf of a cupboard, beside the household store of medicines, and David presumed that his uncle had mistaken the horse powder for cream of tartar.

The judge, Lord Cowan, summed up the evidence and concluded that there had been poison administered by some person, but left it to the jury to decide if David Ross had been the culprit. The verdict was eight to seven in favour of not proven and David Ross walked free.

Breach of Promise

It is not heard of much nowadays, if at all, but in the high Victorian age the courts heard a great number of breach-of-promise cases. These cases usually followed a familiar pattern: a man had promised marriage to his sweetheart, she had allowed him the freedom of her body and then, once he had taken advantage of her, he changed his mind or transferred his affections to some other trusting woman. Duncan MacGillivray, a sheep dealer of Strathnairn, was allegedly one such man. His sweetheart was a teenage girl named Ann Robertson, who lived in nearby Scaniport.

Some few weeks before Whitsunday 1875, MacGillivray approached Ann and said quite bluntly, 'Ann, will you marry me?'

Ann did not reply at first, but kept MacGillivray waiting, either through reluctance to commit herself or simply to tease him. Eventually she agreed, and added, 'But when?'

MacGillivray replied, 'At the term,' meaning Whitsunday in May.

Nothing much happened on the marriage front for three weeks, but the couple pursued the romantic pursuits that have occupied young people since time immemorial. As the term time drew closer, MacGillivray again mentioned his intention to marry Ann, but this time her mother was also present and no doubt listening to every word while pretending not to. On that occasion, MacGillivray also asked if Ann was thinking long-term or perhaps contemplating an early marriage. He also promised, quite soberly, to marry her when the term was over.

A few days after that, MacGillivray drew up a contract of marriage between the two of them and actually brought it over to Ann's house, but in the enjoyment of each other's company, the business of signing was forgotten. He took it away with him when he left, unsigned. However, when the relationship reached its near inevitable conclusion and Ann fell pregnant, MacGillivray denied he had promised marriage. Ann took him to the sheriff court in Inverness in October 1876, and MacGillivray admitted he fathered her child. Ann won her case and hopefully made good use of the financial award to care for her child.

Only the following year there was a similar case in Lewis that invoked much public interest, and again came to Inverness Sheriff Court. In this instance it was a domestic servant named Ann Macaskill from Stornoway, who was pursuing compensation after she had been let down, and a man named Donald Macleod, who was the man involved.

Macleod was an interesting man. He had known Ann when she was only an eleven-year-old girl while he was a working blacksmith of twenty-five. They both lived in Harris at the time and were as friendly as any people of such different ages could be. However, like so many of his compatriots, Macleod found the lure of North America attractive and he spent eight years working for the Hudson Bay Company in Canada.

When he was in Canada Macleod worked with Ann's brother, and they spoke of her from time to time. Eventually Macleod returned to Scotland and settled in Stornoway in Lewis. After a while Ann called on him to hear news of her brother, and Macleod found that she was no longer a child but an attractive young woman of nineteen. The humorous friendship for a man for a young girl blossomed into a fully-fledged romance between a man and a woman. At that time Ann was out of a position, and as Macleod was also looking for work, the couple had plenty of time to spend on each other. They met frequently, walked out together and visited other people as a couple.

One day Macleod put forward a leading question, 'Are you not married yet?'

Ann replied, maybe half in jest and whole in earnest, 'No, I was waiting for yourself.'

There was no more said at the time, but the mention of the topic revealed that the subject was in both their minds. After more than two weeks together, Macleod travelled south and found a job as a blacksmith in Coatbridge but now both people saw their relationship through different eyes. Whereas Ann was quite convinced that Macleod had proposed to her on a number of occasions, Macleod was equally adamant that he had not. He admitted that he had thought about marriage with her, but his mother had persuaded him that she was the wrong girl for him. There were stories of Macleod intending to give Ann a dress and a sealskin jacket that he may have brought back from Canada, and counter stories of Ann pondering taking a job in service in Aberdeen. There was certainly an exchange of letters between Macleod and Ann's brother, although there does not seem to have been any further direct contact between Macleod and Ann herself. Macleod did not write the letters himself as he was no scholar, but he dictated them.

When the case came to court the sheriff listened to all the evidence carefully. In his opinion, there had been a contract of marriage made, although no date had been set. He set damages at £120, payable by Macleod to Ann.

Breach of Promise at Brora

Georgina Elphinstone lived at Strathsteven, near Brora on the north-east coast of Scotland, with the Moray Firth a stone's throw in front and the great brown hills rising behind her. In January 1878 she was a good-looking single woman of twenty-three, and that year she took a fancy to a contractor named Alexander Forbes, who lived at Redburn Quarry near Beauly, a good few miles to the south.

Georgina lived with her father. She was a well-known person in the locality, and got on very well with a man named William Forbes, who walked with her sometimes on the road between Brora and Strathsteven. One cold day, William introduced her to his brother Alexander, who was then working on the railway that snaked its way northward from Inverness towards Wick and Thurso. Alexander was no stranger to the district, as his father was a local man who lived not far from Georgina. Alexander was a handsome and personable man and he was as attracted to Georgina as she was to him. When he saw her at a concert at the schoolhouse by Brora shortly after they met, he signalled to her to wait behind for him.

They walked home together and their friendship grew. Every evening Georgina would go to the house of her uncle Angus Gunn for fresh milk, and Alexander just happened to be walking on the road at the same time. The pair did not make any formal arrangements to meet at this time but certainly they became close. On 1 January 1879 Alexander came to Georgina's house and escorted her to a dance at his father's house. It was a typical Highland Hogmanay dance that continued well into the wee small hours of the next day, and Alexander made the most of his opportunity to get to know Georgina even better. He said that he loved her and invited her outside the house into the cool crispness of the night.

That was the beginning of a new stage in their friendship. They remained close until about mid-April 1880 when Alexander teased her by saying she was in haste to be married and Georgina laughed and said she was very happy as she was. In June that year when Alexander had to travel to Glasgow, he said, 'Trust me Georgie, I will never forget you.'

Alexander spent over a year in the Glasgow area, but the two kept in touch. Georgina sent him a string of letters and had a lock of her hair made into a chain, and sent him that as well. In return, Alexander sent her a book of Burns' poetry, but few letters, if any. He claimed that he thought she would laugh at his letters. However when he came back to the Brora area for a couple of weeks he dropped a bombshell: he had seen another woman when he was in Glasgow. He also accused Georgina of being 'cool in your demeanour'. She replied that she thought he had forgotten her as he never wrote. However, the relationship seemed to survive that blip and they continued as friends.

Before Alexander returned to Glasgow he came to say goodbye to Georgina and said he would 'claim you as my wife' but admitted it could be years before he could do so. Georgina asked if he was sure he knew what he was doing, settling both their lives. Alexander said he was, and Georgina said that she would wait for him.

The Glasgow job ended and Alexander returned north, to work in a quarry near Beauly. Georgina hoped that things would continue as they had before, but unfortunately Alexander had other plans. He had met yet another woman and was writing to her. Georgina heard the stories and confronted Alexander on the road. He was honest enough to admit that he had another girl in Beauly, but as soon as she heard the news Georgina fainted. Alexander caught her as she collapsed; when she recovered he told her in apparent sincerity that she was his only girl and he would never see the girl in Beauly again.

Reassured, Georgina thought that things would return to normal, but instead only a few weeks later she heard that Alexander was once again walking out with his Beauly girl. Shortly after that, she heard that he had asked the girl to marry him. Brave or stubborn, or unwilling to admit the unpalatable, Georgina confronted Alexander in his father's house and he admitted everything.

'All must be over,' he said, 'and you must forgive me.' He offered to pay Georgina, presumably for the hurt he had caused her. The case came to court, but Alexander paid £40 to Georgina to settle matters.

There were other occasions when there were rivals for a lover's affection.

Love Rivals

In early 1899 John Sinclair was a respectable labourer in Inverness. He was a hardworking man and he had a fine-looking sweetheart, with whom he spent as much time as he could. Unfortunately, there was another man who was also interested in the same woman.

Colin MacDonald was also a labourer in Inverness and he had taken a liking to Sinclair's sweetheart. He believed the lady was far too good for Sinclair and told him so, publicly, and with some venom. Naturally, Sinclair objected and told MacDonald that it was none of his business, particularly as MacDonald was a married man with two of a family. MacDonald responded by lifting a poker and cracking it over Sinclair's head. The poker broke with the force of the blow, and Sinclair was knocked to the ground.

After the Northern Infirmary bandaged up Sinclair's wounds, he reported the assault to the police. MacDonald ended up with three months' hard labour to ponder his actions.

Disputed Paternity

In late 1877 and early 1878 Sheriff Hill at Tain Sheriff Court contemplated a perplexing case of disputed paternity. Back in 1874, John Skinner, a fisherman at Inver, married Mary Mackay from the same village. Skinner was a virtuous man and restrained himself from any sexual pleasures until after the marriage. However, only eight months later his wife gave birth to a little boy. Skinner swore that it was impossible for the boy to be his, and as his wife died not long after the birth, she could not be questioned on the matter. However, Skinner claimed that just before she died she had told him he was not the father. He had brought in two kirk elders to listen to her confession, but they both gave slightly different tales. Mackay refused to accept responsibility for the child, who was handed to the care of the parish.

When the child was four years old the simmering dispute reached the sheriff court at Tain, as the parish asked for Mackay to help pay for the child's upkeep. The sheriff listened to evidence from various witnesses, who pointed out that Mary Mackay had worked as a fish gutter before she was married. The female gutters and packers followed the herring fleets around the coast, and it was not unknown for the women to become more than friendly with the fishermen. The witnesses spoke of Mary sharing accommodation with five other women, with some nights spent in singing and dancing, with fishermen keeping them company until the morning. There was no doubt that she had been a loose woman with poor moral standards, but even so the sheriff ruled that Mackay should pay the parish for the child's upkeep.

Sometimes affairs of the heart could take unexpected twists but only in the Hebrides could the following events take place.

Raiders of the Lost Heart

February in the Hebrides can be cold and bleak, or wild and spectacular. It can also be heart-achingly beautiful. Sometimes the weather is crisp and clear and sunshine glints from snow-smeared hills, while Atlantic waves break silver around black skerries and on deserted beaches. On days like that, the islands of the west may be seen as romantic. There was certainly some romance in the February of 1850 when the Isles were the backdrop to one of the strangest sequences of events that ever nineteenth-century Scotland saw.

The principal actors in the romantic play were all local to the area. There was Donald Macdonald of Baliloch in North Uist, Donald Mackenzie of Monkstadt in Skye, and Charles Mackinnon, a fisherman who was also from Monkstadt, as well as Donald Ferguson and William Macdonald. However, there was also Robert Macdonald of Rodel in Harris and Patrick Cooper from Edinburgh. The events of the month of February 1850 affected all these men and more, but it revolved around one young woman.

It all began when young Donald Macdonald of Baliloch had fallen in love with twenty-one-year-old Jessie Macdonald, the daughter of Macdonald of Balranald in Harris. In 1849 Donald was appointed as Lord MacDonald's temporary factor in North Uist. He was friendly with the Balranald Macdonalds, and after a while he and Jessie decided they must become man and wife.

Unfortunately, Jessie's family did not agree with their daughter's choice of suitor. They much preferred her to become attached to an Edinburgh man named Patrick Cooper, who just happened to be Lord MacDonald's factor in Harris. Lord MacDonald was the landowner of huge tracts of the Hebrides, so his factor would be a very powerful and influential man. Cooper knew Jessie Macdonald well and was as attracted to her as Donald was. Indeed, he had also asked her to marry him, and although she had not given a positive answer, he believed she could be persuaded to accept his hand. Jessie Macdonald had said she was in great difficulty and 'never expected the offer'. Not long after he proposed, Cooper was summoned to Portree where a friend was sick.

The Balranald Macdonalds knew that neither Jessie nor Donald would be easy to persuade, and they expected that the two would elope despite the express wishes of Jessie's family. However, the elopement, when it came, was still a shock for them. It was on 15 February 1850 that Jessie's brother brought the family the news that Jessie was missing.

The elopement had been well planned and well executed. Donald's servant, Ronald Macdonald, had taken a dog cart to the lodge at Baliloch, parked outside and loaded their trunks in the back. The lovers came out arm in arm and laughing, jumped in the dog cart and ordered Ronald to mount the horse while they sat side by side and drove through the dark morning of lightning and thunder.

Naturally, the family guessed at once what had happened. They rode from Rodel in the south of the island to Tarbert, twenty-four miles away. Donald and Jessie had fled to Lochmaddy in North Uist. They boarded a vessel named *Eliza MacLeod* at four in the morning, but the weather closed in and the shipmaster, Donald MacLeod, thought it too dangerous to put to sea. Donald and Jessie both wanted to go to Edinburgh to get married, but when they eventually set sail they only got as far as Loch Tarbert. The Balranald Macdonalds arrived around the same time, along with Cooper, who had dashed over from Skye, complete with great anger and two or three braces of

© Author's Collection

Village of Tarbert

pistols. The combined force boarded the vessel and fought Jessie back under their control.

It was not an easy meeting. Jessie had clung to Donald and said she would die rather than part with him, and was crying as if her heart would break, nearly hysterical to remain with her sweetheart, but the family dragged her away and ordered her to forget him. She did not. Accordingly, they sent Jessie to live with her uncle John Robertson Macdonald, commissioner for the Earl of Dunmore, who lived at Rodel House at the south coast of Harris. She was well treated there. Unlike the heroines in romantic novels who were locked in their rooms, Jessie was free to roam. Her only hardship was not having Donald.

In the meantime, the rumours about Cooper grew, including a lurid story that he had come searching for Donald at Monkstadt carrying three braces of pistols, as he wanted to kill his rival to get Jessie for himself. Jessie's family also contacted Angus MacDiarmid, the local policeman for the south of Harris, and had him watch Rodel in case Donald should come looking for her.

However, Donald planned to regain Jessie for himself. He was not prepared to give up after a single setback. He wanted his Jessie. He heard that Patrick Cooper was due to arrive at Rodel on the Saturday, so he determined to reclaim her before his rival came onto the scene. On the morning of Friday, 8 February 1850, he gathered a number of his friends and some of his father's household servants and planned a swift raid over the sea to Harris to reclaim his girl. He asked Donald MacLeod to take them over to Harris in *Eliza MacLeod*. However, the Hebridean seas in February can be stormy, and MacLeod thought it was unsafe to venture out that night.

According to Donald Ferguson, who took part in the raid, the object was purely to 'get a wife for their master's son'. However brave their intentions, the night was stormier than ever, so quite a number of the men returned to Monkstadt without venturing to sea, but others were stouter of heart. There were about a dozen men in the boat when they left North Uist shortly after eleven o'clock that night. They had one object in mind: get Jessie Macdonald away from her uncle and into the arms of her sweetheart, but some carried sticks in case Jessie's uncle or any of his household should try to hold her against her wishes. However, Donald ordered them all to act peacefully.

The twenty-mile crossing to the harbour at Rodel took between three and five hours, so the winter dawn was still some hours away when they disembarked and crunched ashore. Among the men were Donald Ferguson and William Macdonald from Fearn of Kilmuir, who was a sheriff officer and therefore more usually on the side of the law. The whole band took the short walk up to Rodel House, but only Donald and Donald Ferguson came to the porch at the front door. When Donald Ferguson asked the daughter of the house where Jessie was, she told him that Jessie shared a bed with her aunt, Mrs Macdonald.

As soon as he saw the mob surrounding his house, Jessie's uncle, Robert Macdonald, charged out of the house in his shirt and drawers, swearing loudly, and ordered them to go away. Robert Macdonald's attitude is not surprising given the time of day and the number of men who disembarked from the boat, particularly as some were armed with sticks. He demanded to know why they had come to his house.

A Lewis man, Donald Mackenzie, answered for them all: 'We have come to get a wife for Monkstadt's son.'

Donald told Robert quite emphatically that he would not go until he got his wife, but Robert replied, 'There is no wife of yours here,' and grabbed hold of the collar of Donald's shirt. However, the front door had been left open and Donald yanked himself free and pushed in, with Jessie's Uncle Robert close behind. Donald told the rest of his party to remain at the gate and ran upstairs to where Jessie was getting ready. A few of the men followed Donald into the house and they told Robert Macdonald that they only wanted to get Jessie out. If Robert Macdonald did not interfere there would be no harm done.

Still in his shirt, Robert Macdonald dashed for an outhouse where some of his servants lived, presumably to get help to chase away the invaders. Hard on his heels was Kenneth Macdonald, his clerk, who was also only half dressed. Kenneth Macdonald lifted a gun and threatened to shoot the invaders unless they went away.

Mackenzie taunted him. 'If I don't be quiet, are you going to shoot me?' When the clerk raised his gun Mackenzie cracked him on the side of the head with his stick and Charles Mackinnon snatched the gun.

The clerk shouted out, 'Murder!'

He ran to the door of the house but Robert Macdonald had also returned and locked the door behind him.

'For God's sake, let me in,' Kenneth Macdonald pleaded, with blood streaming down his face from where Mackenzie had thumped him. Macdonald opened the door. Then Macdonald, with his clerk, Kenneth Macdonald, and his shepherd, John Macdonald, ran upstairs to Jessie. Robert grabbed hold of his niece while the other two jumped on Donald. For a moment it seemed that the elopement would fail, but Donald struggled free, pushed open the bedroom window and called out, 'Come on, my lads. I am a prisoner in the house.'

Half a dozen men who had been kicking their heels on the ground floor and around the porch clattered up the stairs to help. William Macdonald, the sheriff officer, tried to avoid Robert Macdonald in case he was recognised, but there were enough of the rescuers to do the job. They burst into the room, waving their sticks and shouting loud threats.

Perhaps because he was outnumbered, Robert Macdonald tried to reason with the invaders, but their blood was up and they were intent on completing their mission. Robert Macdonald still tried to hold Jessie back, but Donald would have none of it. Donald faced Jessie and asked, 'Are you my wife, Jessie?' and she said that she was. Donald addressed Robert Macdonald and said, 'Is marriage enough when said before you, a Justice of the Peace?' It obviously was not. Robert Macdonald said he would not listen to such nonsense. He grabbed Jessie around the waist and again tried to drag her away, but Donald and others forced him from her.

There were three other women in the room, Robert's wife Mary and their daughter Ann, together with Miss Landles, the governess. All three were screaming with fear. Robert shouted above the noise and asked Jessie if she would rather stay or go: she chose the latter. Robert Macdonald then suggested she could remain until her father gave his consent. Donald said he would not wait, and Jessie laughed. She was very keen to get away before Cooper arrived.

The majority of the men waited outside the house as lantern light glinted behind the windows, flicked off and then reappeared at different windows. The men muttered that if they got Donald out safely they could do without the woman, but after about ten minutes the window opened and Donald leaned outside.

'Come on in, my lads, and take the trunks. We are ready to be off.'

William Macdonald was one of the men who helped carry Jessie's trunks outside, then Donald and Jessie hurried out of the house. Robert Macdonald's gardener rushed past, as if to call for help to stop them escaping, but Ferguson grabbed him by the front of his jacket and held him secure. The rest of the Uist men carried Jessie's trunks towards the boat, with Jessie herself coming last.

They headed back out to sea after having been only two hours at Rodel House. As a quick hit-and-run raid it had been perfectly planned and executed, with complete success and no injuries. Donald Macdonald had reason to be proud of himself.

The vessel put out to sea, leaving Harris astern. At first they were uncertain where to go. Some suggested heading to a small bay near Borrodale in Skye and anchoring there for the remainder of the day, either in case Jessie's father should find a boat to follow them or until the weather moderated. One of the men in the boat, Norman

MacLeod, agreed to carry a letter from Jessie to her mother. Jessie was smiling as the boat put out; she was very happy to be back with Donald. Eventually they headed east to the mainland and put ashore at Gairloch, where Donald and Jessie disembarked. From there they travelled to Edinburgh and were officially and finally married.

Jessie's father and uncle pressed charges against the raiders and four of them were summoned to appear at Inverness Sheriff Criminal Court. Only Donald Macdonald appeared. He pleaded not guilty to the charge of invading the dwelling house of John Robertson Macdonald and assaulting his clerk and shepherd. Donald put forward the defence that he and Jessie had been separated against their wishes and any subsequent trouble was not their fault, but blamed those who had taken away his intended wife.

Jessie was anything but reluctant to be taken away from her uncle, and the court heard the contents of a number of letters she had written that proved without doubt her attraction to Donald. One of these letters confirmed her prior knowledge and complete approval of her rescue:

'My Dearest Donald' she wrote, 'If the bearer of this letter meets you on your way here, you must return home. It seems that W. Macneil suspects or else has heard what we have been intending to do. As he had no opportunity of telling Papa of it, he deputed John Macdonald to do so, which he did last night, and Papa immediate wrote William to find out all he knew of the matter. I heard this from the grieve's wife. John Macdonald told her husband of it. Now my own Donald, we must be off this night. You had better not come till half past eleven o'clock. I shall be quite ready to start with you.'

When the letter was read out, most of the people in the court started to applaud, much to the annoyance of the sheriff. It was only when Donald Macdonald got her letter and learned that Cooper was due at Rodel the next day to persuade Jessie to alter her romantic interest that he decided to rescue Jessie.

The jury only took ten minutes to find Donald not guilty and he returned to his wife.

Incest

Crimes are much the same the world over, so the Highlands had its share of sexual crime in proportion to its population. Rape and sexual assault were not unknown, but in 1836 there was one crime that caused tongues to flap throughout the region. Together with child abuse, incest may be called the secret crime. When incest occurred between brother and sister and one of the participants was a minister, then things were worse.

It was November 1836 and Miss Kennedy was playing her piano at the manse at Logie, Inverness-shire. She had been sick for some time past but nobody, probably least of all her, knew what the matter was. However that day she collapsed. At the time her brother, Donald Kennedy, was in a neighbouring parish but a speedy horseman galloped to fetch him and he hurried to his sister's side. The sister was taken to bed but it was soon obvious she was in great pain. A doctor was called and gave the unbelievable news that the minister's unmarried sister was about to have a child. When she was delivered, she refused to say who the father might be.

As she lay, subject to intense questioning and a scandal to the parish, Donald Kennedy quietly disappeared. His parishioners wondered if he was so ashamed of his sister's behaviour that he could not face them. After all, his father had been the minister before him and Donald had only been admitted as minister two months previously.

A week or so later, the mystery was solved. Hiding in Aberdeen, Donald Kennedy wrote a long letter to the Moderator of the General Assembly of the Church of Scotland, admitting that he was guilty of an incestuous relationship with his sister and he was the father of her child. In the same letter he resigned his position in the church.

In the meantime, Miss Kennedy had fled the parish and headed west to escape censure and whatever penalties the law felt appropriate for her crime. However, she was pursued and caught, to be dragged into the jail at Dingwall, county town of Ross. After being held there for a while, a sheriff officer bundled her and a female friend into a chaise and whipped up for the road to Tain. When they arrived there, the officer left the chaise for a moment and the sister and her friend took the opportunity to flee.

Whether their escape was deliberately engineered to forestall the intense scandal of a court appearance or not, there was no more heard of the Logie incest case.

Murdering the Wife

Sometimes the circuit courts were faced with a case that seemed so obvious that they had no option but to find the accused guilty, even when there was no hard evidence. Such a case occurred in Inveraray in the autumn of 1804. The accused was Duncan MacArthur from Dail in South Knapdale and the victim was his wife, Elizabeth McKinnon. Her body had been found at the Crinan Canal, with her upper body on the bank and her feet under the water in October 1803. She had been strangled.

The evening before her body was found, McKinnon had accompanied MacArthur on a visit to Lochgilphead. She had not been seen alive since. There were no witnesses to the murder and no other evidence pointing to MacArthur, but still the jury found him guilty of murder. The judge, Lord Cullen, decided that MacArthur should be fed on bread and water until 31 October, then carried to the murder spot and hanged. His body was to be publicly dissected and anatomised.

There was some unease that the verdict was reached purely through circumstantial evidence, so the jury was relieved when MacArthur confessed.

Murdering the Husband and Father

In the Inverness Circuit Court of April 1852, Sarah and James Fraser were convicted of poisoning William Fraser, an innkeeper near Tain, by arsenic. That was bad enough, but Sarah was William's wife and James was his son. Sarah was forty years and James was just seventeen. Both pleaded not guilty but there was a great deal of evidence against them. They were proved to have bought the poison, and medical evidence showed arsenic in William's stomach. James Fraser had also said that he hoped to kill his father, which proved he had a loose tongue and little sense.

The jury found them guilty by a majority and recommended mercy, but without saying on what grounds they wanted mercy. There was some doubt as to the sentence when a packet of poison had been sent to Edinburgh to be checked and had been pronounced sealed when it was open, but after that point of law was sorted they were sentenced to death without hope of reprieve.

Lord Cockburn, an influential High Court judge, political reformer and author, mentioned this case in his book *Circuit Journeys*, and said of the murderers: 'I never saw a couple of less amiable devils. The mother especially had a cold, hard eye and a pair of thin, resolute lips producing an expression very fit for a remorseless and steady murderess. She saw her daughter, a little girl, brought in as a witness and heard her swear that there were no rats in the house and that her father's sufferings were very severe with a look of calm, savage ferocity which would have done no discredit to the worst woman in hell.'

Overall, relationships were much the same in the Highlands as anywhere else. Most marriages would jog along with good days and bad, some would be tainted with discord and others were simply hell on earth. There is no doubt that Highlanders experienced the same problems as other people, and sometimes had the same violent solution.

10

Savage Assaults

Assault is one of the crimes that never disappear. It was common in the nineteenth century and it is common today. Whatever the image of the peaceful Highlands, there were assaults committed there as well, both on the streets of the towns and in the quiet glens.

Assault by the Army

On 5 July 1804 James Speirs, a cotton spinner at Cromwell Park, had gone to the fair at Perth. It was quite late when he left, walking back home along the turnpike road. He passed the toll bar just outside the town shortly after eleven when he became aware of rapid footsteps behind him. Before he could turn, three men dressed in the red coats of soldiers were around him. One punched him to the ground, and as he lay there, all three rifled his pockets. They snatched a silver stopwatch and his pocketbook and purse with fifteen shillings in silver and banknotes, then ran away, leaving him dazed on the road. The stopwatch did not belong to Spiers but to his foreman, who had loaned it so that Speirs could check and regulate a piece of machinery.

When Speirs recovered, he woke up the toll keeper, who helped him into Perth to report the attack. The authorities asked the usual questions and arrested three soldiers who had been out of barracks that night – Corporal John Battersby and Privates James Kean and Patrick Connor.

The three soldiers had been drinking in Millar's public house in Perth until late on the fifth, leaving just before eleven o'clock at night. For the next hour or so their movements were unknown, but around midnight they came to the brothel of Mrs Jones and demanded entrance. Mrs Jones' daughter Mary and another friendly lady brought them to the garret, where they bought five mutchkins of whisky. Miss Jones noticed that the corporal paid for the whisky from a purse in which there was also a silver watch.

All five left Mrs Jones' house, but Connor wandered away before they came to an equally unsavoury establishment run by a man named Taylor, and drunk porter and more whisky. When they were here, Battersby dropped and then hastily scooped up a red pocketbook. They returned to Taylor's pub and once again Battersby dropped the pocket-book. At around five in the morning, when drink had chased all sense from the soldiers, Battersby began a fight with Kean. He accused Kean of stealing five shillings and a watch from him. Kean denied everything and when two constables arrived, Battersby withdrew the charge.

On the morning of the sixth, a small boy saw two soldiers throw something over a garden wall, and being a boy and therefore naturally inquisitive, he investigated and found two silver coins. He told his elder brother, who informed their father. Next morning both boys climbed over the garden wall. They found a purse, a silver watch and a small collection of silver coins, which they gave to their father. The father was an honest man and handed everything to the authorities. At that time, every quality watch had an identification number, which showed that the legal owner was Mr Speirs' foreman. Battersby, Kean and Connor were arrested and clamped in Perth Jail; there was not enough evidence against Connor so he was released, but Kean and Battersby were locked up. They were to be tried at the September Circuit.

However, neither soldier was inclined to meekly await his fate, and a few days before their trial, they broke free and ran. Kean was never seen again, but Battersby was recaptured at Bridge of Earn and hauled back to jail. His trial took place in January 1805, but despite all the evidence, the jury could not reach a verdict and the case against him collapsed.

Horsewhipping a Magistrate

Sometimes cases of assault captured the attention of the propertied classes. This was more often the case when one of the persons involved was from that strata of society. When both parties were gentleman and the case involved a public whipping, then they read the accounts with fascination and no doubt there were discussions around the breakfast table as to just how much the newspapers missed out and the gossips put in.

On 9 March 1831, George Cameron, an Inverness solicitor, brandished his dog whip outside the front entrance to the Northern Infirmary. He waited until Lachlan Mackintosh of Raigmore walked past, then took the whip and lashed Mackintosh over the head and shoulders. Mackintosh, a magistrate, tried to defend himself as best he could with his umbrella, so the good people of Inverness had the entertaining spectacle of two respectable gentleman fencing with dog whip and umbrella in a very public place. After just a few moments, both men had lost their hats and a dozen people had gathered to watch the fun.

Eventually a number of the spectators decided to intervene and pulled the combatants apart. Cameron called Mackintosh a 'low scoundrel' and told him to remember that he had been horsewhipped and to 'take that for the abominable lies he put in his paper'.

As usual, there was a backstory to the assault. In this case, Cameron thought he had been sufficiently provoked to retaliate in such a manner.

Mackintosh had written a letter to the *Inverness Journal*, in which he attacked Cameron's person and character in strong terms, but signed the letter 'A Subscriber', which was not entirely accurate as he was the proprietor and editor. Cameron had stalked up to Mackintosh and demanded to know if he was the author of the letter, before he launched his assault.

Despite the whip and umbrella, neither man had been injured. Mackintosh entered the infirmary to take part in a manager's meeting, and no doubt Cameron continued on his way with a feeling of smug satisfaction and having meted out retribution. However, Mackintosh did not let matters rest there and took Cameron to court.

The case came to the Inverness Circuit Court in May 1832. The Lord Advocate decided he could not prosecute a case where he knew the contestants, but the jury were told that the offending letter had handwritten amendments in Mackintosh's writing. They heard that Cameron was a man of sterling character, and then they heard the contents of the letter. It mentioned that Cameron had tried to unite the two Inverness newspapers, but said that he had done it for the worst possible motives.

When the Lord Justice Clerk summed up, he called the letter 'the most scandalous libel' and the jury must have agreed for they found Cameron not guilty, despite the testimony of the men who had witnessed the assault.

Free-Fighting Seamen

In the nineteenth century British seamen had a reputation for drunken violence when ashore. The dock areas of most port towns and cities were places best avoided by respectable women and men, and Inverness was no different. At the beginning of January 1884, seamen from the London-registered steamer *Morvern* met in a serious affray that ended up with a mass brawl, a stabbing and two arrests. *Morvern* had arrived at Thornbush Pier in Inverness on Wednesday, 29 December 1884.

As was not uncommon with British seamen, the crew spent the next few days drinking, so by the time they had returned on board and were ready to depart for Leith, the drink had taken hold of them and some began to quarrel. John Tyndall, the mate, gave an order, some of the crew refused to obey, strong words became harsh and the mate threw a punch. Within a few seconds there was pandemonium as most of the crew joined in, punching, kicking and swearing nautical oaths.

When he saw the fight was becoming serious, Captain Whittaker slipped ashore to get assistance, but John Macdonald, one of the crew, followed and knocked him to the ground. Whittaker struggled free and managed to find the police.

In his absence the fight became even fiercer. A group of the hands followed Tyndall below and attacked him. Outnumbered and out-muscled, the mate drew his knife and lashed out, stabbing John Douglas of Glasgow in the back. Shortly after the stabbing the police arrived and arrested both Tyndall and Macdonald. Macdonald was fined £5 for assaulting both the master and mate, while Tyndall was released on a £10 bail.

The Army Again

From 1859 when there was a scare that the French might invade, the Volunteer movement swept the length and breadth of the country. For many of the men, joining the Volunteers was a social event, while some perhaps genuinely believed they were serving Queen and country. However, it was not always harmonious within the ranks, and sometimes there were disputes. In the summer of 1891 some of the Volunteers of the Kirkhill area of Inverness had a minor dispute with Colour Sergeant MacFarquhar. At that time, the colour sergeant's house doubled as the unit's armoury and the men were gathered there. Three of the privates – Thomas Fraser, Andrew Fraser and William Chisholm –

attacked MacFarquhar with fists and boots. The colour sergeant drew his sword but still the three privates pressed hard on him.

The sergeant backed off a little, but reached for one of the rifles that were handy in their ranks. He pointed it at the nearest private and squeezed the trigger so there was a massive bang and a flare from the muzzle. As the weapon was only loaded with blank cartridges, there was no major harm done, except to further anger the privates.

Chisholm also grabbed a rifle, levelled and fired, which precipitated more shots from MacFarquhar, so the house was a crashing crescendo of rifle fire and reeked with smoke. Chisholm was the angriest of the privates and shouted out that they should load with ball cartridge and finish off the business there and then, but the arrival of the police put an end to things before there were any serious casualties.

The three privates were arrested and charged with assaulting MacFarquhar, but when the case reached the sheriff court in Inverness, Sheriff Blair sided with the privates. He found them not guilty of assault, but fined Chisholm seven shillings and six pence for breach of the peace. He also said that MacFarquhar's behaviour had been 'highly reprehensible' and wished he was in the dock in place of the privates.

Chasing the Attackers

Charles Robertson was a hardworking carter from George Street in Inverness. On Tuesday evening, 9 December 1884, he visited a public house after his work. As he emerged, two young men approached him – John Taylor and Alex Kessock – and demanded he give them money for whisky. Robertson refused and tried to push past them, but they knocked him to the ground. When another man appeared, all three of them tried to go through Robertson's pockets. He fought back and held them off until a passer-by shouted.

The three attackers fled, but Robertson was not content to leave it there. He got off the ground and chased them, caught Kessock and

George Street, Inverness

held him secure until a policeman arrived. Kessock was given a £3 fine at the Inverness Burgh Police Court with the alternative of seven days in jail.

Football players in the late Victorian period were also capable of rash actions. In 1896 John Macdonald was a baker but he also played football for the Caledonian Football Club. On 18 November that year he attacked a woman called Catherine Noble, threw her to the ground and laid into her with his boots. He was arrested and appeared before the police court, where Bailie Smith fined him £5.

Given the sometimes foolish actions by some footballers of the twenty-first century, Macdonald's actions are a reminder that people do not change. Violent crime is probably as common in the twenty-first century as it was in the nineteenth, and for the same reasons. However, religion could also lead to disputes.

11
Crime and Religion

Although Protestants and Roman Catholics share the same Holy Trinity and basic Christian beliefs, sometimes their doctrinal disagreements led to physical confrontations in nineteenth-century Scotland. These disputes could be over major points of religion or over the route of a march, but there can be few such encounters over which denomination should hold sway over the last few minutes of a dying man.

A Priest Tried for Assault

The situation arose from a long-standing friendship and a genuine desire to help. Captain Ross was an elderly man. He was seventy-eight years old, lived in Fort Augustus and was married to Elenora. He was also a long-standing member of the Church of Scotland, but was very friendly with the Reverend John Macdonald, the local Roman Catholic priest. Macdonald had often attempted to convert Ross to the Catholic persuasion but Ross rebuffed him every time. However, as Ross grew older his mind began to wander a little and Macdonald pressed ever harder as he tried to gain a convert for his faith or, as he believed, tried to save a soul for heaven.

On 10 September 1869 Macdonald called at Ross's house 'to have a crack about the old folks'. Elenora allowed him in, thinking nothing of it, until her husband suddenly announced, 'Mr Macdonald, I wish to become a Roman Catholic.'

Of course the priest was very pleased to hear that and grasped his opportunity, but Elenora was a bit concerned. She knew her husband was not himself, for if he was rational he would not have considered such a thing. Elenora thought this new desire was 'nonsense' but did not interfere as Macdonald had Ross say some prayers and kiss a ribbon. As the priest began to move onto more elaborate matters, Elenora stepped into the room and called a halt. Macdonald did not object and left immediately.

When Ross's mind returned to reality, he could not recall the priest's visit. He became afraid and asked his wife, 'Will you protect me and keep the priest and these Roman Catholics away from me? That priest has been trying to convert me for years.'

Elenora agreed, of course. She wrote to the Reverend Macdonald, asking him not to call any more, and she thought the matter was closed. However, at about nine in the evening of 13 September, she was in her husband's bedroom when she heard quick but quiet footsteps, and the priest slipped stealthily through the door. He was not alone, as Alexander Macpherson, a gamekeeper, and Donald Maclellan, an army pensioner, were with him.

Undaunted, or more likely angered by the intrusion of three men, Elenora at once stepped forward and put out her hands and told them they were not allowed in. Alexander Macpherson had other ideas. Placing his hand on her breasts, he said, 'I'll force my way.' He grabbed her arms and pushed her aside as he tried to storm into the captain's bedroom. Elenora staggered, but she was not a woman to tamely submit to such bullying. She reached out, caught hold of Macpherson by the collar of his coat and his luxurious whiskers and held on tight, completely blocking his access into the captain's bedroom. As the gamekeeper and the elderly woman struggled for mastery, Macdonald the priest said, 'Lay hold of her and hold her fast.'

The priest thrust into the bedroom as Macpherson twisted Elenora's arms behind her back and held her there, in pain and with her nose scratched and bleeding. Not surprisingly, Elenora yelled for help, and John Fraser, the local lock-keeper and a near neighbour, ran in to the house. Macpherson may have been brave when fighting an elderly woman but he was not so tough against a man, and Elenora was soon free again. A second man named John Shaw had also heard Elenora calling for help and arrived just then. The third of the intruders, Maclellan, grabbed hold of him and knocked him onto a chair, where they wrestled.

John Shaw's wife heard her husband shouting and piled in to help him, so the room was a shambles of fighting men and women. As somebody grabbed hold of Mrs Shaw, she shouted, 'Oh, my arm,' and her husband said angrily, 'Loose the woman! Do you want to kill her?'

When Fraser had freed Elenora from Macpherson's grip, she rushed to her husband's bedside. The priest was already there; busy with his converting, and Elenora asked her husband if he wanted the priest to leave. When Captain Ross said yes, the priest said, 'You see that? He wants me!'

Elenora asked again, 'Do you want the priest?'

'No, no,' said Captain Ross.

'Do you want the priest to go away?' Elenora repeated.

Captain Ross said yes, but again the priest either misunderstood or twisted the captain's words, and said, 'You hear? He wants me!'

At that point, Elenora began to get angry. 'You lying scoundrel,' she said. 'Don't dare you say to me that he said that.' She again asked the captain if he wanted the priest, and again he said, 'No!'

John Fraser was next to ask Ross if he wanted to become a Roman Catholic and again Ross replied, 'No, no.'

Elenora took charge again, asking the Protestants to 'rally round my husband's deathbed' to keep him safe from the Catholics. They obeyed her, facing the priest and his followers across the recumbent form of Captain Ross, and then Elenora dashed to the fireplace and grabbed the poker. She moved to the head of the bed, brandished the poker and said loudly, 'You Roman Catholics can leave the room.'

Macdonald was not yet ready to submit. Rather than obey Elenora, he stepped to the Protestant side of the bed and said he had something to say to the captain. That was enough for Elenora. She hefted the poker and gave him a mighty swipe on the shoulder, and when Maclellan lunged toward her, she thumped him as well.

Elenora realised the Catholics were afraid of her, so she followed them as they left, threw the poker after their retreating forms and slammed the door on their backs. A few moments later, a doctor arrived to attend to Ross, but also treated the cut on Elenora's nose where Macdonald had caught her and the extensive bruising on her arms caused by Macpherson. Captain Ross died a short while later, with his wife ensuring he remained resolutely Presbyterian to the end.

When the case came to Inverness Sheriff Court, the sheriff fined Macdonald £10 with the option of thirty days, while Macpherson and Maclellan were fined £2 or ten days.

Misconduct in the Kirk

The nineteenth century was a time of intense religious feelings in Scotland. There was the Great Disruption of the Church of Scotland in 1843 when the Free Kirk was formed from churchmen who could not agree about patronage, there were fears of the industrial towns being anything but Christian, and there was the furore that Darwin's theory of evolution created. In the midst of all that, individuals challenged the authority of the local churches in various different ways. On 10 June 1838 a schoolmaster named Hugh Fraser created his own mini dispute in the church at Kirkhill, between Inverness and Beauly.

It was the time of Communion in the church, but only those parishioners with a Communion token were permitted to sit at the Communion table. Although he lacked the necessary token, Hugh Fraser sat down with some force among the Godly. The minister, Reverend Alexander Fraser, reminded him he should not be there and asked him to leave. When Hugh Fraser remained just where he was, two of the elders, William Campbell and Alexander Sinclair, tried to persuade him to go, but still he remained. When Campbell and Sinclair repeated their demands, Hugh Fraser said he would stay and would fight back if they tried to use force.

The minister and the elders tried to hold Holy Communion as normal, but as the cup of wine was being passed around, Hugh Fraser lunged at it while the congregation recoiled in horror. What made it worse was that Hugh Fraser had performed exactly the same actions the previous two years, and each time the elders had forcibly hustled him away. He was charged with breach of the peace, profanity and illegally disturbing the congregation.

At the circuit court of September 1839 he was found not guilty of the first two charges but guilty of the third, and the judge, Lord Medwyn, ordered that his moveable possessions be escheat to the Crown: the law allowed no other course of action.

Accusing the Minister

Christina Thomson was a domestic servant by profession. In May 1884 she became the cook for the Reverend James McHardy, Church of Scotland minister at Latheronwheel in Caithness. About three months later, McHardy began to take physical liberties with her. Despite that, or because of it, Thomson remained as his cook for the next three years. From May 1887 to May 1889 she lived at home with her father, but McHardy had not forgotten her. He passed her in the village and surreptitiously passed small messages to her, informing her when she could visit him in the manse. When she obeyed the summons, McHardy always let her in himself and brought her into the study to continue their relationship.

In 1889 Thomson re-entered McHardy's service as a housemaid. As McHardy continued to be more than friendly, it was nearly inevitable that she should become pregnant. However, when she informed the minister of her condition he suddenly lost interest in her, ordered her back to her father's house and told her not to say who the father was. Thomson said she was not inclined to go back home, but she would like to go to America to hide her condition. McHardy gave her a generous £13 to cover her expenses for the trip, but Thomson's brother persuaded her not to emigrate, so she remained in Latheronwheel.

At least, that was the tale that Thomson spread around.

McHardy had another version of the story, and written proof to back him up. As well as strongly denying the charges of an intimate relationship, he produced a couple of letters, one from his wife to Thomson that read:

December 26, 1890

Dear Tina, I am very sorry to hear of your condition. I suppose you will have heard from home that there is a fearful suspicion that it is Mr McHardy that has put you wrong and that it is likely to ruin him, if it has not done so already. Would you write by return to say who the father is, or if you will not, to clear Mr McHardy.

Yours Sincerely,

E. McHardy.

The second, purported to be Thomson's reply to Mrs McHardy, read:

Orwell Place, Edinburgh
December 28, 1890

 Mrs McHardy, Madam, I had your letter last night and was very much surprised. My people never mentioned such a thing to me. There is no doubt that I am bad enough, but the very idea of a married man. It was in terror of Mr McHardy that I left the place. I thought that if I escaped his knowing I was all right, because I know how desperate he was at any girl who went wrong. I am not compelled to give up the father, but I am quite prepared at any time to go to any Court in Scotland and clear Mr McHardy. I never told my own people the real father so I decline to tell you.

 I am your humble and obedient servant,
 Teanie Thomson

Thomson added to her claims. She said that on one occasion the governess of the house, Miss Spence, had come into the room and found her sitting on the minister's knee, with him pressing his face to her breasts. However, the governess gave a less colourful version of the incident, when she came across Thomson and McHardy together in the parlour. According to Spence, the minister was listening to Thomson's heart after she had been in bed with influenza.

The case was heard before the sheriff court at Wick at the beginning of January 1892. William Henderson, a servant of the McHardy's, said that Thomson had always behaved with 'perfect propriety' at the manse, while another witness claimed to have seen her out with a man. Worse for Thomson, Dr Burn of Latheron stated that in the summer of 1895, when Thomson said McHardy had become intimate with her, the minister was actually seriously ill. The minister's financial affairs were also examined and there appeared no cheque for £13. When two young men appeared as witnesses and admitted they had been sexually intimate with Thomson, and there was talk about an abortion, the case was virtually decided.

Sheriff Mackenzie ruled that Thomson had not proved that McHardy had fathered her child. He thought that the story was improbable and that Thomson had lied frequently and contradicted herself throughout the hearing. The minister won that case.

The Disruption Disruption

The Church of Scotland has an interesting history. Born in the turbulent sixteenth century, it was heavily involved in the civil wars of the seventeenth and was riven by disputes in the eighteenth. In the nineteenth the worst troubles occurred in 1843, when there was a major schism over the issue of patronage. The crux of the matter was whether the landowners should appoint their own minister into the local church, or whether the congregation should select the minister they wanted: autocracy or democracy.

The issue came to a head at a meeting in Tanfield in Edinburgh, when over 600 ministers left the meeting in protest and founded their own church, the Free Church of Scotland, which was perhaps stricter in Presbyterian practices but was also free from interference from the landlord class. This incident was known as the Disruption. However, the labour pains for the birth of this baby Church were painful, and even after the event there were troubles and grief. One case in point was the riots that rocked the church and parish of Resolis, on the north coast of the Black Isle, in September 1843.

When the incumbent minister, the Reverend Sage, had seceded to join the Free Church, the Presbytery of the Church of Scotland decided that the Reverend John Mackenzie should be the new minister. However, many of the parishioners and others from the surrounding area did not agree with a Minister of the Established Church. Being Highland and of strong opinions where religion was concerned, they decided to show their displeasure in the old-fashioned way, with loud words, stones and sticks. There was no secret about their desire to prevent the Church from placing their preferred man in position, and on Thursday, 28 September 1843, around 300 of them picked up whatever weapons they could and prepared for battle.

However, the Presbytery was quite determined in their choice and took strong steps to defend it. Colonel Hugh Baillie, MP, the Lord Lieutenant of Ross, sent messages to the local Justices of the Peace requesting their presence at the inauguration of the new minister. He also ordered the Cromarty-based coastguard to prevent the ferries from Invergordon, Alness and Fowlis carrying Free Kirk supporters to help the Resolis protesters. All these precautions proved fruitless.

About eleven in the morning, a group of young men scrambled up a ladder and began to ring the bell of the simple church. As a crowd of mainly young men and women gathered on the slopes of the small hill on which the church stood, Sheriff Jardine, Andrew Shaw McKenzie of Newhall, the main landowner, Hugh Fraser, another local landowner and Colonel Baillie, George Gillanders, Provost of Fortrose and a host of supporters of the established church rolled up in their carriages. The crowd had been busy heaping up piles of stones of various sizes, ready to repel any advance by the Established Church supporters.

The Sheriff Clerk of Cromarty, John Taylor, bravely stepped forward and tried to soft talk the crowd, but the reaction was less than favourable. A woman named Eppy Aird indicated the stones she held in her apron. 'If you try and put in that minister,' she said, 'we'll find a use for these.'

The newcomers tried to push through but failed to make any impression against the crowd. As the forces of authority withdrew, the parishioners celebrated by tolling the bell. When Mr Innes Cameron, the Procurator Fiscal and a supporter of the Free Church, arrived in a two-horse phaeton, accompanied by a sheriff officer and tried again, a shout of 'Moderates!' came from the Free Kirkers, and it was not long before the first stones began to sail through the air.

Leaving the women safe in the carriages, the Lord Lieutenant led an entourage of about 100 of the great and the good towards the church, but the stone-throwing increased, volley after volley pelting down upon them. Somebody felled Provost Gillanders with a stick, and others who went to his help were also downed by Andrew Holm and some other Free Churchmen. Gillanders told Holm he would be marked, to which Holm remarked, 'I will mark you, you bastard.'

The Lord Lieutenant asked what the trouble was all about, and was bluntly told that the crowd would 'not let yon man' into the church. Deciding that discretion was safer than bruised valour, the Lord Lieutenant and Sheriff Jardine withdrew from the church and sent for help. Lieutenant Thomson and a party of men from the Coast Guard Preventative Service hurried over from their base at Cromarty. They were armed with pistols and cutlasses, while those men who supported the Lord Lieutenant had one double-barrelled musket and a few pistols for defence, plus whatever sticks and staffs they could find locally. The sight of weapons only served to aggravate the crowd. Stones flew in increased volleys.

Still determined to position the minister in the church, the forces of law and authority formed an orderly body, placed the revenue men in front with drawn cutlasses and prominent pistols, and marched steadfastly towards the crowd. The Free Kirkers responded with their own tactics: the women, or possibly men dressed as women, were at the front of the crowd, baying for blood, and the men were behind, throwing stones in an incessant hail.

The Established Churchmen tried to outflank the multitude by going through a field of stubble at the side, but the Free Church crowd again repelled them with volleys of stones. The Lord Lieutenant tried to intervene personally and lunged into the crowd to try and arrest one of the most active of the protesters, but when somebody struck him a savage blow on the arm, he retired. A stone crashed against the sheriff's thigh, while stones bounced from the carriage of Mr Cameron, the Procurator Fiscal. The carriage windows were broken and one of the panels was dented and battered. When Cameron tried to remonstrate with the crowd they replied with a heavy volley of stones that sent him scurrying for cover.

At that point the sheriff decided that enough was enough and read out the Riot Act to try and calm the crowd down. Once it was read, he tried to explain its purpose and meaning. He had just said, 'God save the Queen' when a large stone whizzed past his head. It was ten to three in the afternoon.

The coast guard drew their pistols and fired a volley over the heads of the crowd, but then hastily reloaded as the crowd surged towards them. The shots must have been badly aimed, or perhaps intended only to warn, for there was only one minor injury when a man was struck in the leg. Thomson led a desperate charge at the Free Church people, but was felled by a large stone that broke a rib, and a second tore open the back of his neck. Special Constable Munro from Fortrose was also injured. Some of the members of the Establishment party also resorted to stone throwing, so at times the missiles crossed and re-crossed the air between the two opposing parties.

Despite his own injuries and the numbers of the crowd, Lieutenant Thomson and the sheriff decided not to continue firing in case somebody was seriously hurt or even killed. One of the leaders of the crowd was a woman named Margaret Cameron. She was a tall, active, well-made women with a powerful voice and even more powerful arms, with which she threw a fusillade of stones. Margaret Cameron had a personal reason to be involved in the riot as she was the dairymaid to the Reverend Mr Sage, the minister who had seceded to join the Free Church.

The authorities waited on the fringes of the crowd for some time, and then withdrew from the church without having achieved their objective. There were rumours of more Free Church supporters waiting in the woods that the church backed onto. Margaret Cameron led the pursuit of the retreating authorities. As she was cheering on the others, Provost Cameron saw his chance to make an arrest. He grabbed hold of the woman and both overbalanced and tumbled into a ditch.

As the crowd and the coastguard watched, quite amused, a man named Watson rushed up and between them they managed to subdue Margaret Cameron and drag her away, despite a spirited rescue attempt from the crowd. When the woman was securely held, Watson and Cameron bundled her into a gig, where a sheriff officer named Dingwall arrested her, the driver whipped up and they rattled away to the jail at Cromarty.

Dingwall was a brave man, but the crowd had him in their sights. When Dingwall slipped into a house at the village of Jemimaville, the crowd rushed forward to get revenge, but he slithered through a back window and fled into the woods of Poyntzfield. As he ran to the safety of Avoch on the south of the Black Isle, the crowd took howling revenge on his gig instead. They smashed it to fragments. In the meantime, the Reverend Mackenzie was inducted at the inn at Fortrose rather than at the church in Resolis.

Having repelled the Lord Lieutenant, the sheriff and all his men, the crowd at Resolis enjoyed a noisy party. They spent the night in cheering and singing, clattering the bell and laughing. However, they had not forgotten Margaret Cameron. A large group marched to the jail in Cromarty, alarming the jailer and the local authorities. The Lord Lieutenant was aware that there was the distinct possibility of similar scenes at Knockbain, also in the Black Isle, where the minister had also seceded. He sought military support from Sir Neville Douglas, who commanded the military forces in Scotland. However, even that was not easy. Although the nearest garrison was at Fort George, there was only a skeleton force there.

© Author's Collection

Resolis Church, Black Isle

At about four on Friday afternoon, 29 September, around 100 people marched to Cromarty, brandishing staves and other weapons. They tramped in by the western road, camped around the jail, and two spokesmen demanded the release of Margaret Cameron. Naturally, the magistrates refused. The Free Church supporters stated that the people inside the jail had five minutes to change their minds, or they were coming in to get her. The magistrates still refused, but sent for the Reverend Stewart, a Free Church minister, who tried to persuade the crowd to go home. They listened politely, nodded and then proceeded to rescue Margaret Cameron.

Led by two men named Murray and a Free Kirk elder named Andrew Holm, the men rushed into the courtyard into which the prison door opened. They used huge rocks to splinter a panel of the front door, finished the business with clubs and hammers and surged into the lobby of the jail. However, there were two further doors between them and the prisoner. Margaret Cameron was held in a small cell, twelve foot by eleven, with a wooden floor. This cell was known as the Black Hole and had a single, barred but unglazed window at the level of the ground. The crowd spent less than ten minutes in breaking through to Cameron, using a log as a battering ram to crash through the door of the cell. They snatched the prisoner and carried her shoulder high through the streets before they returned to Resolis. Although the mob also smashed open other cell doors, the three prisoners preferred to remain where they were.

On the next day, Saturday, 30 September, a crowd gathered outside the house of Mr Mackintosh, the most prominent person in Resolis and a man who had refused to switch his allegiance to the Free Church. Rather than wait for the assault, Mackintosh and his wife fled, with Mrs Mackintosh in disguise. The mob rampaged through their home. The Mackintoshes ran to Braelangwell, the house of Sir Hugh Fraser, but Sir Hugh also had his troubles. He had sent his carriage away to pick up a lady guest, but a crowd intercepted it and pelted the coachman with stones.

In the meantime, the Reverend Mackenzie tried to preach at Logie, but once again a hostile crowd confronted him. They had barricaded the entrance to the church and a crowd seethed outside. When Lady Ross of Balnagown drove up in her carriage, the mob closed ranks to deny her access. They repelled her with foul language and when Lady Ross came out of her carriage and tried to speak, a woman lifted a stick and whacked her across the arm. Her Ladyship retreated to loud abuse and the expected volley of stones. The church bell was tolling all the time, a clattering background to the pandemonium.

A gentleman by the name of Ross was next to try to get to church, and when he was chased away he drove to Tain and fetched Sheriff Cameron. By the time they reached Logie the Reverend Mackenzie had already departed. Cameron spoke to the crowd, some of whom told him that all they wanted was a site to build their own church, and then they all drifted away.

The authorities offered a reward for information about other anti-Established Church actions, such as the people who cut off the rope for the bell at Tongue church and filled the keyhole of the church door with gravel. The insurrection against the landlords' intrusion into the religion of the people was spreading all across the north. There were injurious remarks scrawled on walls, coal tar smeared on the homes of Kirk Elders and other petty acts of vandalism that showed the deep feelings of the Free Church people.

There was further trouble at Rosskeen, five miles north of Alness, on Sunday, 1 October, when a rumour spread that the Reverend Mackenzie was due to preach there. A crowd waited to bar his entrance to the church, and when he did not turn up they turned their spleen on Donald Fraser, the precenter of the Established Church, instead. They were chasing him through the churchyard when a soldier, Lieutenant MacLeod stepped in and saved him.

On Tuesday, 3 October, four sheriff officers came to Invergordon with warrants for two men who had been leading players in the riots. However, word soon spread, a man ran through the town clattering a bell to gather a crowd and forestall the arrests. The suspects were hustled to safety and the mob confronted the sheriff officers. 'Go home,' they said, 'or we will stone you to death.' The sheriff officers left; the suspects were not arrested.

For the remainder of that long Tuesday, crowds surrounded the church at Rosskeen in case the Reverend Mackenzie should arrive to take his place. The entire area was controlled by the followers of the Free Church. They had men watching all the local gentry, who remained faithful to the Established Church with its police of patronage, and were aware of every movement. They sent threatening letters to many of the men who remained with the Establishment and made no attempts at disguise.

There were troubles and rumours of troubles at other places in the area. The Lord Lieutenant had heard a rumour that there would be trouble at Kiltearn on Wednesday, 27 September, so tried to forestall it by posting a notice to the local magistrates commanding in the King's name that they all attend at the church. The gathering took place, with many of the seceding ministers also there to help keep the peace. The established minister was inducted without any trouble.

After the partial success at Invergordon, the seceding ministers preached the doctrine of non-violence wherever they could. The Reverend Macdonald of Ferintosh preached to the congregation at Evanton, with the message that anyone who used violence to try and stop the induction of new ministers would not be welcome in the Free Church. The Free Churchmen sent a request to the Duke of Sutherland, one of the largest landowners in Scotland, to supply land on which to build Free Churches, but he refused, saying that the Church of Scotland was the persecuted party and if he consented he would be seen as 'giving his countenance to its opponents'. He did agree that he might consider giving land for a church if there was no religious building in the area, but any subsequent church would have to follow the rules of the Established Church of Scotland.

Sutherland was not alone in denying the Free Church any scope on his land. In January 1844, MacLean of Ardgour had an interdict served on the Reverend John Mactavish, prohibiting him from erecting a tent and preaching to a gathering of people at Ballachulish.

By Thursday, 5 October, the authorities were retaliating. When two young men from Tain had travelled south to Inverness to watch proceedings at the court, Superintendent John McBean recognised them as being involved in the agitation and hustled both to the jail in Dingwall. The Constabulary Committee of Inverness-shire met to decide a course of action and see if the Inverness Police could be employed to help out in Ross-shire.

Even more emphatically, 200 men of the 87th Foot, the Royal Irish Fusiliers were sent from Paisley to Leith and then by sea to Ross to keep the people in order. Led by Captain Keate, they disembarked at Invergordon from the *Duke of Richmond* steamer on the morning of Wednesday, 4 October. A crowd watched them march up to their temporary barracks at an old hemp factory, but there was no trouble. Later that same day, Superintendent McBean of the Inverness-shire Police and Superintendent Mann of the Elgin Police arrived with an officer and fifteen men of a revenue cutter. They were there to execute arrest warrants on the people thought to have led the riots.

Once they had force behind them, the authorities moved quickly. They arrested seven men that same evening and locked them in the guard room under the watchful eyes and glittering bayonets of the Royal Irish. A body of soldiers escorted the prisoners to the jail at Tain.

The arrival of the military sucked the spirit from the people of Tain. Some asked the soldiers if they would fire at unarmed civilians if they were ordered to, and the Irishmen replied, 'If you resist, we'll cut you down like the standing corn.' There was obviously no pan-Celtic sympathy from the Irish soldiers to the Highland Scots.

On Saturday, 7 October, the Lord Lieutenant swore in hundreds more Special Constables, many of them tenants of the landowners. There were fifty men from the estate of Sir John Mackenzie alone. Perhaps 300-strong and escorted by a body of the 87th, the combined force crossed the firth from Invergordon to the Black Isle and marched to Resolis to swear in the new Established minister. The soldiers did not approach the actual church but the sixty or so people who gathered made no attempt to intervene this time. The people of the Highlands very seldom opposed the army.

That same evening, three more suspected rioters were arrested as they lay in bed in Jemimaville, and were taken to the jail in Dingwall. A few days later, three men were arrested in Cromarty, suspected of being involved in the jailbreaking there. Others who were known to have taken part in the riot fled the area. The authorities debated raising a force of constables or even a troop of yeomanry to keep order in the north of Scotland.

After about a week the bulk of the infantry were withdrawn to Fort George, east of Inverness, and only a token force of thirty under the command of Lieutenant Turner remained at Dingwall, ready to march wherever they were required. A steamer named *Modern Athens* berthed at Invergordon, in case she was needed to carry the troops at Fort George to any possible trouble spot.

By December, six of the arrested men were out on bail, but were summoned to the High Court of Justiciary in Edinburgh. Their trial took place on Wednesday, 10 and Thursday, 11 January 1844. On 10 January, John Urquhart, Donald Urquhart and a fisherman named Robert Hogg were put on trial for breaking open Cromarty Jail and freeing Margaret Cameron. Others also appeared. There was Andrew Holm, a fisherman and labourer of Ferrytown in Resolis parish, a labourer named Andrew Fraser, the stone-thrower Elspet Aird, a shoemaker named William Fraser and David Mackenzie, a crofter from Bog of Cullicudden. The latter three chose not to appear and were subsequently outlawed.

Andrew Holm and Alexander Fraser pleaded not guilty to a charge of mobbing and rioting and disturbing the Presbytery of Chanonry. When witness after witness reported seeing them heavily involved in the riot they changed their plea to guilty. They both were given six months in jail, while John Urquhart was given nine months for his involvement in breaking Margaret Cameron from the jail at Dornoch.

Overall, the sentences were fairly moderate considering the trouble and expense the government had been to, but the moral seemed fairly clear: be careful when meddling with the religious feelings of the Highlanders.

12

Poaching

Poaching was endemic across the nineteenth-century Highlands and Hebrides, but there were many different types of poaching. There was the refined hunting of deer with rifles; there was the less refined driving of deer into ambushes. There were a dozen methods of poaching for salmon and trout, from using lanterns to 'burn the water' to hooks and nets. The movement of game birds such as partridge could be studied, for if disturbed but not panicked a covey would follow a recognised path and into a skilfully laid net. Nets could also be used for rabbits, while there could be wholesale attacks on pheasants, which roosted fairly close to the ground. Highland poachers probably utilised all of these methods at some point in the century. Most poaching was small-scale and simple.

The Highland historian Dr I. Grant mentioned poaching in her classic book *Highland Folk Ways*. Grant stated that she was 'lucky enough to have been given the rifles of three noted poachers': one was a long-barrelled flintlock, another a weapon that could be broken in two so the barrel was concealed down the owner's trouser leg and the third was an ex-army rifle from the mid-1850s. She also mentions various methods for poaching for trout or salmon, such as using torches on the surface of the river; using leisters, or three-pronged iron forks; or an otter board, a board with lines attached; wickerwork traps; or simple guddling, when somebody would lie on the bank of a river, place both hands in the water and tickle a fish into submission. There follows a number of examples of Highland poaching.

Destroying the Yairs

There was a stir of interest at Inverness Circuit Court in September 1833 when a number of fishermen from Ullapool appeared for poaching. They were Alexander Matheson; Donald Mackenzie, also known as Andrew Roderick Macgregor; Allan Campbell, also known as McIvor; Murdoch Urquhart; Colin Macleod; and John Cameron, known as Castle, together with Donald Fraser, who was the agent for the British Society for the Encouragement of Fisheries at Ullapool; Norman Macdonald; and Colin Ross. All were charged with destroying the yair, or fish trap, on 24 September 1832 on the shore of Loch Broom that belonged to Sir George Mackenzie of Coul and removing the materials that made up the yair. The yair was designed to catch salmon. They were also accused of destroying a yair at the mouth of the River Broom that belonged to Reverend Thomas Ross, the minister of Loch Broom.

Only Colin Ross, Norman Macleod and Allan Campbell appeared and pleaded guilty. The others were outlawed. The defence said that the offences were committed at a time of extreme poverty and the men were facing starvation and they were not aware they were breaking the law. To his credit, Sir George Mackenzie agreed that the men had not realised they were breaking the law, and the judge, Lord Meadowbank, ordered them to have two months' imprisonment in Tain.

Famous Poachers

Two of the most famous poachers of the central Highlands were John Farquharson and Alexander Davidson. The careers of these two men spanned the central decades of the nineteenth century, with Davidson in the '20s and '30s and Farquharson in the '40s and '50s.

Davidson was a gamekeeper turned poacher who roamed the braes of Atholl, yet he was also a man of honour. Before he encroached on anybody's land, he would send warning in advance. He died in 1843.

Like Davidson, Farquharson was a name redolent of the sweet heather of Badenoch, and like Davidson, he poached at will around Atholl. Another keeper turned poacher, he was an expert shot but fell foul of the law from time to time. In 1884 he was caught shooting and selling grouse and fined £25, six months' wages for a skilled man. He lived until 1893 and died in his own bed.

Two Small Examples

On the night of 25 October 1874 an old man named William Jack was poaching in the Perthshire hills. He roamed the fields around Kilmadock and Lecroft with nets and sticks and eventually slipped onto the farm of Thomas Reid. However, Reid was a watchful man and recognised Jack as a habitual night poacher. In April next year Jack stood before the circuit court in Perth. The Lord Justice Clerk awarded him two months in jail.

At the beginning of August 1886, a gang of salmon poachers fought with Lord Middleton's gamekeepers at the mouth of the Applecross River in Wester Ross. The poachers were local crofters from Lochalsh and had put a splash net across the mouth of the river to catch the salmon when the keepers arrived. Both sides fought and the result was a draw; the keepers prevented any salmon being poached and got possession of the net, but the poachers escaped.

At other times what started out as a simple attempt to lift game could end in bloody violence, and gamekeepers were known to carry weapons for their own defence.

Poaching Lord Lovat's Lands

In one case in February 1887, Donald Macdonald, Lord Lovat's gamekeeper, was patrolling the Inchberry Estate near Inverness. He had experienced trouble with poachers, and a few days previously somebody had sent him hate mail and a death threat, so he carried a revolver. Nevertheless, rather than live cartridges, he had it loaded with blanks; his purpose was to scare and capture the poachers, not kill them. He did not patrol alone, for William Logan, the coachman and gamekeeper to another local landowner, Major Gordon, and a third keeper named William Fraser, also came to help.

Macdonald was not just doing his normal patrols but was actively searching for poachers on Lovat's land. It was a dark night, sharply cold, and not long after midnight he heard the sound of footsteps. He peered through the dark and saw a large group of men, nine or ten strong, about 100 yards away. They were walking slowly and purposefully into a field. As the keepers hid behind a drystane dyke and watched, the men began to set a net across the field, with the obvious intention of trapping rabbits.

Despite the odds against them, Fraser and Logan dashed into the field and grabbed the nearest two of the poachers. As soon as the gamekeepers came into the field, the poachers began to throw stones at them. Two or three hit Logan on the body and one split open his skull so he was nearly blinded by the blood that poured over his eyes. In that state it was difficult for him to see who had thrown the stones, but nevertheless, he lifted his stick and closed with the poachers. As he grappled them he identified one as a plasterer named Robert Johnston, while the others were John Carr and James Chisholm, all three from

Inchberry House on Inchberry Estate, where Donald Macdonald fought the poachers in 1887

Inverness. He thumped one poacher with his stick, knocking him down, and then heard the triple bark of Macdonald's revolver.

While Logan and Fraser had been battling against odds, Macdonald had snatched the centre of the net from the field. He had no sooner done this when he heard the sounds of combat from his two companions, and he hurried to help them. Dim in the dark, he saw two of the poachers lying prone on the ground; one was Robert Johnston, but he could not recognise the other.

Macdonald arrived at the scene at the same moment as five of the poachers, and a second battle began. The poachers lifted stones and again began to pelt the gamekeepers. One poacher named Allan Johnston threw a large rock that smashed into Macdonald's mouth and knocked him, bleeding, to the ground. He spat out a dislodged tooth. As he lay there, one of the poachers, possibly Carr or a man named William Downie, shouted, 'Finish him! Finish him!'

Not surprisingly, with half a dozen angry and violent men surrounding him, Macdonald became frightened. He pulled out his revolver and fired a couple of shots. The poachers hastily retreated into the dark, but Macdonald heard them arguing, with one man accusing the others of cowardice. 'He's firing blanks,' somebody said.

Macdonald shouted to Logan to also use his gun, and Logan fired into the ground to make sure the poachers did not recover their courage; there was a lull and the gamekeepers withdrew to Inverness. They told the police and Macdonald had a doctor see to his injured mouth.

That was not the only time poachers struck at the Inchberry Estate. About ten days later Macdonald was again on patrol and he found a game bag concealed in a ditch. When he opened the bag he found over thirty poached rabbits.

When the poaching case came to the circuit court in spring 1887, all the accused – James Chisholm, John Carr and Robert Johnston – denied poaching at the Inchberry Estate. They put forward various alibis that neither the judge nor the jury found credible, so all were handed nine months in jail.

The Glenelg Hunt

The Highland Clearances are well known, with the indigenous population being evicted by the hundreds to make way for sheep. However, there is an even more sinister side to the Clearances than alterations to farming practices.

When the Australian wool industry erupted in the nineteenth century, demand for Scottish wool plummeted and the landowner had to search for an alternative source of income. Sometimes the people were cleared so the landowner could indulge in a pastime that was growing in popularity in the nineteenth century. The people were removed so the upper classes could enjoy the sports of deer stalking and grouse shooting. Land that had been carefully tendered for generations was allowed to descend into moorland so bracken and heather spread over the countryside. It is deeply ironic that heather is now often seen as a symbol of Scotland when it was once kept under control by hardworking Highlanders.

Deer were probably as unpopular as sheep had been, possibly because the landowners prevented the crofters from defending their crops from them. Deer were nearly as sacred to the landowners as cows were in Hindu India. However, there was resistance. There had always been poaching in Scotland, but in the Highlands it now increased.

In 1887 in Glenelg in Skye the local crofters combined in a massive deer hunt that drove hundreds of deer into the sea. Naturally, the landowners sought revenge and had the leaders of this resistance movement arrested. The High Court in Edinburgh found them not guilty and a crowd carried them down the high street of the capital, chanting, 'Down with the tyrants.' It was a long way from the early days of Clearance.

The Pairc Deer Raid

Although some aspects of Highland crime are similar to crime else-where in Scotland, others are unique to the time and place. The deer raid on Pairc, Lewis, also known as Lochs, was one such. It is unfair to call the raiders poachers, for at no time did they hide their actions.

In 1887 the Gaelic communities of the Hebrides were no longer willing to accept the abuses that had been piled on their ancestors. They had seen the results of land grabs in Skye and Tiree, while the Crofting Act of 1886 had created a measure of stability and security of tenure. However, things in the Crofting Counties were far from perfect. The people of Pairc in Lewis were a case in point. For generations their land had been squeezed by the local landowners. In their case, it was the Matheson family who were turning large acreages of what had been productive farmland into deer forest for the sporting interest. The 1880s was a bad decade for the Hebrides, with crop failures, foul returns at the fishing, falling cattle prices and fewer jobs on the mainland. People in the overcrowded crofts faced destitution.

Donald Macrae, a schoolmaster from Balallan and formerly a maths teacher at Inverness Academy, was allegedly the leader of the six men who decided to fight against the loss of their land. Retaliation of some sort was necessary. With a growing population and a limited supply of land, the crofters and cottagers were living on the cusp of starvation. As the indigenous population suffered, Lady Matheson leased another twelve square miles of hill to a sportsman named Joseph Platt. The local crofters believed this land would be better utilised for crofting and they had hoped to have it returned to ease the burden of overcrowding and lack of land. The Pairc forest had been started at the beginning of the century but as deer hunting became a popular sport for the wealthy, the landowners had gradually expanded the forest at the expense of the surrounding crofts until thirty crofting communities were cleared.

After generations of such attrition, Macrae organised a raid on Matheson's deer forest, with the intention of killing or poaching the deer, and more importantly of drawing attention to the plight of the crofters.

The raid was well prepared, with the crofters gathering enough food for three days and carrying spars and sails from the fishing boats to act as makeshift tents. They left the scattered townships around the Pairc area, some carrying flags and most carrying guns of various vintages. The high skirl of the pipes announced that the men of Balallan Township and all the rest were no longer prepared to be persecuted. Others of the deer raiders were gathered by the sound of the horn, which seems to have been the way in the Highlands.

At dawn on Tuesday, 22 November 1887, the crofters rendezvoused between Balallan and Eishken. It was a beautiful day, but the number of men who gathered can only be estimated; the figures quoted varied from a few score to as many as 2,000. Mrs Jessie Thorneycroft-Platt, wife of the tenant, greeted the raiders, but she spoke in English and they replied in Gaelic. Her head gamekeeper was a Gaelic speaker, but rather than support the raiders he said, '*An Annam a Dhia bheil an caothadh oirbh?*' – 'In the name of God, have you gone mad?'

With the gathering complete, the raiders split into small groups and moved into the forest. What happened next was a determined, organised attempt to exterminate the deer population in the area that had once been cultivated land and was now a wilderness. The men were divided into occupations: some were stalkers, some were marksmen, others were porters who carried the sections of tent or were ready to carry the dead deer. Matheson's gamekeepers tried to minimise the damage by driving the deer away from the raiders, but they were competing with experts who were also fighting for their families.

On the first night, the raiders gathered at Airidh Dhomhnuill Cam, at the site of what was said to be one of the last clan battles in Lewis, where MacAuleys and Macleods slaughtered each other centuries before. The night was as interesting as the day. As pipers played cheerfully, the men feasted on venison from some of the deer they had killed, then prayed for God to bless this 'Holy Crusade'. Many men slept under the stars, others under canvas as if they had not a care in the world.

In the meantime, the tenant of the shooting estate contacted Sheriff Fraser and Procurator Fiscal Ross.

As rain threatened the next day, the hunt resumed, with more cottars drifting in from the surrounding area. By that time the authorities were determined to end proceedings. With so many people involved, the local police were helpless so Sheriff Fraser had resorted to what seemed the usual tactics in dealing with unhappy Highlanders, and had called for overwhelming backup. As well as whistling up police from the mainland, he had asked for Royal Marines, while a company of the Royal Scots were also on their way from Maryhill Barracks in Glasgow. While he waited for this support, Fraser and Ross took a steamer from their base in Stornoway to the seat of trouble. HMS

Ajax sailed north to support the law, but the Hebrideans could also use sea power, and Harris fishing boats carried away the carcasses of deer. In this case the islanders were more effective at sea than the Navy, for *Ajax* broke down in the Clyde. In the meantime, a party of raiders shared their venison with Douglas Thornycroft, Mrs Platt's brother.

By Thursday, 24 November, with an estimated 200 deer killed, the raid was finished and the men gathered at their camp. The flames of huge peat fires reflected from the lowering sky, while the bright music of the pipes contrasted with the dark, still waters of Loch Seaforth. The camp centred on a huge tent of canvas sails and cabers, filled with the scent of stewing venison. The crofters lounged amidst the heather, some mouthing Gaelic songs. They listened to the tale of Donald Mackinnon. He had been pursued by the police and on an impulse turned at bay, gun in hand. However, rather than become a fugitive, Mackinnon was to turn traitor and give the authorities the names of the leaders of the raid.

Retaliation began. Sheriff Fraser visited the township of Eishken and read the Riot Act to the forty quiet crofters who gathered to meet him as they were on their way home. When Superintendent Gordon led twenty police from the mainland to Stornoway, scores of people gave them a cold welcome, but there was no violence when the police charged five men with mobbing, rioting and intimidation. The five men were Donald Mackinnon, son of a crofter; Murdo Macdonald, a married cottar; Murdo Macleod, a landless squatter; Roderick Murray, who was arrested when attending drill with the Royal Navy Reserves; Malcolm Mackenzie and Donald Macmillan. They walked quietly into custody.

Donald Macrae was also arrested for inciting to mobbing and violence, and for pointing a firearm at the police superintendent. He had stated that the raid was to bring public attention to the plight of the poor of Lewis. The publicity did just that. A newspaper called *The North British Daily Mail* sent a reporter to Lewis and started a fund to relieve the poverty. Sympathisers in Scotland and descendants of those exiled in the Clearances contributed until the sum totalled more than £4,000, but in the meantime, the arrested men travelled to Edinburgh to face their trial.

The Lord Justice Clerk summoned up the case very much on the side of the landowners, but also stated that deer and grouse were wild animals and not private property. The jury found all the accused not guilty. They believed that the men had not been mobbing, as they were scattered over 144 square miles of wild hills. They had intimidated nobody; they had treated the sheriff with respect and even shared their food with Mr Thornycroft. It was a massive victory for the crofters and a crowd carried Macrae shoulder high down the High Street, crying, 'Down with the tyrants.'

The raid had gained publicity, but the Pairc remained a deer forest even after the raid and the trial, but there is a much later postscript. In 2011 Rosanna Cunningham, the Environment Minister, granted permission for the people of Pairc to buy the estate under the 'Right to Buy' provisions of the 2003 Land Reform Scotland Act. The crofters continue to fight.

Other poachers had less high ideals and their actions led to tragedy.

The Poacher from Patagonia

Every country in the world has its wild areas, the Badlands, no-go areas, places where for a while the rule of Law does not run. Nineteenth-century Scotland was no exception. In the 1890s the forests and hills of Abernethy became notorious for extensive and aggressive poaching. The police and gamekeepers were hard pressed to keep things under control. Of all the poachers, one of the most notorious was Allan Macallum.

Allan Macallum was a rogue, a wanderer, a poacher and a wild man of the hills. Born on the shores of Loch Ericht in Perthshire, he was bred to the outdoor life. His father was a gamekeeper who soon took his family to Lochaber, where Macallum grew into active youth. His father tried every means he knew to cure him of the habit, but neither kind words nor stinging blows had the desired effect, and father and son worked outdoors but on opposite sides of the fence of legality. As would be expected, there were frequent family conflicts, as well as encounters between Allan Macallum and the other local gamekeepers. When his father died, still in the Fort William area, Macallum's mother moved to Coylum Bridge, working for her older son, Donald, who in turn worked for the Grants of Rothiemurchus. By that time Allan Macallum was an experienced poacher and had left Scotland years earlier to try his luck elsewhere.

For seven years he worked as a shepherd in the Falkland Islands and in neighbouring South America, where he wandered in Patagonia. Although rumours of wild days and heavy drinking reached Scotland, there were no details. Around 1890 Macallum returned home and lived with his mother and gamekeeper brother. He had earned a little money and was quiet for a while, but he soon took to wandering into the quiet solitude of the hills for days at a time. He did not look out of the ordinary, a stocky man with a neat moustache, who wore a bonnet and a tweed or tartan jacket, but he returned to his poaching way of life. Soon he was to be notorious throughout the Highlands.

Macallum relished the life of a poacher, especially as he had a huge area in which to operate, from the Nevis range by Fort William all the way east to the granite plateau of the Cairngorms. He was a natural outdoors man, agile, fit and used to being alone. He lived by poaching the wildlife and selling the produce to game dealers the length and breadth of the country, sending his catches from the railway station at Boat of Garten.

About 1892, Macallum's mother returned to Lochaber. Perhaps Macallum went with her, for he vanished for a few months. It is possible he was employed as a shepherd in Aberdeenshire or in the far north, but by late 1893 he was living with his brother in Glenmore. Despite his brother's occupation, Macallum and the gamekeepers were old adversaries, and he had been fined and jailed on more than one occasion. He was notorious for abusive language and having allegedly threatened both gamekeepers and policemen in the past.

Eventually Macallum and his brother Donald argued about the extensive poaching, there were harsh words exchanged, and Macallum threatened violence. In return, Donald suggested that Macallum was insane, and then they went their separate ways. Donald reported his brother's threat to the police, and a constable travelled from Aviemore to Macallum's cottage, but by the time he arrived, the place was securely fastened and there was no way in. The constable returned to Aviemore, reported his failure and returned with reinforcements, but with no better luck.

Perhaps encouraged by the presence of the police, the local people began to voice their opinion of Macallum the poacher. They told the police he was dangerous and agreed he was probably insane; they claimed they were frightened when they knew he was roaming free.

At this time, Macallum was forty-three and a deadly shot. He was a touch over five foot ten inches tall, broad in the shoulders, deep in the chest and powerful of arm and leg. Overall, he was a formidable man to cross but he seemed to have no close companions, except for a very faithful dog.

The poaching continued. Macallum failed to appear at a court in Inverness and was sentenced to a fine of five shillings in his absence, with seven days in jail if he failed to pay. Constable Thomas King of Nethy Bridge Police Office was sent to arrange payment. King was an equally powerful man, with fifteen years' experience in the police. He was over six feet tall, muscular and was married with eight children.

Since the disagreement with his brother, Macallum had moved in to Marjory Macpherson's cottage at Milton of Tulloch in Abernethy parish. Macpherson was known locally as Black May; her daughter, Christina

Grant, also shared the cottage, which was little more than a wooden shanty with a porch in front. It was a typical but and ben with the front door leading into a small lobby or hallway. The kitchen and the bedroom both opened off this lobby. There were no other rooms in the house.

King contacted Constable John MacNiven to help arrest Macallum. The two policemen met on Wednesday, 20 December 1893, and arrived at the cottage at nine in the morning, but there was no Macallum. Macpherson was there with her daughter; both were in bed. King and MacNiven remained in the cottage for three quarters of an hour in case Macallum returned, but when Macpherson said she thought he was outside, the police left to look for him, each going their separate ways, and with Macpherson watching.

MacNiven strode toward Tulloch Public Park and walked straight into Macallum, who carried a rifle or a shotgun. MacNiven thought he was drunk or had been drinking.

Macallum pointed the gun at MacNiven. 'I will put this through your heart,' he said.

'Why would you put anything in my heart?' MacNiven asked. 'I have no ill will against you and you can have none against me.' Not surprisingly, MacNiven was scared, in case Macallum should carry out his threat.

'I suppose you have come after me about the fine,' Macallum said. 'I will pay the fine but I'll be damned, but I will fight for liberty this time.'

MacNiven did not come close but said he would accept the fine in instalments if Macallum signed a document to say he would pay that way. Macallum still held his gun in both hands and walked toward Macpherson's cottage without answering.

MacNiven did not follow him directly but walked in the same direction, keeping a little distance between them. On a number of occasions, Macallum turned to face him and pointed the gun in his direction, but that may have been a coincidence due to the manner in which the weapon was held. Perhaps because of the gun, MacNiven did not try and arrest Macallum alone.

By eleven in the morning MacNiven and King were reunited and they returned to Macpherson's cottage, but once again Macallum was not there. They left and waited for him outside throughout that dark day of cold and sleet until half past three in the afternoon, when a young labourer named Peter Grant told them that Macallum was back in Macpherson's house.

They returned to the cottage once more and King shouted out, 'Hulloa, Macallum!'

Macallam answered at once: 'Yes, what have you to say to me?'

King said nothing. The police entered the cottage together, with MacNiven going into the tiny bedroom and King into the kitchen. As soon as MacNiven entered the dark bedroom, he heard Macallum's dog growl and thought it might attack him. Instead, he thumped it with his baton. As the dog yowled and backed off, MacNiven heard the sound of gunfire. The room was so dark and the sound so loud that MacNiven thought that Macallum was shooting at him and shouted to King for help, but there was no reply. Still believing that Macallum was in the bedroom, MacNiven left to find King. He crossed the lobby, entered the kitchen and stumbled over something on the floor.

Only when he lit a match did he see the body of King lying face downward on the floor with a single-barrelled muzzle-loading gun over his legs. The barrel of the gun was warm, as if it had been recently fired, and King had been shot through the heart. MacNiven tried to ascertain whether King was alive or dead. As he stooped, he saw a man in the cottage doorway and recognised Alexander Grant, the postman.

He called out, 'Watch the door; he is in and King is shot.'

'He is not in,' Grant said. 'He is away down the road.'

MacNiven then tested to see if the gun was still loaded by blowing down the barrel and then thrust his finger in the barrel. His finger was black when he withdrew it, which was a sure sign that the gun had been recently discharged.

Once MacNiven and Grant ascertained that King was dead, they carried the body to the nearby cottage of Betsy Geddes to wait for Dr John Grant from Grantown. Dr Grant came that same evening. As soon as King was taken out of the house, MacNiven borrowed a spring cart and drove to Nethy Bridge to raise the alarm.

Alexander Grant explained his side of the story. He had been outside the cottage when Macallum returned. He saw the police enter a few moments later, heard the door slam and a voice call, 'Allan,' then there was the sound of a shot and he saw Macallum running away from the house. Macallum was not wearing his boots, but his dog followed him.

As was usual in such cases, the police asked for another medical opinion and Dr William Barclay of Grantown also examined King's body. He said the shot had passed between the seventh and eighth rib, fired from close range. After the murder, the police were now involved in a manhunt.

Chief Constable McHardy sent telegrams to all the police in Speyside and the surrounding area, ordering them to search for Macallum. Superintendent Hugh Chisholm, the deputy chief constable, led the hunt for the fugitive murderer. There were reports of Macallum from various places.

About nine on Wednesday night, 20 December, Macallum called at the house of John Stewart at Tonterie, about a mile from the shooting. Stewart was an old friend and fed Macallum and gave him an old pair of boots. On Wednesday night Macallum called at the lonely cottage of Angus Grant at Clachaig and took as much food as he could. The Grants knew who he was but were too afraid to resist him, yet when he asked them how Constable King was, they realised he was not aware the policeman was dead. That same night Macallum borrowed a match from a tramping shoemaker near Skye of Curr, so he was making to attempt to hide from the police. As always, Macallum's dog accompanied him, but a day later the dog was seen back at Macpherson's cottage, alone.

The police followed Macallum's trail. They found the impression of a human body in an outhouse at Lurg Farm, about a mile from Clachaig, and guessed Macallum had been there. The police suspected he was heading for Donside, either by Tomintoul or by Inchrory, over the wild, bare hills. Chisholm sent nine policemen to pursue him and had another fifty casting a wider net around the countryside. There were stories that he had been seen between Balmoral and Ballater, and rumours he may run into Deeside, but the police concentrated on the Don area.

Chisholm led Sergeant Fraser of Kingussie and Constable McBeth of Inverness to follow the trail of Macallum. On Saturday, 23 December, a farmer named William Bell told the police that Macallum was at his farm at Tomachrochair, which ironically means 'the hangman's knoll'. The next morning the police caught him. Four police found Macallum in the barn, covered in straw. Chisholm arrested him on the charge of murdering Constable King. Surprisingly for such a reportedly violent man, Macallum did not resist. The police searched and handcuffed him.

Macallum was brought back to Aviemore, from where he was then taken to Inverness. There was a crowd waiting to see him at Inverness railway station, some pointing as he left the train, handcuffed to a policeman. He was tired, weather-beaten and ragged as he was bundled into a cab and carried to the jail. He appeared before the sheriff that same day but did not plead. All the time he was held in custody, Macallum had kept a guard on his tongue and rarely spoke to anybody. Almost the only thing he said was to ask about the welfare of his dog.

Macallum was tried at the circuit court at Inverness Castle on Wednesday, 15 February 1899, in front of a large crowd. As usual, the circuit court opened with a show of ceremony. The Cameron Highlanders provided a guard of honour for Lord Trayner, the Provost, magistrates and the town council as they travelled to the court. The defence tried to claim that Macallum had been temporarily insane but a string of witnesses, including three doctors, testified to his sanity. All said he was of a naturally quiet and sullen disposition. The defence said he had changed since he came back from the Falklands and Patagonia, but the jury decided he was guilty of culpable homicide and the judge sentenced him to fifteen years' penal servitude. He was sent to Peterhead shortly after.

Constable King was buried at Abernethy Churchyard and a subscription fund was raised for his widow and family. By 12 February 1899 it had raised £12,000, mostly in small amounts of money, which shows the public interest in the case. The murder of Constable King was big news in the Highlands at the time. The newspapers carried inches of column space and a poet named Arthur Francis Paterson wrote about it:

> While the snow caps the brow of Cairngorm
> And the red deer to Glenmore repair
> A ghost and a legend shall linger
> Round the steadings of Tomachrochair
> For black was the heart of Macallum
> As the breast of the black-cock in air
> But blacker the curse he has muttered
> On the farmstead of Tomachrochair

Mccallum was obviously an extreme case and most poachers were much more small-scale. However he is an example of how what may seem to be an innocuous or even a victimless crime could escalate into murder deep in the Highlands. Poachers came in all shapes and sizes, and not all were simply countrymen out to bag a single rabbit for the pot.

13
Children and Crime

It seems common for adults to complain about the younger generation, but there is no doubt that in the nineteenth century, children were involved in a great variety of crimes, and children in the Highlands were no exception. The jail at Inveraray in Argyll holds the records of over 4,300 prisoners, including children, and shows that children such as seven-year-old James McCulloch could be sent to an industrial school for five years, while nine-year-old Charles McHaig was sent to prison for fourteen days for housebreaking.

However, the penalties when they were caught could be much harsher, particularly at the beginning of the century.

Transportation and the Birch

On 2 May 1836, at the circuit court at Inverness, James Gillespie, otherwise known as James Young, was only sixteen when he was charged with theft and forgery. Despite his youth, he was sentenced to be transported for life. Only a month later he was aboard *Lady Kennaway* with 300 of his fellow sufferers on their way to New South Wales.

© Mary Evans / Classic Stock / H. ARMSTRONG ROBERTS

Children also played their part in
some crimes of the century

At the beginning of the century, children were treated much like miniature adults, as far as the courts were concerned. They could be transported for long years, sent to adult prisons and even hanged for what today would be considered relatively minor crimes. By the latter decades of the century the situation had altered; children could be sent to industrial schools if their home life was deemed likely to lead them into greater trouble, they could neither be transported nor hanged. However, there were other punishments that errant boys would not have enjoyed in the slightest.

On 14 January 1877, at Inverness Police Court, thirteen-year-old John Allan was found guilty of stealing £1 and three shillings from the pocket of a woman who was visiting his mother's house. It was obviously not Allan's first offence, for his mother said she could no longer control him and was willing for him to be sent to a reformatory. The Dean of Guild, Mr Falconer, sentenced the boy to ten days in prison, followed by five years in a reformatory. Not surprisingly, young Allan was unhappy at this harsh sentence; he cried and bawled out to his mother to 'pay the fine' as he was wrestled away. Other youngsters were given a different type of sentence.

In the Inverness Sheriff Court on 7 April 1886, two young boys faced Sheriff Blair. Joseph Robertson was aged thirteen and his companion, John Robertson, was aged fourteen. They were accused of having stolen a pair of boots from Neil Cameron of Ballifary, Inverness. Although they both pleaded not guilty, the evidence was pretty conclusive against John Robertson. The case against Joseph was found not proven. Sheriff Blair ordered John to be given six strokes of the birch. Although the sentence was mild compared to what it might have been, it is unlikely that John felt particularly happy as he lay across the birching bench with his trousers around his ankles.

At the same court a thirteen-year-old girl named Jessie Stewart pleaded guilty of stealing a half sovereign from the school at Kingussie. Sheriff Blair let her off with an admonition.

Despite the threat of the reformatory and the birch, in November 1887 the Inverness Police faced a mini crime wave by a group of children. There were break-ins throughout the town and four boys were arrested and sentenced to be birched. However, only a month later the crimes began again, worse than before; the police scoured the town for every young lawbreaker they could find and hauled them before the burgh police court. Eleven boys faced Bailie Macdonald across the bench and heard him pronounce painful sentences on them. John Long, Hugh Munro, Alexander Shaw and Alexander Macpherson were found guilty of stealing two bonnets from a shop in Academy Street, twelve boxes of cigarettes from the railway bookstall, and hatboxes and pheasants from the railway. Bailie Macdonald awarded them nine strokes of the birch each.

At that same court sitting William McPherson and John McNeill were found guilty of stealing a sheepskin and a fleece from Macdonald, Fraser and Company's Auction Market. They were only given three strokes each. Angus and Christopher Mair, David Macdonald, John Fraser and Duncan Mackenzie had broken into Inverness Bowling Club and left with a sixty-foot tape measure and forty-eight Chinese lanterns. The bailie thought they deserved five strokes of the birch for their behaviour.

The birch was not just used in Inverness but all over the area. At the beginning of October 1883 Jeremiah Nicolson, a thirteen-year-old boy in Lerwick, was sentenced to nine strokes for cutting a girl called Christine Hay on the head with a knife. The girl had run up to him to beg 'a sweetie' and he claimed he had accidentally cut her. Sheriff Rampini also gave Nicolson twelve hours in jail, possibly to recover from his ordeal.

A Medieval Landlord

Children could be victims as well as perpetrators of crime and occasionally cases occurred that showed the landlords to have a mentality that belonged more to the Middle Ages than to the nineteenth century. Such was the situation at Fodderty, between Dingwall and Strathpeffer, in September 1856.

Finlay Noble was twelve years old and lived in Dingwall. On that day, he had gone up the steep hillside above the farm at Fodderty and cut a quantity of bracken, a plant which was more of a nuisance than a blessing but which Finlay wanted for a pet lamb. As young Finlay was carrying the bracken back to Dingwall, he met Charles Master, the tenant of the shootings of Castle Leod; Master lived at the lodge at Fodderty. The Marquis and Marchioness of Stafford owned the area, but the farm at Fodderty was leased to a third man named James Dudgeon.

Master was displeased to see Finlay carrying bracken, which he claimed was his property, and he forced the boy to carry it back over half a mile to the lodge house where he lived and place it at the front door. On his journey back to the lodge, Master called at the house of Mackenzie, who was a ghillie in his employ, to give him some support against the twelve-year-old Finlay, and once at the lodge he sent for a whip. By that time Finlay was in tears and promised not to take any more ferns if he was let go. With Finlay suitably frightened, Master shoved him inside one of the compartments of his dog kennel, with dogs confined in the space at his side, and left him there in the dark for an hour or so. After that Master asked Finlay's name and address before moving him to the larger laundry for two hours before finally setting him free. Finlay only got back to his father's house at six at night.

The ordeal affected Finlay so he slept badly for the next few nights. His father, Lieutenant Alexander Noble, brought Master to court and the sheriff-substitute decided that the imprisonment was illegal and ordered Master to pay £10 and costs.

Children and Education

In the nineteenth century Scotland was proud of an education system that ensured that the vast majority of children were able to at least read and write. However, sometimes there were flaws and, as usual, it was the most vulnerable, the children themselves, who paid the highest price. In 1872 the Education Act ordered that all children had to attend school, by law. This act intended to install universal education for all, but there were a few parents who attempted to avoid the compulsion.

One such was George Frances, the factor for Mr Baillie of Dochfour. In June 1877 he appeared before the sheriff court at Inverness, accused of refusing to send his thirteen-year-old son Benjamin to school. Frances pleaded not guilty and gave documentary proof that he was educating his son at home. The same document also claimed that Donald Fraser, the local schoolteacher, had an immoral character and was therefore not suitable to teach the young. The teacher was due to stand trial at Inverness Sheriff Court on a charge of adultery. He was suspected of living with the wife of a shoemaker named Donald Mackinnon.

At the court Fraser was called as witness. He had been the schoolteacher at Glenelg for fifteen and a half years and said young Benjamin had not attended school there for some three and a half years. The defence based their case entirely on Fraser's supposed adultery, but the sheriff did not think that was relevant and found Frances guilty of neglect and fined him £1, with a pound expenses as well.

Cruel and Unusual Punishment

In the past, Scottish schoolteachers had the power of the tawse over their pupils. Sometimes they were known as 'skelp-doups', and there had been a well-known, if possibly apocryphal, statement in Scotland when a parent handed over her son to the care of the school: 'Here's our Jamie; be sure you lick him weel.' By the nineteenth century this image was beginning to be challenged, as some schools became more humane and the process of education by repression eased a little. There was even the occasional case where teachers were brought to court accused of cruel practices. Such an accusation was only part of a case that came before the sheriff court at Inveraray in March 1894.

The schoolmaster accused was William Smith, who was the teacher at Lochgoilhead in Argyll. He had been a schoolteacher since 1855 and the board appointed him to Lochgoilhead in 1891, but after some time there were doubts about his efficiency. A number of matters came to the attention of the school board of Lochgoilhead and Kilmorich, mainly concerning Smith's failure to keep proper registers and records of his classes.

On 26 January 1892 William Adams and James Blair, two members of the board, arrived for an inspection to see if the reports were correct. They had notified Smith in advance that they were coming, but as soon as they entered the school and reminded him of their purpose, Smith became very agitated. He first grabbed hold of Adams and threw him out of the building, and then advanced angrily on Blair, who was counting the number of pupils present. Smith grabbed hold of Blair and ordered him out of the school. Rather than be assaulted, Blair obeyed at once, and the board members fled, leaving the school and the pupils in Smith's tender care.

The board checked up their records and accused Smith of falsifying the school records. They claimed that although thirteen pupils had left the school in March 1891, Smith had retained the names on the register. This seems a small matter, but the amount of grant the government paid depended on the number of pupils. Smith denied the allegation. The board also accused Smith of assaulting Blair and Adams to prevent them from inspecting the old registers and comparing the present registers with the actual attendance of pupils. Smith denied that allegation as well. Finally, the board accused him of immoral conduct by assaulting board members in the presence of his pupils and of fraud by adding false names to the school register. The immorality came about because it was Smith's duty to teach morals to the young, and acting as he did, he was bringing the children up the wrong way; there was no question of lewdness. Not surprisingly, Smith denied any such immorality.

In response, Smith said there were some members of the board who were disappointed with the examination results of 1891 and who refused to fill in the official forms for the education and probate duty grants. As a result, Smith's wages were dramatically reduced. Smith also claimed that some of the board members made false statements to the education department about him and that they planned to remove him from his position without giving him the retiral grant to which he was entitled.

The board now turned the screw. They said that for twelve years before the passing of the 1872 Education Act the people of Lochgoilhead had refused to send their children to the local school because of Smith's poor reputation. Only Smith's own children and a few paupers attended his school, while the local people hired another teacher for their children. Equally worrying, the board also spoke of excessive and unusual punishments, with

Smith issuing regular doses of castor oil to the children in his care. One of the children who were so punished was the son of Duncan Blair. On 16 November 1883 he was also excessively caned on the hands and the face, with 'numerous strokes' being inflicted. Not surprisingly, Blair had withdrawn his children from the school after that.

The court did not agree that the punishments were excessive as 'no serious results to the children had followed', so there were no damages due to be paid to the parents, but they also agreed that Blair had the right to withdraw his children and no fees should be paid to Smith after that date.

Child Cruelty

Every area of the world has its quota of people who bully those weaker than themselves, and the nineteenth-century Highlands were no different. Child cruelty is arguably the worst kind of abuse, as the victim is completely unable to defend him or herself, while any complaints are likely to be ignored.

Sometimes cruelty took on a sexual nature. On 1 August 1878 Sheriff Thoms presided over a court at Wick. The man in the dock was a druggist named James McCann, who was accused of indecently assaulting an eleven-year-old girl. The jury found him guilty and he was sentenced to nine months in prison. At other times the offence was more drawn out.

In 1850 David Greig was ten years old, the son of Alexander Greig, the schoolteacher at Inchberry in Rothes, on the northern fringe of the Moray Highlands. His father had remarried, and his stepmother, Elizabeth Moir, was not happy to have to care for her new son. The Greigs, man and new wife, did not want young David to sleep in the same house but forced him to spend his nights in a makeshift crib in the schoolhouse, with loose straw for a mattress and a rug for covering.

He was fed on potato peelings, when he was fed at all, and lacked either a shirt or shoes. The only time his trousers were removed were when his stepmother found an excuse to whip him with a rope. To add to his sufferings, David was unwashed, so lice and other vermin tormented him by night and day.

He weighed less than 30lb when he was rescued from his tormentors, and the adult Greigs were hustled into cells. They pleaded guilty to 'culpable and cruel neglect of a child' and were each sentenced to fifteen months in prison.

The Unwanted

Some crimes involving children showed the best side of human nature, as well as the worst. Such a case involved the bachelor James Grant. On 30 August 1882 James Grant lived a solitary life. He farmed a parcel of land near Fort George, a few miles to the east of Inverness, and he had no inkling that he was about to become a new father. He may have seen the train steam into Fort George Station from the east that evening, but it is unlikely he would pay much attention. Perhaps he should have, for a mysterious lady disembarked from the train and handed a metal biscuit box to the station porter, asked him to deliver the box to Farmer Grant and paid him six pence for his trouble. Then the lady boarded the Inverness-bound train and vanished from history.

True to his occupation, the porter duly handed the metal box to James Grant. If Grant was surprised to receive an unexpected gift, he was even more surprised when he opened the box and found a newborn baby girl. The story became a bit garbled as it travelled, and there were ugly rumours of child murder, but in reality Grant cared well for the girl. The identity of the mother was never ascertained, but possibly Grant had met her some nine months previously and the relationship had terminated in an unwanted pregnancy. In this instance, the story had a happy ending as Grant took easily to fatherhood.

Cruelty to children is one of the worst possible crimes as the victim is nearly always too young to retaliate or perhaps even to understand what is happening. In some ways, the Highlands may have been less prone to such things, as the communities were small and often close-knit, so there was less opportunity for hidden abuse. Unfortunately that did not preclude every case, and no doubt there were many instances of hidden cruelty. Perhaps someday the world will grow beyond such monstrosity.

14
Women and Crime

Although the majority of crime was committed by men, Highland women were eminently capable of breaking the law. They were heavily involved in the anti-Clearance riots, sheep stealing and illicit distilling, but could also take part in more mundane crimes. For example, in May 1802, Janet Catnach, a widow who lived at Braemar, was banished from Scotland for seven years for housebreaking and theft.

In the Inverness Circuit Court of April 1823, Isabella Urquhart was found guilty of fraud and forgery and handed a sentence of seven years' transportation. On hearing the sentence she broke down in tears.

At the same court, Margaret Grigor was given twelve months in jail for concealing her pregnancy, which was a crime common among unmarried mothers. However, one of the more spectacular and sadly widespread crimes was child murder. Highland women were no different to those in any other part of the country.

The Dead Dog in Thurso

There was nothing extraordinary about James Campbell. He was a typical thirteen-year-old boy who went to school and played with his

Not all nineteenth-century women were as cheerful as this

friends. Late in the afternoon of 20 April 1876 he was playing marbles with a friend, William Sutherland, beside Carnaby's Close in his home town of Thurso, when one of the marbles rolled into a pile of straw. William Sutherland walked over to retrieve it when he saw something interesting.

'Come and see this dead dog,' Sutherland called out, and Campbell came over. He looked closer and saw a body half covered in stones. When he poked around a bit he realised it was not a dog, but the body of a baby boy. Campbell ran to tell his neighbours, who quickly fetched the police.

The constable uncovered the child and examined him, hoping for life, but he was stone dead. The police called Dr Craven, who said the baby had been born after full term and killed after birth. The police began making enquiries to see if any local women had recently had a baby. Susannah Wilson said she remembered that just after the Wick herring season the previous week a woman named Christina Reid had claimed she was pregnant, but there was no sign of a baby. However, a jury at the circuit court in October were either not so sure or sympathetic to the mother and returned a not proven verdict.

Others cases were more clear-cut.

Death in the Black Isle

Jane Bain was a nineteen-year-old mother with a problem. She was unmarried but had a small son. In 1890 such a combination made for an unhappy woman, for as well as the obvious financial difficulties in raising a child alone, Bain also had the stigma of not being respectable. In any case, even if she did manage to raise her child to manhood, he would also have to carry the burden of illegitimacy all his life.

On 12 January Bain and her sister, Isabella, came to stay with her aunt, Ann Docherty, at their house on the Braes of Kilcoy in the Black Isle, north of Inverness. Bain had her child with her, a boy about eighteen months old. The Bains stayed with Docherty for about three weeks, during which time Jane offered Docherty ten shillings a week if she would look after the child. Docherty said she would not accept any money but would bring up the child if she had to. On Thursday, 30 January, a little after midday, Jane Bain took her son with her as she walked on the road to Dingwall.

Bain said she was walking to a place about a mile away. She claimed she had a job sowing there, and would take her son with her. Docherty pointed out that it was a wild, wet day for such a walk and by the time Bain arrived there would not be much daylight left for sowing anyway. In January the light would fade shortly after three. However, Jane was adamant.

It was well after nine on a dark night before Bain returned, and she came alone. Docherty asked where her son was, Bain said she had put him in the Inverness Poorhouse, but Docherty did not believe her and pressed for more information. She said there had not been the time to walk from Kilcoy to Inverness, hand over the boy and walk back. She knew her niece was lying and on the Friday she applied all the pressure she could, but Bain put her head on the table and refused to say anything. Docherty suspected that Bain had abandoned or even drowned the infant and asked in a score of different ways. She continued to ask until the Saturday morning when Bain, worn down, told her another story.

'I did it,' she said, again and again. 'I did it. My dear darling boy, I did do it.' Bain confessed that she had drowned her son. She said she had gone into a wood beside the road and walked until she had found a lochan. She had ducked the toddler's head into the water and then taken him out again. She wrapped the boy in her shawl and tried to bring him to life again but his face frightened her. She put him on the ground and kicked him on the head three times and put him back in the water.

Docherty informed the police about what Bain had said and on Sunday, 1 February, Bain guided Constable Alexander Mackay to a small pool inside the wood. She showed him her dead son at the foot of a tree beside the pool and blamed it all on her mother.

The case came to the circuit court in Inverness in May that year and the jury found Bain guilty of culpable homicide. Lord Kincairney sentenced her to seven years' penal servitude.

Witchcraft

Much less common than the disposal of an unwanted child was an accusation of witchcraft, although it was not unknown in the nineteenth century. Although it was an intensely religious period, pockets of superstition still lingered in various places. In one case in the police court in Inverness in December 1883, Isabella Macrae, an elderly woman from Muirtown Street in Inverness, was charged with assaulting a young girl. Macrae said that the girl had verbally abused her and that her grandmother was a witch. Most of the court's time was taken up with the names the child had called Macrae, but before Bailie Mackay gave his verdict the old lady produced a *corp creagh*. A *corp creagh* was a clay image shaped like a human and was used in witchcraft. This one was around four inches long and had the legs broken off. There were pins thrust through the place where the heart would be and green worsted threads tied around it. The spell, Macrae believed, was held within these threads. It is perhaps significant that green was the sacred colour of the Celts, used by fairies and possibly witches. Macrae believed that the image represented her, and since the legs had been broken off she was losing the strength in her own legs.

As usual, there was quite a crowd of spectators in the court and they were highly amused as they listened to Macrae's talk of witches and clay images. One man offered to buy the *corp creagh* but Macrae objected strongly. She claimed that if the image was damaged or broken she would die, so she had to care for it herself, as she was not yet ready to die.

Macrae had recently lost her husband and three horses, and blamed the deaths of all four on witchcraft. Bailie Mackay listened to all the evidence, as well as Macrae's beliefs, but preferred to stick with the initial charge and handed the old lady a choice of a fine or imprisonment. He did not mention the witchcraft.

As in every other part of Scotland, Highland women were involved in different types of crime. They could be thieves, they could be fraudsters, but the most tragic crime was also the unhappy killing of their own children. It was not uncommon throughout the nineteenth century but every case carried its own tragedy.

15

A Mixed Bag of Crime

The police were not only responsible for curbing the obvious crimes such as assaults, murders and theft. They also had to cope with a whole host of different offences. Some would be instantly recognisable to the officers who patrol the streets and roads today. For example, there was sexual crime, such as the case of Coll McDonell, who was found guilty of assault with intent at the circuit court at Inverness in May 1810. He had tried to rape young Janet McPherson, and Lord Armadale gave him three months for his misplaced lust.

Other crimes were seen as more serious at the time.

Blair the Forger

In the early nineteenth century forging banknotes was regarded as a very serious crime. That was possibly because a skilled forger would find notes relatively easy to copy, and the authorities thought if they did not act firmly the country would be swamped with false money, which could ultimately damage the economy. In February 1814 a forgery case from Argyll came to the High Court of Justiciary in Edinburgh.

Nathanial Blair was the man accused, although he usually travelled under the alias of Nathanial Sawers. On 15 October 1813 he had been at Kilmore Market in Argyll and had agreed to buy a horse from a man named Duncan McGregor. They had arranged a price of £10, with five shillings discount, or 'luck money' as it was known, for a cash purchase. Both men met at the house of Kenneth Douglas, with a fourth man, Hugh McCorquadale, also present. Black counted out three £2 notes of the Bank of Scotland, four Falkirk Bank notes of small denominations, one British Linen Company note and two notes from other banks. The notes were counted out by candlelight at seven in the evening, with the light flickering across the faces of the men and the wind rattling the window behind them. Immediately when the deal was concluded Blair left the house and vanished into the dark of the October night.

As soon as Blair was gone, McGregor handed over one of the British Linen Company twenty-shilling notes to McCorquadale as payment for a previous debt. The next morning, McCorquadale left the house and returned to his sister's house in Oban. He gave her the banknote in return for change, and everybody seemed happy. His sister's husband, Andrew McIntyre, a Writer in Glasgow, was taking his morning dram at the time and somebody came to the door. McIntyre saw the visitor and came back to McCorquadale, saying that the note was forged. They checked with McGregor and decided to have a word with Blair.

Picking up a man named Colin McNab, McGregor and McIntyre tried to find Blair. They followed his trail to Portsonachan at Loch Awe, and saw him arrive with a few horses and a small girl. One of the horses was the one McGregor had sold him. Without any hesitation, McGregor and his companions grabbed hold of Blair and took him to the magistrates to be examined.

Blair gave his own story. He said he was a horse dealer and when he was by Loch Lomond he sold a horse to a man he did not know and was given a bundle of notes. Shortly afterward he met the girl and they travelled together.

The jury at the High Court did not think much of Blair's story and found him guilty of forgery, so he was sentenced to be hanged in Edinburgh on 9 March 1814.

The Science of Phrenology

Fraudsters could penetrate to every corner of the nation. In January and February 1863 Shetland was graced by a Professor Duncan, who gave public lectures on the then popular science of phrenology. However, he was also collecting goods and clothing for himself from unsuspecting shopkeepers. When one reported him to the authorities, the learned professor appeared before the court at Fort Charlotte in Lerwick. Sheriff-Substitute Bell discovered that his real name was Duncan McLean and it was as his proper persona as a flesher from Arbroath that McLean was awarded forty days with hard labour.

Impersonating Sir Charles

In the nineteenth century railways made travel to the far corners of the country far easier. However, they also facilitated crime. In August 1881 Sir Charles Cuffe of Kilkenny House in Ireland arrived at the railway station at Thurso. He was not a happy man. He was visiting some of the landed gentry of Caithness but was hampered, as his luggage had been stolen. Sir Charles said he had been in Inverness and had boarded a train he thought was heading north, but inadvertently had climbed into a carriage bound for the west instead. He had left the train at Dingwall, but the goods van, with the bulk of his luggage on board, had continued onward to Thurso. When Sir Charles arrived the following day, his luggage was nowhere to be seen. As Sir Charles was obviously a gentleman and had such good relationships with the local gentry, nobody questioned his story and a search began for the luggage, without results.

Sir Charles was a cheerful, good-natured man, small of stature and fluent in French and German. He looked as if he may have been an ex-army officer, as he carried himself well and spoke with authority. He was not shy, and befriended a number of people, including Sergeant Miller of the Thurso Police.

The luggage theft was news for a while, but was forgotten after a few days. Interest was revived in October when Sir Charles reminded the world that his possessions had never been recovered. He had induced the local landowners to grant him hospitality for the past weeks, but unfortunately he was unable to pay as the Irish Land League had persuaded his tenants to withhold their rents, so he had no disposable income at present. However, things were not all black. His background and breeding was enough to make him friends, and one of the obliging gentlemen from Thurso drew up a letter of recommendation to an Edinburgh bank, allowing Sir Charles to draw cheques up to the value of £60, backed by the Royal Bank of Ireland.

Unfortunately, the Royal Bank of Ireland refused to pay any money, saying Sir Charles's note in their name was a forgery. An Edinburgh hotel found that Sir Charles had fooled them with a £15 cheque on the Bank of Ireland as well. The police began a thorough investigation of Sir Charles Cuffe and discovered many interesting things. They discovered that his friendship with the gentleman from Caithness was not at all longstanding; in fact, it had only begun a few weeks ago when the supposed Sir Charles met the gentleman on the P & O steamer *Australia*, on passage from Malta to Great Britain.

The police delved a little more and found out that the real Sir Charles Cuffe was actually on the Continent, seriously ill. The imposter

This inscription is on the wall of the prison in Fort George

was in great demand, particularly by the law, who wanted him to answer questions on fraud, forgery, falsehood and wilful imposition. However, the imposter was never caught.

Superstition

In late 1871 superstition was still prevalent among some of the inhabitants of Lewis. That year a crofter only sixteen miles from Stornoway, the largest town of the Hebrides, accused his neighbour and his wife of witchcraft. He said they were thieves, as they had used the black arts to steal the substance out of his cow's milk. Sheriff Mackenzie and the audience of the court were vastly amused and fined the man five shillings.

An Embezzling Bank Clerk

As well as crimes peculiar to the rural areas and the sea, the Highlands had its share of ordinary white-collar crime, including embezzlement. One instance that attracted some interest at the time was centred on Norman Macdonald, a bank agent from Redbank, near Creagorry in Benbecula, who was accused of breach of trust and embezzlement in September 1883.

Macdonald was the bank agent at Creagorry and also the clerk and treasurer for the school board of South Uist. It was a position of trust, as it involved dealing with money in an organisation that incorporated the prospects of every child on the island. Macdonald held the position from May 1875 and it seemed he was steadily draining the funds from the board into his own wallet. This was only a few years after the Education Act had made it compulsory for every child to have at least a modicum of learning. Between May 1873 and April 1883 Macdonald embezzled £1,530, nine shillings and sixpence from the board. Not only that, but he was also the Inspector of the Poor for the parish of South Uist and embezzled £348 intended for the poor, and kept it for himself.

Macdonald pleaded guilty but had a defence that there was no malicious intention, he was only a slovenly accountant. He claimed he merely confused money that was due to him and money that was due to the various funds he was responsible for. All the money he embezzled was replaced by Macdonald or by his friends. All the same, he was sent to penal servitude for five years.

Reckless Driving

Although the advent of the internal combustion engine undoubtedly made Scottish roads more dangerous, there were occasions when horse-drawn vehicles could also be fatal. Such a case occurred on

Sunday, 12 March 1820, when James Jordan drove the North Mail Coach between Port Gower and Berridale.

Mail coaches were much like the later postbus in that they carried passengers as well as letters and parcels, so the driver was in a very responsible position with the Royal Mail and people's safety under his care. As well as the four passengers who sat inside the coach and shuffled their feet in the straw on the floor, there were others who balanced on the roof outside; they paid less for the privilege of enjoying the bracing Scottish weather and views.

Jordan was probably a good driver when he was sober, but unfortunately he liked his drink too much. He had been drinking that day, so when he approached the Bridge of Langwell at some speed, his passengers were alarmed. They had cause to be. Jordan's speech was slurred, he was driving far too fast for the darkness of the night, and to make matters worse, only one of the coach's two lights were working so the driver and passengers could hardly see the edges of the road. When Jordan negotiated the sharp turn that led onto the bridge he lost control of his horses, the coach swayed, tipped and overturned, with its entire body coming apart from the wheels. The outside passengers were tumbled off; some were thrown over the parapet of the bridge into the water below, and one unfortunate man named James Sutherland was killed.

The passengers were not quite sure what had happened. Some thought that Jordan had clattered the coach against the parapet, others said the road had huge ruts that toppled the coach, but everybody had felt a sudden jerk a moment before the accident. However, it was not until the coach was inspected after the accident that people realised just how badly it had been maintained. The mortices were decayed and the woodwork of the body was rotted through. It was an accident waiting for the right time to strike.

When the case reached the circuit court in Inverness in May 1820, the jury needed very little time in finding Jordan not guilty of culpable homicide.

In that same court on that same day, there was a second case involving a coach accident. That one took place on the mail coach between Inverness and Fochabers on the Nairn to Forres stretch of road. William Evenes was the driver, with George Jenkins the guard, and the prosecution alleged that on 8 November 1819 they drove in such a 'careless and culpable manner' that when they were a mile west of the Bridge of Findhorn they did 'throw down David Laing' and run over his body so he died of his injuries a short time later. However, once again a brief examination found that there was no case to answer.

Change for a Shilling

Some crimes seem so petty that today they might be laughed off, but at a time when poverty stalked many households and even a single penny might mean the difference between mere hunger and utter starvation, small amounts of money meant much more than they do now. In late November 1868 a man in his early twenties entered a shop in Inverness and asked the shopkeeper if he could have change for a shilling. In this case, the man was perfectly innocent, but asking for change was a common method for forgers to rid themselves of false money, and the shopkeeper was instantly suspicious.

He took the shilling, examined it and thought it appeared a bit spurious, but rather than merely refuse the request and hand it back he decided to make his own test. Accordingly, he fetched a hammer and smashed it on top of the coin, bending it in half so it was unusable. The owner was naturally unhappy at this cavalier treatment of his money and demanded either change or another shilling to replace the ruined one. The shopkeeper refused both requests. The coin owner called the police, who hauled the shopkeeper away, and the coin owner sued him for damages of £5.

The matter was settled out of court; the owner got his shilling's worth of change and a small amount to compensate for his trouble.

Vandalism

For much of the nineteenth century the cause of progress was deemed much more important than the care of historical artefacts and monuments. City improvements and modernisation to farming practices saw the demise of thousands of irreplaceable ancient buildings, but in 1882 the Ancient Monuments Act gave a measure of protection to some of the thousands of castles, brochs and duns that give silent tongue to the history of Scotland. Naturally, some people continued the work of destruction and fell foul of the law. The first case in Shetland was in April 1888, when a Lerwick flesher named Hugh Mackay decided to build a new stable.

Unfortunately, he was near to the Broch of Clickinim, which was then thought to be a Pictish castle. The broch seemed to supply a ready-made reservoir of building material for his stable, and Mackay happily quarried away until he was caught. He appeared before Sheriff Mackenzie, who thought his actions were 'wanton destruction of an ancient monument' and fined him the maximum of £5 with costs of £4 and ten shillings to pay for the stones being returned.

Highland crime then was as varied as crime anywhere in the country. Despite the more scattered population and the distances between centres of population, forgery, deception and fraud could be encountered in the north.

16
The Arran Murder

Arran is the holiday island in the middle of the Firth of Clyde. Travelling there has been the highlight of the year to many thousands of city dwellers from the height of the Victorian age until the present time. It is an island for all tastes, with high granite peaks, curved yellow beaches, luxuriant gardens, tropical palms, rolling uplands castles, lonely cottages, herds of deer, fish in the burns and lochs, and ten picturesque villages with a plethora of hotels and bars. However, in 1889 it was also the scene of an alleged murder.

Edwin Rose was not a typical example of a person who holidayed on Arran. The majority of the holidaymakers were from industrial west central Scotland, hardworking manual workers from the shipyards, mills and factories who took their annual holiday 'doon the watter'. Rose was a Londoner and a builder's clerk in an office, a thirty-two-year-old man who planned to stay in the Glenburn Hydro in Rothesay in Bute but also visit the neighbouring island of Arran. Rose was not alone; he travelled with two men from Linlithgow, Francis Mickel and William Thom.

At the height of the Victorian period, the Clyde was very well served with steamers that crossed and criss-crossed the waters in frantic competition. On 12 July, Rose and his companions from Linlithgow caught the *Ivanhoe* steamer from Bute to Arran. While on board, Rose met a twenty-five-year-old man from Glasgow, who gave his name as John Annandale. His real name was John Watson Laurie. He had been born in Coatbridge and he had his own reasons for travelling to the Clyde Coast.

Laurie was slender but with a good set of shoulders. He walked with a confident roll and, like many Glaswegians, was fashion conscious, wearing knickerbockers when he walked the roads and hills. Laurie was a pattern maker – a mould maker – for Springburn's Atlas Iron Works in Glasgow and had been happily engaged, so life seemed pretty rosy for him. But apparently in 1889 things started to go wrong. He allegedly stole some money from his work, which caused a scandal, and although his family repaid the cash, his girl had broken off their engagement. Laurie believed the girl had gone to Rothesay in the Isle of Bute with a Coatbridge schoolteacher. He caught the ferry over and began to search for her. He did not find her and his money ran out, and then along came Rose.

As often happens on holiday, the two formed a friendship. While the Linlithgow men had no time for Laurie, he and Rose travelled together to Arran, and Laurie booked them both for a week with a Mrs Walker at Invercloy in Brodick, staying in an outhouse. While here, Laurie also met a friend of his called James Aitken, who must have wondered why Laurie used the name Annandale. However, he did not ask too many awkward questions, and Laurie and Rose continued on their holiday. After a day in Arran, they returned to Rothesay for the night.

The next day all four men sailed back to Arran, but while Rose shared Laurie's lodgings in Invercloy, the other two stayed at a yacht that was moored offshore. Morning saw Laurie and Rose wandering in

Glen Rosa, and for much of the next day the four men were together, but the pair from Linlithgow left by the half past three ferry. So far they had walked the hills and generally behaved just like any other holidaymakers in the island.

However, the Linlithgow two were not quite as enamoured with Laurie as Rose was. Before they left Arran, they warned Rose to be careful of his new companion. Despite the warning, when Laurie suggested to Rose that they climb Goatfell on Monday, 15 July, he agreed. So that day they set off up Arran's highest mountain. They left with some secrecy. They did not tell Mrs Walker where they were going, and she thought they had fled without paying their bill. When Laurie came down he was alone, and Rose was never seen alive again.

It was some time before his disappearance was noted. By 18 July it was known that Rose was overdue, but he was a grown man and may well have decided to stay longer in the Scottish Highlands. On 22 July some of the Rose family travelled north to Rothesay, and on 27 July, twelve days after his climb, Rose's brother Benjamin came over to Brodick to look for him. He made enquiries and found out about the Goatfell climb, so helped organise a search.

Around 200 men gathered at the kennels of Brodick Castle, divided into three groups and scoured the granite slopes of the mountain. Their search was made harder by a mist that swept over Goatfell, but when the sky cleared after an hour or so the searchers took out binoculars and telescopes and peered into every crack and cranny. The searchers were thorough, inspecting overhangs, probing scree slopes, putting their lives at risk in the search for Edwin Rose.

They found Rose's cap, walking stick and various other knick-knacks in a long line in a corrie that led to the top of the hill. They continued to search and eventually found a body hidden in a makeshift howff, a rough rock shelter in *Coire nan Fuaran* above Glen Sannox on the lower slopes. His skull was splintered, his spine broken, ribs smashed, buttock ripped, and he had been robbed. Although the body

Goatfell from Brodick Bay

was decayed and partly eaten by insects or birds, the clothing was enough to identify the body as that of Rose.

Police enquiries continued. A number of witnesses had seen Rose and Laurie on the summit of Goatfell about twenty past six in the evening, but none knew exactly what happened after that. A shepherd remembered seeing a weary-looking man coming down the hill alone after nine o'clock that same evening, although others thought he was mistaken in thinking that was Laurie. Others were convinced Laurie had been seen drinking at the Corrie Hotel about ten that night, and somebody else remembered seeing Laurie leaving on the seven o'clock ferry the next day, after which he caught a train to Greenock. He had been wearing a striped jacket – Rose's jacket. Laurie's liking for fancy clothes had worked against him.

Laurie returned briefly to his lodgings in North Frederick Street in Glasgow and then travelled back to Bute. From there he shipped to Glasgow, where James Aitken challenged him in the street.

So far the police were looking for the non-existent Annandale, but James Aitken knew both names and informed the police. Laurie promptly sold his work tools, told his colleagues he was off to Leith and then he disappeared.

As the hunt for Annandale ended and that for Laurie began, Rose was buried at the lonely graveyard at Sannox, near where his body was found. For a while it became a popular destination for the curious visitor, and the credulous believed his ghost walked the hills.

Details and rumours of Laurie began to emerge. Laurie was a good singer, he earned twelve shillings a week, and his father had kicked him out of the family home in 1886. Laurie was a womaniser; he was reported as having been seen at Rothesay and Dunoon, both times in the company of women. Around the same time there were a number of men in the West of Scotland who claimed that their daughters had been romantically attached to Laurie, which, if true, would have made him a very busy man indeed. The police made a number of arrests in the Glasgow area but released them all. There was a momentary stir when they found the body of a suicide on the shores of Loch Lomond, but it was another unfortunate and, according to the *Glasgow Herald* of 9 August, 'a religious maniac' and not Laurie. An abandoned pit shaft near Coatbridge was inspected when somebody found a scrap of paper with the words 'I am the murderer' scrawled on it lying nearby, but Laurie was not inside.

In August a letter was written to the *North British Daily Mail* with a Liverpool postmark and purporting to come from Laurie. It said, 'I rather smile when I read that my arrest is hourly expected. If things go on as I designed then I will soon have arrived in that country from whose bourne no traveller ever returns.' The letter gave details of Laurie's past, with detailed references of his abortive love affair with a teacher who cheated on him by 'encouraging the attention of another man', who was also a teacher and who spoke ill of Laurie at every opportunity. Laurie, if indeed he wrote the letter, claimed that he travelled to Rothesay 'to watch her audacious behaviour' but in so doing he met 'another young lady'. More significantly, Laurie also said, 'As regards Mr Rose, poor fellow, no one who knows me will believe for one moment that I had any complicity in his death.'

Witnesses saw Laurie sail from Glasgow to Liverpool on the steamer *Owl*, and while on board he was very charming and sang 'The March of the Cameron Men'. There were also rumours of a man of 'wild and reckless appearance' who caught a train to London, was followed by a gentleman but disappeared into the crowd. He was also reported at Longniddry, Shotts and Kilmarnock.

In reality, the Glasgow Police were soon on Laurie's trail, but he slipped out of the city and south to Liverpool. The police moved in on his lodgings but he was gone; all they found were a number of shirts that belonged to Rose. The police continued to hunt, having railway stations and shipping ports throughout the country watched.

On 3 September the painstaking scrutiny proved its worth, as Laurie was seen boarding a train at Ferniegair, south of Hamilton. The local policeman proved tenacious and followed Laurie, chasing him into a patch of dense woodland. Laurie rolled under a bush, tried to commit suicide here by slashing his throat with an open razor, but he failed and was arrested, bleeding from a shallow cut.

With the Victorian love of the macabre, local entrepreneurs made the most of the occasion. They cut sprigs from 'Laurie's bush' and sold them at a penny an inch, and even made a number of walking sticks from the wood, which sold for stupidly inflated prices.

The trial was held in the High Court in Edinburgh on 8 November, with people queuing outside to hear the details. The Lord Justice Clerk, Lord Kingsburgh, was the presiding judge. Laurie's trial was unique in that it was the only accusation of murder between two hillwalkers, which, given the opportunities for murder in these lonely places, is quite significant. Murder trials were a great public entertainment before the advent of radio and television, and this one seemed to have some fine gory details. He appeared before the bar looking fairly well dressed and with a silk scarf concealing the cut on his neck where he had tried to kill himself. He had a new short beard and stared steadfastly at anybody who looked at him.

Laurie agreed he had begun the ascent of Goatfell with Rose and admitted he had robbed the body, but denied murder, claiming that Rose had met two other men on the ascent and had fallen down the mountain. The prosecution claimed that Laurie had murdered Rose with a rock, but the nature of the wounds negated that. There was no blood on Laurie's clothes, which was interesting, as to murder Rose in such a brutal fashion as the prosecution claimed would have meant great quantities of blood being spattered around. It seemed more likely that Rose had fallen while negotiating the col between North Goatfell and Mullach Buidhe, two of the peaks on the summit ridge. The position of Rose's possessions may strengthen this argument, although the fact that Rose's cap was neatly folded is curious, unless one considers that Laurie may have been mentally unbalanced and deliberately folded and placed the cap.

'I robbed the man but I did not murder him,' Laurie claimed. The evidence may suggest that his statement was correct.

There was one further strange piece in this course. The Arran Police buried Rose's boots in the sand in the belief this would prevent his ghost from walking. Even in 1889, and in an island only an hour's sail from the Scottish mainland, old superstitions remained with even such a respectable man as a police officer.

Despite the fact that all the evidence was circumstantial, the prosecution used Laurie's subsequent behaviour and the robbery as the basis of their case. The judge insisted that the case be decided on the Saturday, one day after it started, so pushed and harassed the jury to reach a quick verdict. The jury agreed with the prosecution, but only just: they spent a mere forty-five minutes in debate and decided by eight men to seven that Laurie was guilty. The judge sentenced him to death, but the sentence was later commuted to life imprisonment. He was held in Peterhead for a while but escaped and was transferred to Perth and died in Perth Criminal Asylum in 1930, after nearly foty-one years in jail, making him Scotland's longest-ever serving prisoner.

The case provoked quite a lot of reaction, and there was even a doggerel song composed and sung in Glasgow:

I do believe and shall believe
That Laurie killed poor Rose
And on Goatfell he shed his blood
And stole away his clothes

The mystery of the Goatfell murder, or accident, remains unanswered. Did Rose fall, or was he pushed? After this length of time it is unlikely that the truth will ever be known.

17

The Ardlamont Mystery

'Not proven' is a uniquely Scottish verdict that means exactly what it says: the jury could not decide whether the accused man or woman was guilty or not. They thought there was insufficient evidence to convict the accused of the crime, but enough doubt remained that they were not entirely convinced of their innocence either. Arguably the most high-profile 'not proven' case in the Highlands was the Ardlamont Mystery. It may have been murder, it may have been a tragic accident; the facts and fiction of the case were argued all over Great Britain. However, after being presented with all the available evidence, a jury of fifteen reasonable people could not decide, yet public opinion, fuelled by newspaper speculation, seemed to believe it was murder.

The Ardlamont estate is in the Cowal Peninsula in Argyll. In 1893 it was an 11,000-acre sporting estate, catering for shooting parties that walked the hills and fished or hunted the local wildlife. Most of these sportsmen came from outside Scotland; mainly English from the middle and upper classes indulging in a spot of outdoor living amidst the truly spectacular scenery, while the house staff, gamekeepers and ghillies were usually locals. The estate centred on classical Ardlamont House, with roots back to the seventeenth century.

That year Alfred George Monson had hired Ardlamont with the supposed prospect of teaming up with a young man named Windsor Hambrough to buy the property. Monson was not a particularly prepossessing figure, being under average height and slightly built, with a shock of fair hair and a large nose, but he also looked intelligent. He was a man with a history, having been on the verge of financial trouble for much of the past decade. He had been born in May 1860, the third son of the Reverend Thomas Monson of Kirkby-under-Dale in Yorkshire, and was distantly related to the Viscount Oxenbridge. His grandmother was married to the 5th Viscount Galway and the family was closely related to Baron Monson, so Monson would certainly be considered a gentleman, but there were dark shadows in his life, despite his family background and being married with three children. He had rented a house once, had watched it burn and claimed a considerable amount of insurance money as a consequence. Nevertheless, in 1891 he had managed to find a job as a military tutor to a young gentleman named Windsor Dudley Cecil Hambrough. The two would be together until Hambrough's death in 1893.

Hambrough was related to New York bankers and had a fortune due to him on his twenty-first birthday from his grandfather's estates. Monson found him a post as lieutenant in the 4th Battalion Prince of Wales Own Yorkshire Militia. His father had been in the Isle of Wight Rifle Volunteers and hoped that his son would have joined the Hampshire Militia. A London financial agent named Tottenham had introduced Monson to Hambrough's father, but Tottenham was also a man on the edge of respectability.

Cecil Hambrough came from and was heir to Steephill Castle, a castellated mansion built in 1835 by his grandfather, John Hambrough. The mansion was near Ventnor on the Isle of Wight, and Hambrough

© Crown Copyright: RCAHMS.
Licensor www.rcahms.gov.uk

Ardlamont House

was fast approaching his twenty-first year. His father was the Justice of the Peace for Hampshire and lived at Houghton, Stockbridge.

Monson was lucky, for Hambrough's father, Major Hambrough, could not have checked his background very thoroughly. The salary for the mentoring position would have come in immensely handy, as he was on the cusp of destitution. Monson seems to have enjoyed living the life of a gentleman, but had not the resources to support it, or to support his wife. A few weeks after accepting the position as tutor, Monson was declared bankrupt.

Leaving his Harrogate home to rent a property named Risely Hall, Monson paid merely with empty promises until he was challenged, then borrowed money and headed north. His charm had worked on Hambrough, for despite his father's newfound scepticism, he remained as Monson's ward. Monson hired out Ardlamont, depending on his undoubted charm and the reputation of an English gentleman for honesty and integrity, in lieu of the more usual rental of actual cash. Monson forged the signature of a man named Jerningham, with a footman as the witness. Cecil Hambrough, twenty years old in 1893, would have gloried in the life at Ardlamont for the season, which was a common way for the wealthy to spend the late summer.

Monson had a little bit of paperwork to do and asked Hambrough to sign a number of forms and documents that insured his life. The young man seemed completely under Monson's spell and did as he was asked, but it is doubtful if he understood anything that was going on. However, by 8 August they were both safely ensconced in Ardlamont. Hambrough had invited a group of his friends to join them as paying guests.

In August a man named Edward Scott arrived. He was also known as Edward Sweeney, and sometimes as Edward Davis, but now posed as Edward Scott, an engineer. He was about twenty-seven years old, delicately built with narrow shoulders, about five foot nine tall and dark-haired. Sweeney was a bookmaker's clerk and would not take part in any shooting but would carry the guns and take home whatever game they bagged. He was a friend of Monson's and had not met Hambrough before he arrived at Ardlamont.

On 9 August Monson hired a boat from local man Donald McKellar. Monson and Sweeney took it out on Loch Fyne in the morning, after which Sweeney left on a mission of his own. Loch Fyne is a spectacular arm of the Firth of Clyde, whose waters caress the shore of Ardlamont Estate. That same evening, Monson and Hambrough took the boat out in Ardlamont Bay on the loch. For some reason the boat began to leak and capsized. Both men were thrown into the sea. Monson was fairly safe as the summer seas were calm and warmed by the Gulf Stream, but Hambrough was a non-swimmer. Luckily they were not far out at the time and managed to struggle ashore safely.

In the early morning of 10 August, a day of high wind and driving rain, Monson sent the gamekeeper away on an errand before he, Sweeney and Hambrough walked out to the woodland. It was about six o'clock. The three men spread into a line, as people did when they were out shooting. However, only Monson and Hambrough carried guns, and Sweeney was in the centre with the game bag. While Hambrough carried a long-barrelled twelve-bore shotgun, so was presumably after birds or rabbits, Monson had a short twenty-bore.

Running around the edge of the plantation was a drystane dyke about two and a half feet in height, covered in turf and with a ditch at the side. Once they reached the trees the men split up, and that was the last that Hambrough was seen alive. If any local workers heard the sound of a shot, they would have expected it and took no notice.

A few moments later they heard the sound of running men and saw Monson and Sweeney dashing down from the trees. There was no sign of Hambrough. The two men retreated into the gun room. James Wright, the butler, looked in to see if all was well. Wright was a self-effacing man of around twenty-two. Monson and Sweeney were busy cleaning the guns but were unhappy, with Monson in particular seeming upset. The butler asked if everything was all right and if Mr Hambrough would be along later.

Monson told them that they had separated in the woods and he heard the sound of a shot. He had shouted out, asking Hambrough what he had killed, but there was no answer so he had hurried over. Hambrough was lying in a ditch with a gunshot wound behind his left ear and his brains on the ground beside him. It was obvious that there had been a tragic accident and Hambrough had accidentally shot himself while climbing over the dyke. The blast from the shotgun had smashed into his head and he was already dead when Monson found the body, apparently on top of the dyke.

At first the estate was in shock and then people wondered how he had managed to shoot himself in the back of the head, and what happened to Hambrough's gun. All the same, they called for help and Dr McMillan came from Tighnabruaich. Around the same time as the doctor came, Sweeney left Ardlamont house in a pony and trap. He said he had business to 'take him away' and would leave a forwarding address at the Central Station Hotel in Glasgow. The policeman at Tighnabruaich approached him as he waited for the ferry and asked him not to leave, but without authority to hold him, they could only watch when Sweeney caught the boat.

The Procurator Fiscal in Inveraray sent Sub-Sheriff Sharp and Mr Naughten, the deputy Procurator Fiscal, to investigate the case, but he had no doubt about Monson's version of events. He even reported sympathetically that Monson would now be in financial difficulties as his employer was dead. Two weeks later, Monson travelled to Inveraray and reported to the Procurator Fiscal that Hambrough had insured his life for £20,000, with the Mutual Insurance Company of New York. There was also talk of another policy for £10,000 with the Scottish Provident. Monson's wife was the beneficiary. That led to some suspicion, particularly as the last of the forms had only been completed two days before the death.

The story gradually emerged. Monson had attempted to obtain insurance with a number of companies but most had turned him down when he mentioned the size of the amount he wanted to insure Hambrough for. Monson had discovered that Hambrough was about to inherit a fortune on his twenty-first birthday, and he invented a story that he wanted to buy the estate of Ardlamont. Parts of the family estates on the Isle of Wight had been sold during an agricultural depression and the money would be paid to Hambrough very shortly. Until his money came through, Mrs Monson would lend him the money and the life insurance ensured that she could do so. Monson's story was a lie, but like the best lies, it was based on truth.

The police visited Ardlamont and began to question the staff. Sweeney had vanished and was never seen again. When they heard about the near drowning incident on Loch Fyne, the police suspicions increased and they inspected the boat. There was a small hole drilled in the hull. That in itself could be innocent enough; it might have been made to help drain the boat, for every open boat takes in water from spray or large waves, but if so the hole would have a bung. There was nothing in it; the hole was open for the sea to enter and to judge by the state of the wood, it had been recently bored. The police suspected that Monson had tried to drown the non-swimming Hambrough.

They also inspected the spot where Hambrough's body had been found and wondered anew how a man with a long-barrelled shotgun managed to shoot himself behind the ear. They also wondered how nearby trees, particularly a rowan over six feet away and a lime tree seven feet away, could be riddled with shotgun pellets. It was possible, they surmised, that Hambrough could have been shot by somebody else from a distance away, hence the spread of the shot. If he had shot himself at close range the shot would not have had time to spread. However, the woods were often used for shooting so the scars could have occurred at any time. The police busied themselves experimenting with different types of shotgun to test the effects of gunfire on trees from different ranges.

In the meantime, Hambrough's body was taken south and buried at Ventnor in the Isle of Wight. The burial was a splendid affair, with all the pomp and ceremony the Victorians lavished on the dead. Strangely, there were rumours that the missing Sweeney accompanied the coffin, but the police did not pursue him. The stories were false, as the mystery man was the Ardlamont factor, a man named Steven. Monson was also at the funeral and met Major Hambrough. Hambrough was buried in a brick grave near the family vault. A few days later he was exhumed in the presence of McCulloch, the Procurator Fiscal; Dr Littlejohn from Edinburgh; Dr McMillan; and a couple of London surgeons. Littlejohn was a major figure at the time, being the medical officer for health in Edinburgh and a man whose advice helped convict Dr Pritchard, the Glasgow poisoner, and Laurie, the Arran murderer. The autopsy merely confirmed that Hambrough had been shot in the head. There was the usual crop of rumours concerning the case. On 25 September the *Aberdeen Journal* carried the story that a poacher had seen the whole thing. Most stories were either exaggerated or completely false.

Suspicion, however, spread. Monson was placed under police surveillance and tried to live as normally as possible while two police stalked him everywhere. On 28 August Chief Constable Fraser of the Argyllshire Police drove a pony and trap from the Royal Hotel at Tighnabruaich towards Ardlamont. About five miles into his journey he met Monson, who was also driving a pony trap, with a guest at his side and his constant escort, Police Sergeant Ross sitting in the back of the trap. Fraser said he had some business with Monson, who passed the reins of the horse to his companion and transferred to the captain's trap. Sergeant Ross followed him and the guest drove on alone. As soon as Monson was in Fraser's trap, Fraser drove back to Tighnabruaich. 'You may consider yourself under arrest for the death of Mr Hambrough,' he said.

Rather than act upset, Monson coolly asked to see the warrant, which he read through word for word with a show of unconcern. From Tighnabruaich Monson was bundled into the *Lord of the Isles* steamer and taken to the jail at Inveraray. Shortly afterward, he appeared before Sheriff-Substitute Shairp at the sheriff court. He pleaded not guilty to the charges of attempted murder and murder, and was lodged in the cells at the courthouse pending a full trial. His previous calmness had gone by that time and he appeared agitated. While in the cells he lived as a gentleman, with meals brought to him from the George Hotel.

Mrs Agnes Monson became something of a celebrity, with her movements being watched and commented on. When her husband was arrested and placed in Greenock Prison she sailed north in Cecil Hambrough's splendid steam yacht, built for him on the Clyde but never paid for. She visited her husband and stayed at the Argyll Arms Hotel and the Western Temperance Hotel. In September the forging of Jerningham's signature came to light when Major Lamond, the owner of Ardlamont House, asked him for the rent that was due. Naturally, Jerningham knew nothing of the case, and said he did not even possess a footman.

The case came before the High Court in Edinburgh with only Monson at the bar. It was a high-profile case, with the Lord Justice

Clerk presiding and possibly Scotland's premier defence lawyer, John Comrie Thomson, acting for Monson. Police guarded every entrance to the court. There was a crowd in Parliament Square but Monson was held in a cell beneath the courthouse and taken directly to the court. He arrived dressed very smartly, even flashily, but he looked pale. He spoke with his wife for some time before two tall policemen escorted him to his position before the judge. On his first hearing when he was accused of attempting to drown Hambrough and with murdering him by shooting, Monson said, quietly but firmly, 'Not guilty.' He left the courthouse in a cab for Calton Jail, with crowds watching for a glimpse of what was really a celebrity murder case. Sweeney was summoned but did not appear for his trial.

One of the witnesses for the crown was the Edinburgh forensic scientist Dr Joseph Bell, who was the prototype for his townsman Conan Doyle's Sherlock Holmes. Dr Bell informed the jury that, in his opinion, Monson was guilty of murder. There were doubts, though. There was no proof that Monson or Sweeney had bored the hole in the boat, and no witnesses to the actual death. More crucially, the insurance policy would not be paid to Monson but to his wife, who was not even slightly implicated in the killing. There were expert witnesses who testified to the type of powder in Hambrough's cartridges and others who had been with him on previous shooting expeditions who stated he always carried his gun carelessly, even when negotiating fences and walls, and a gentleman named Philip Day, who testified that Hambrough had once shot a fox terrier by accident. A Colonel Tillard testified that when snipe shooting he had once stumbled and shot off part of his own ear, so Hambrough's death could well be an accident. The defence also asked what could possibly be the motive. After ten days of intense scrutiny, the jury failed to reach a verdict and the result was not proven.

That was not the verdict that Hambrough's friends wanted. Year after year on the anniversary of Hambrough's death they tried to rebuild interest in the case by having the following notice published in the national press:

> *Sacred to the memory of Cecil Dudley Hambrough, shot in a wood near Ardlamont, August 10th 1893. 'Vengeance is mine, I will repay,' saith the Lord.*

The case left a feeling of unease among many in the country. To an extent it exposed the hollow mockery of many of the supposed upper-class of society who posed as superior beings while they lived on charm, non-existent funds and the charity of friends and money-lenders. The fabric of Victorian society was looking porous in the closing years of Her Majesty's reign.

The following year, Monson was again in court, this time as he sued Madam Tussaud's waxwork museum for erecting a model of him carrying a shotgun outside their Chamber of Horrors. The court ruled in Monson's favour and awarded him damages of one farthing, quarter of a penny. The legal profession used this as a test case of 'libel by innuendo'. In 1898 Monson was in court once again, being jailed for five years for fraud, but the mystery of what happened that sunny day in Cowal has never been satisfactorily resolved.

Epilogue

There is still crime in the Highlands and probably always will be. The area has changed a great deal since the nineteenth century. Gaelic is spoken less and there are many incomers from other parts of Scotland and from other countries. The threat of mass eviction has gone and there are no more convoys of whisky smugglers wending over the hills. Murder is not common but still occurs, but there is a new worry about drugs in communities from Arran to Wick and the usual Scottish problem with alcohol abuse remains a worry. Child abuse is as hidden as always, the driving can be atrocious on narrow Highland roads and fishermen have been known to participate in the Black Economy rather than follow the perhaps too-stringent EU regulations.

The events of the nineteenth century cast long shadows: many of the glens remain desolate despite the struggles of the tenants to retain their land. The population of the Isles is in decline as the youth seek better opportunities elsewhere. Inverness grows and thrives as one of the fastest growing cities in Europe, but more people may lead to rising crime rates in future.

The tourist trade, which spawned hotel robberies, Rose's murder and steamboat races in the nineteenth century, ebbs and flows; the large estates continue to host shoots for deer and game, and crofters farm as assiduously as ever. There is more prosperity than before but there are still pockets of poverty in the small towns and deep in the remote glens. Second homes have drained the vitality of many communities, but incomers have also brought new ideas.

According to the Northern Constabulary's own Public Performance Report for 2011 and 2012, their detection rate is 67 per cent, which is 12 per cent higher than the Scottish average, and they had the lowest level of domestic housebreaking, with the Western Isles particularly safe. Glenlivet now produces legal whisky; there are no pitched brawls in the streets of Wick, and windsurfers play in Gott Bay where the Tiree Expeditionary Force landed to enforce the law. However, the police are still vigilant and fight a daily battle against both residents and visitors who have criminal tendencies.

The Highland hills remain, watching, as the people live out their lives in the blue shadows and along the seething coast. The countryside looks passive beneath a summer sun, but there is always the chance of an eruption if something raises the spirit of the indigenous population, for that is the Highland way.

Select Bibliography

Aberdeen Journal.

Barrie, David. *Police In the Age of Improvement: Police Development and the Civic Tradition In Scotland, 1775–1865.* Devon, 2008.

Burt, Edmund. *Burt's Letters from the North of Scotland.* Edinburgh: Birlinn, 1754, 1998.

Caledonian Mercury.

Cameron, Joy. *Prisons and Punishment in Scotland from the Middle Ages to the Present.* Edinburgh: Canongate, 1983.

Chesney, Kellow. *The Victorian Underworld.* London, 1970.

Cochrane, Lord. *Circuit Journeys.* Edinburgh, Hawick, 1888, 1983.

Cochrane, Lord. *Memorials of His Time.* Edinburgh, 1856.

Devine, T. M. *Clanship to Crofters' War: The Social Transformation of the Scottish Highlands.* Manchester: Manchester University Press, 1994.

Donnelly, Daniel, and Kenneth Scott (eds.). *Policing Scotland.* Cullompton: Willan Publishing, 2005.

Fenton, Alexander. *Country Life in Scotland: Our Rural Past.* Edinburgh: John Donald, 1987.

Fraser, Derek. *Power and Authority in the Victorian City*. Oxford: Blackwell, 1979.

General Police Act 1862.

Godfrey, Barry and Paul Lawrence. *Crime and Justice 1750–1950*. Cullompton: Willan Publishing, 2005.

Glasgow Herald.

Grant, I. F. *Highland Folk Ways*. Edinburgh: Birlinn, 1961, 1995.

Grimble, Ian. *Clans and Chiefs*. London, 1980.

Haldane, A. R. B. *The Drove Roads of Scotland*. Edinburgh: Birlinn, 1997.

Hamilton, Judy. *Scottish Murders*. New Lanark, 2006.

Hughes, Robert. *The Fatal Shore*. London, 1987.

Hunter, James. *The Making of the Crofting Community*. Edinburgh: Birlinn, 2000.

Inverness Courier.

Jones, David. *Crime, Protest, Community and Police in Nineteenth-Century Britain*. London: Routledge and Kegan Paul, 1982.

Knepper, Paul. *Criminology and Social Policy*. London: Sage, 2007.

Livingstone, Sheila. *Confess and Be Hanged: Scottish Crime and Punishment Through the Ages*. Edinburgh: Birlinn, 2000.

MacKenzie, Osgood Hanbury. *A Hundred Years In the Highlands*. Edinburgh: Birlinn, 1995.

McLaren, Duncan. *The Rise and Progress of Whisky Drinking in Scotland and the Working of the Public Houses (Scotland) Act, commonly called the Forbes McKenzie Act*. 1858.

Minto, C. S. *Victorian and Edwardian Scotland*. London, 1970.

Murray, Patrick Joseph. *Not so bad as they seem: The transportation, ticket-of-leave, and penal servitude questions*. Glasgow: Knowsley Pamphlet Collection, 1857.

Murray, Sarah. *A Companion and Useful Guide to The Beauties of Scotland*. Hawick: Byway Books, 1982.

Murray, W. H. *The Islands of Western Scotland: The Inner and Outer Hebrides*. London: Eyre Methuen, 1973.

Rafter, Nicole. *The Origins of Criminology: A Reader*. Oxford: Routledge, 2009.

Ross-Shire Journal.

Scott, Sir Walter. *Northern Lights or a voyage in the Lighthouse Yacht to Nova Zembla and the Lord knows where in the summer of 1814*. Hawick: Byway Books, 1982.

Smith, Gavin D. *The Secret Still: Scotland's Clandestine Whisky Makers*. Edinburgh: Birlinn, 2002.

Smout, T. C. *A Century of the Scottish People: 1830–1950*. London, 1987.

Smout, T. C. *A History of the Scottish People: 1560–1830*. London, 1969.

The Herald.

Tobias, J. *Nineteenth-Century Crime, Prevention and Punishment*. London, 1972.

Whitmore, Richard. *Victorian and Edwardian Crime and Punishment*. London, 1978.

Whittington-Egan, Molly. *The Stockbridge Baby-farmer and Other Scottish Murder Stories*. Glasgow: Neil Wilson Publishing, 2001.

Wordsworth, Dorothy. *Recollections of a Tour Made in Scotland*. London: Yale University Press, 1997.

Selected Websites

Riot at Wick. http://hansard.millbanksystems.com/commons/1847/
    mar/04/riot-at-wick
Inverary Jail. http://www.inverarayjail.co.uk/
Convict Transportation Registers Database. http://www.slq.qld.gov.
    au/resources/family-history/info-guides/convicts
National Library of Scotland Digital Gallery. http://www.nls.uk/

Acknowledgements

I would like to thank the following people and institutions for their help in creating this book. The staff at Inverness Library; the staff at the Highland Archive Centre at Inverness; the staff at North Highland Archives in Wick; the staff at Inveraray Jail, Inveraray, Argyll, the staff at the A. K. Bell Library, Perth; my editor, Kristen Susienka; and finally and mostly, my wife, Cathy, who has endured me writing and talking of nothing but Highland crime for some months.